Across Sicily with Garibaldi's Thousand

An Adventure in Landscape and Italian Memory

Tim Parks

ALMA BOOKS

ALMA BOOKS LTD
60 High Street
Wimbledon Village
London SW19 5EE
United Kingdom
www.almaclassics.com

Represented by:
Authorised Rep Compliance Ltd
Ground Floor
71 Lower Baggot Street
Dublin, D02 P593
Ireland
www.arccompliance.com

Across Sicily with Garibaldi's Thousand first published by Alma Books in 2026

© Tim Parks, 2026

Tim Parks asserts his moral right to be identified as the author of this work in accordance with the Copyright, Designs and Patents Act 1988

Cover: Nathan Burton

Maps: Bill Donohoe

Printed in Great Britain by CPI Group (UK) Ltd, Croydon CR0 4YY

ISBN: 978-1-84688-475-7

All rights reserved. No part of this publication may be reproduced, stored in or introduced into a retrieval system, or transmitted, in any form or by any means (electronic, mechanical, photocopying, recording or otherwise), without the prior written permission of the publisher. This book is sold subject to the condition that it shall not be resold, lent, hired out or otherwise circulated without the express prior consent of the publisher.

Contents

Across Sicily with Garibaldi's Thousand	1
About This Book	3
Chronology	5
PART ONE: A RISING TIDE	**7**
Quarto	9
Talamone	17
Sea and Islands	31
Marsala	37
Towards Salemi	43
Salemi	55
Pianto Romano	65
PART TWO: SWIRL AND FLUX	**85**
Calatafimi Segesta	87
Alcamo	95
Partinico	103
In the Mountains	107
In the Golden Bowl	117
La Portella	121
Piana degli Albanesi	131
Marineo	139
Misilmeri	149
Gibilrossa	157
PART THREE: TAKEN AT THE FLOOD	**165**
Descent on Palermo	167
Barricades	179
Bombardment	189
Stalemate	201
Truce	221
Portraits	235
Secrets	247
Departures	261

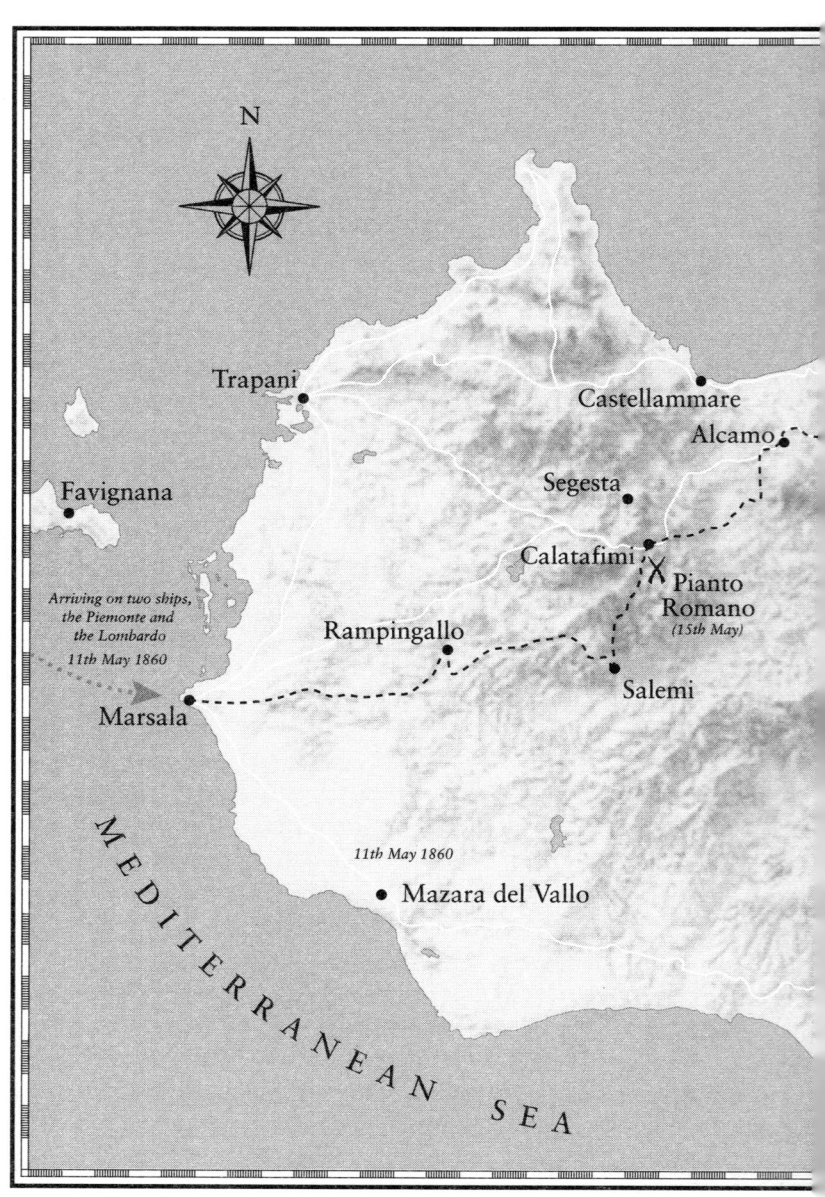

Map 1: Route of the Thousand

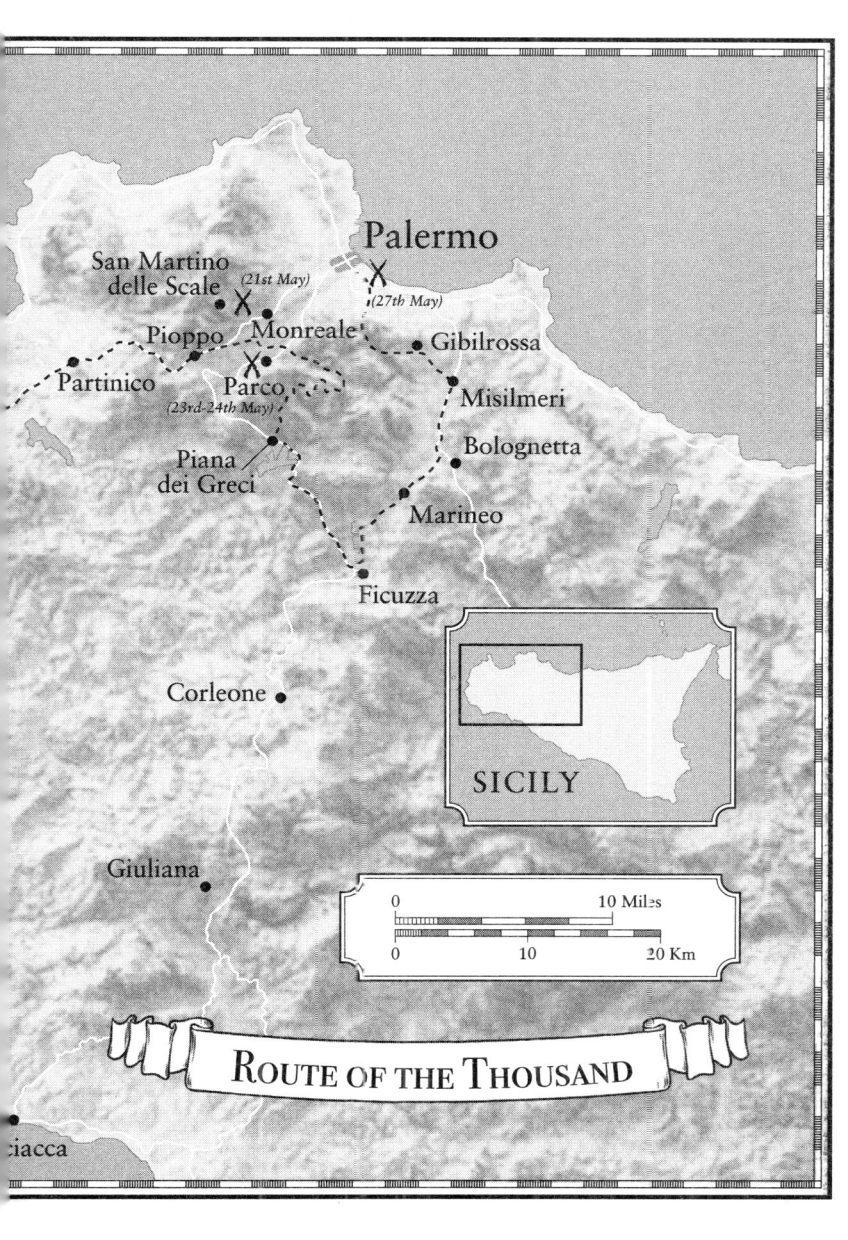

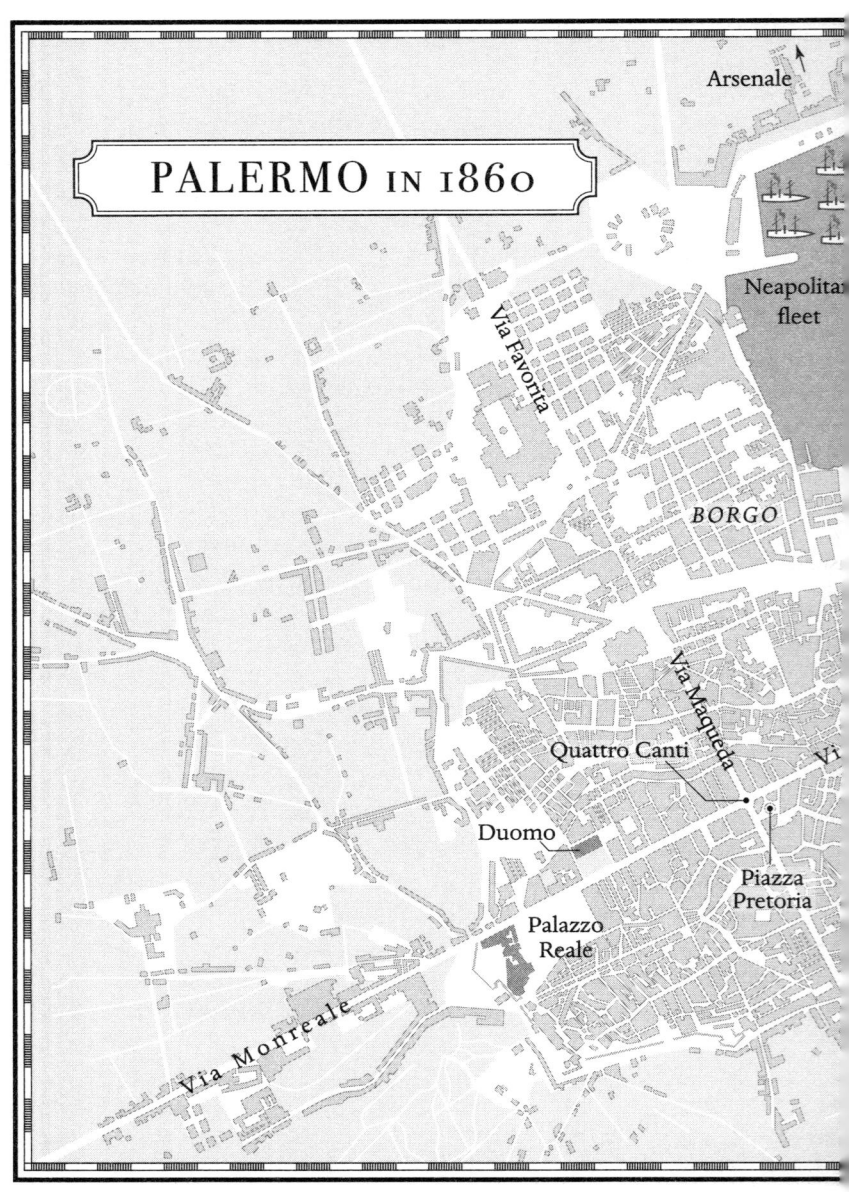

Map 2: Palermo in 1860

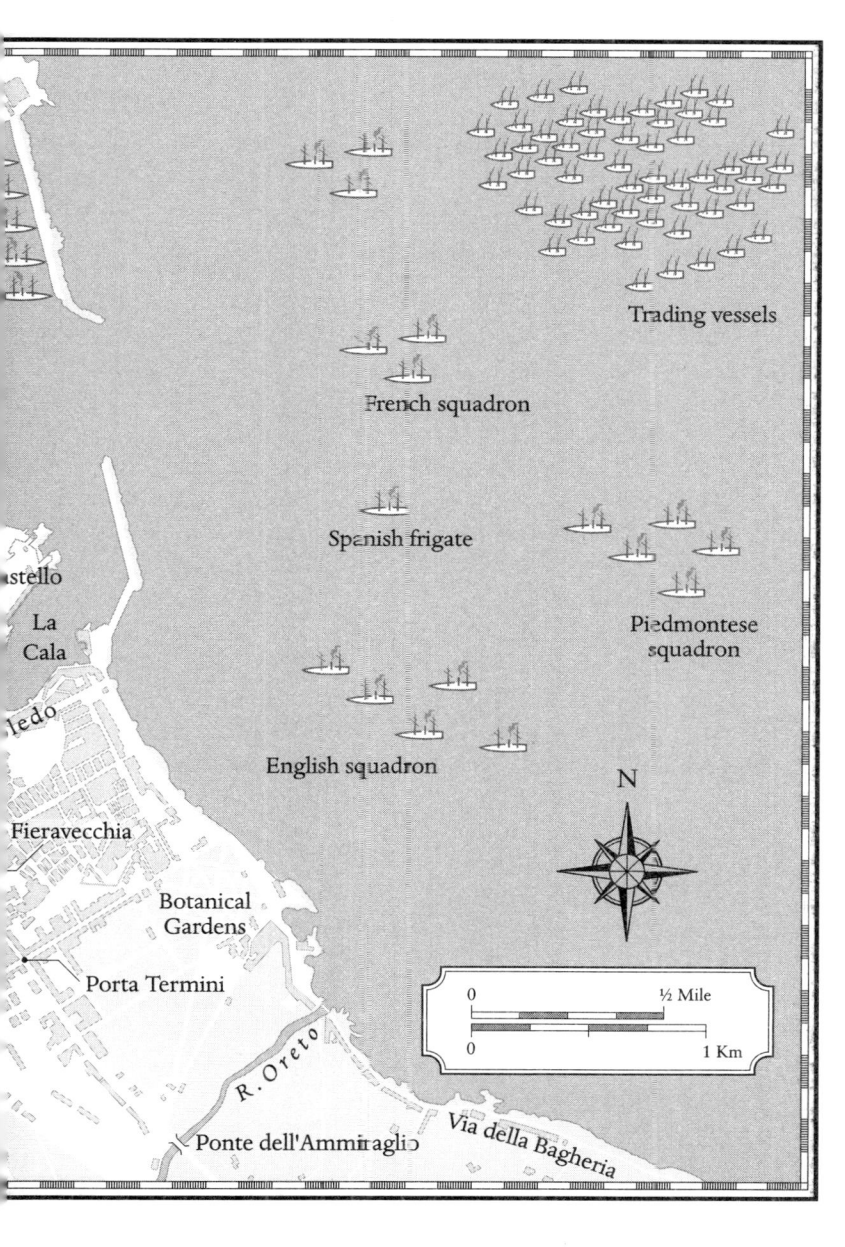

ACKNOWLEDGEMENT

I would like to express my gratitude to Alex Gallenzi, who believed in this book and helped make it so much better than it was.

*Across Sicily with
Garibaldi's Thousand*

About This Book

"It is, indeed, one of the most astonishing military feats of the century," wrote Friedrich Engels in June 1860 of Garibaldi's capture of Palermo. And that was before the Thousand went on to take the whole of Sicily and then southern Italy, allowing for the unification of Italy in 1861. "Garibaldi," claimed the historian A.J.P. Taylor, "is the only wholly admirable figure in modern history."

All this has been written about any number of times. So what can I add? History lives in so far as we engage with it afresh. Just as an old translation – Dryden's *Aeneid*, Pope's *Iliad* – begins to draw as much attention to the time it was written as the original it translates, so historical accounts can grow dusty or distract us with assumptions and presumptions that are no longer ours.

Then the Thousand's exploits in Sicily have always been the object of fierce political controversy. For the pro-unification camp, Garibaldi and his men were saints and heroes. Endless statues were raised, endless streets named after them. But for their enemies who wished (and still wish) that Italy remain divided in separate states, Garibaldi was a pirate, his men ruffians and his supposed military victories bought with masonic gold as part of an international Anglo-American conspiracy.

Where there is not controversy there is indifference. The experience of Fascism, which had always sought to appropriate the legacy of Garibaldi, inoculated Italians against all rhetoric of military triumphalism, or any idea that the world might be positively changed by taking up arms. An article in *Corriere della Sera* in 2010 estimated that half of the country's museums dedicated to the Risorgimento had closed, while most of the monuments celebrating unification had fallen into disrepair. People no longer knew nor cared how the nation state had formed.

I first found myself studying the Risorgimento in my teens as my special subject for A level. So I learnt about Mazzini and Cavour, Victor Emmanuel and Garibaldi. Not long afterwards I married an Italian and came to live in the country those men struggled to create.

Over my forty-five years here I have always retained a fascination for the *then* as opposed to the *now*, always continued to think and read and write about their ideas and efforts, our scepticism. This book is an experiment: how close can we get now to the events and mindset of the past? It is based on diaries, personal accounts, letters and archives, rather than other history books. Fortunately, many documents have come into the public domain in recent years. Crucially, I follow the Thousand on their campaign, walking the distance they walked, the way they walked, from Marsala to Palermo, across western Sicily in the same early summer heat, exploring the places where their adventure unfolded, putting together a chorus of voices, theirs and their enemies', and those of the people of Sicily.

The story culminates in the Sicilian capital, where the citizens rose up against a Bourbon regime that sought to bomb them and Garibaldi into submission, reducing whole quarters of the city to rubble, killing and maiming hundreds, destroying magnificent works of art and architecture. Inevitably, reading vivid eyewitness accounts and visiting the sites of the catastrophe, it was hard not to think of similar carnage going on in the world today. Modern Italy was forged in blood.

I say "I followed... I walked" – in fact, I was with my wife, Eleonora, who hails from Taranto, a southern town where many people share the view that things were better before Italy was unified. If readers find it surprising that I occasionally include our discussions, with each other and with people we meet, it is because my aim is not to produce the illusion of a definitive account – there can never be a definitive account of such complex and momentous events – but to bring history to life as a matter for debate now, between people with different opinions, different aspirations, something that is, paradoxically, part of our world, albeit in stark contrast to it, familiar yet exotic. If the past is a country that issues no passports, nevertheless we are all its citizens.

Readers can view a photo gallery of the journey at
https://timparks.com/non-fiction/across_sicily

Chronology

5th/6th May, night-time. The Thousand depart in boats from the town of Quarto, three miles south of Genoa, boarding two steamers, the *Lombardo* and the *Piemonte*, offshore at dawn.

8th May. The expedition stops at Talamone for arms and ammunition.

9th May. Leaving Talamone before dawn, the expedition stops briefly at Santo Stefano for coal.

11th May. The Thousand disembark at Marsala.

12th May. March towards Salemi.

13th May. Arrival in Salemi.

14th May. Garibaldi proclaimed Dictator of Sicily.

15th May. The Battle of Calatafimi at Pianto Romano. Bourbon army retreats towards Palermo.

16th May. Arrival in Calatafimi. General Lanza is appointed Lieutenant General of Sicily and arrives in Palermo. Giuseppe La Masa leaves the Thousand to recruit local Sicilians.

17th May. March to Alcamo.

18th May. The Thousand march to Partinico, then climb to the heights of the Renda Pass on the mountains above the Golden Bowl, twelve miles from Palermo.

19th/20th May. The Thousand camp in the Renda Pass under heavy rain. La Masa sets up camp for his volunteers at Misilmeri and Gibilrossa, east of Palermo.

20th May. Evening. Descent to Pioppo, nine miles west of Palermo.

21st May. Skirmishes on the road between Pioppo and Monreale, five miles west of Palermo. The Bourbon troops, under the command of Colonel Mechel and Major Bosco, advance. The Thousand retreat to the Renda Pass. Rebel leader Rosolino Pilo is killed.

21st/22nd May. Descent through the night under heavy rain from the Renda Pass to Parco (now Altofonte), eight miles south-west of Palermo.

22nd May. Defensive fortifications built in Parco.

23rd May, afternoon. Brief engagement with advancing Bourbon troops below Parco.

24th May. The Bourbons seek to encircle the Thousand in Parco. Garibaldi orders an instant retreat, and the Thousand fall back in disarray on Piana dei Greci (now Piana degli Albanesi). Colonel Mechel informs General Lanza that Garibaldi is defeated.

24th/25th May. Night-time withdrawal from Piana dei Greci along the road to Corleone. During the night the column splits. Colonel Orsini takes all the carts and cannons onwards to Corleone. The main group circle back to Marineo, sixteen miles south-east of Palermo, where they arrive at 10 a.m. on 25th May. At dusk the men leave Marineo and march to Misilmeri, near the coast, ten miles east of Palermo.

26th May. In the early hours Garibaldi meets La Masa and other rebel leaders in Misilmeri. In the morning the Thousand climb to the heights of Gibilrossa, where they are united with La Masa's 5,000 Sicilian volunteers, the *picciotti*. At dusk they begin their descent on Palermo. During the same day, Von Mechel and Bosco set off in pursuit of Orsini, in the direction of Corleone, thirty miles south of Palermo.

27th May. Shortly after dawn, the Thousand and the *picciotti* begin their attack on Bourbon defences, entering Palermo at Porta Termini at 6.30 a.m. After some hesitation, the people of Palermo join the struggle and begin to build barricades. Bourbon troops shell the city indiscriminately.

28th–29th May. Street fighting all over the city. Continued Bourbon shelling. High civilian casualties. Colonel Mechel marches back towards Palermo from Corleone.

30th May. Lanza invites Garibaldi to negotiations on the British warship HMS *Hannibal* anchored off the Palermo waterfront. Colonel Mechel enters the city at Porta Termini with 4,000 soldiers, but halts his advance when he learns that a one-day truce has been declared. Garibaldi asks the people of Palermo if they wish to accept Lanza's terms for surrender or to fight on. They raise the cry of "*guerra*" – war.

31st May. The Bourbons request a three-day extension of the truce.

3rd June. An armistice is declared, with no time limit.

7th June. The Bourbon army of around 20,000 men retreats from Palermo to the north of the city before embarking on ships for Naples.

PART ONE

A RISING TIDE

Quarto

How to change the world? It's not enough to be ready for the task. You must choose your moment. Have the right collaborators. Believe. Be lucky.

Through the spring of 1860, in a friend's villa above the fishing village of Quarto, three miles south of Genoa, Giuseppe Garibaldi hesitated. Was the tide running his way? It was hard to say. In the spring of 2021 I visited the place: Villa Spinola. It's a decaying, pink-stuccoed building standing fifty yards from a hectic four-lane road. At the front is a police station, and round the back a dilapidated two-room museum where the relics of Risorgimento glory look like they have just been unearthed from your grandfather's attic. I struggled on the steps, recovering from a bout of sciatica "I do not enjoy good health," Garibaldi wrote in a letter at the time – his problem was crippling rheumatism – "and hope I can use what's left of me on behalf of my country before I am quite done for."

Italy was drawing closer to unity, but the final outcome was still uncertain. Piedmont had signed a pact with France to chase the Austrians out of Lombardy and the Veneto. But in the war of 1859 Napoleon III bailed out after the Battle of Solferino, with only Lombardy won. War was bloodier than the emperor had imagined. Nevertheless, he insisted on his reward: the passage of coastal Nice and the mountainous region of Savoy from Piedmont to France. Nice was Garibaldi's hometown. "I'm like Jesus," he complained to Augusto Vecchi, owner of Villa Spinola, "I have nowhere to lay my head."

Other recent events must have compounded a sense that every step forward would be thwarted by a greater step back. In 1859 Garibaldi had been allowed to participate as a Piedmontese general in the war against Austria, but was given just 3,000 poorly armed, older men and sent off on a diversionary mission in the lakes and mountains, where his surprising successes could have little influence on a war that was mainly fought on the plain. Made a general in the Tuscan army immediately after the conflict, he had been planning an invasion to free the Papal

States from Church rule, when the Piedmontese authorities intervened shortly before the action was to begin. Their French allies would not have approved. Garibaldi resigned his commission. In January 1860 he had been allowed to launch a "Million Rifles Appeal" to arm a patriotic volunteer force, but in April when he asked for some of the rifles, now purchased and held by the Piedmontese government, they were denied him.

Another thing Garibaldi had done that January was to marry, at fifty-two, the eighteen-year-old Contessina Giuseppina Raimondi, only to be told days later that she had a lover, by whom she was pregnant. Determined to divorce, he claimed the marriage had never been consummated, but admitted in private that the two had had sex before the wedding. In any event, he had made a fool of himself, which was not good for a man who relied on an aura of invincibility. Planning a raid to destroy the ballot boxes of the referendum that was to legitimize France's annexation of Nice, he was distracted by news that a revolutionary uprising in Sicily might at last prove the spark for a decisive action to unite the north and south of Italy. This was early April 1860. Two hundred men were quickly assembled. That was when his rifles failed to materialize. Then came word that the Sicilian revolution had fizzled out. It was disheartening.

Villa Spinola stands high above the rocky bay of Quarto. Garibaldi did a lot of vigorous digging in the villa's grounds to keep himself battle-fit. Most of the land has been built on now, but behind the villa there is a Veterans Club with a place to play bocce and a small trattoria that operates from a back room of the villa. In fact, the couple who cook and serve in the trattoria are the same who open the museum for you, free of charge. The atmosphere is pleasantly proletarian, which seems appropriate for a down-to-earth man like Garibaldi. My wife Eleonora and I sat under a pergola and ordered gnocchetti and capers. The cook prepared the food in a tiny outhouse. "Not many people visit," his *signora* told us, bringing our plates. She was eager that we sign the museum guestbook. Perhaps some government subsidy has to be justified.

Few men can ever have been in the curious position that Garibaldi found himself in at this point. Nobody doubted that there was a certain momentum towards Italian unity. Various groups and movements wanted it in various forms. The Piedmontese monarchy wished to lead it. Lombardy had been won on the battlefield, and the smaller duchies previously under Austrian protection – Tuscany, Parma and Piacenza, Modena and Reggio Emilia – had all agreed to be annexed by Piedmont and thus subsumed into a larger Italian state. Romagna, one of the papal territories, had also been captured and annexed. Yet the pope, whose remaining states covered most of central Italy, was determined to block unification and could rely on a strong French garrison in Rome to guarantee his sovereignty. To the south, the vast territories of Campania, Puglia, Basilicata, Calabria and the island of Sicily were ruled from Naples by a young Bourbon king, new on his throne, who had no intention either of relinquishing power or of entering a federation with other Italian states. His well-equipped army was 90,000 strong.

So there was no legal path to unity. The only development that might sanction further steps in that direction would be a popular uprising. Such things were not unheard of. It had been Sicily which in January 1848 sparked off the dramatic wave of liberal revolutions that swept through Europe that year. Naples had seen revolutions in 1820 and 1848. Rome had had its short-lived republic of 1849. But such insurrections were hard to predict and notoriously precarious. Their leaders had conflicting goals, some republican, some monarchists, some supporting a federal state, others a centralized kingdom. They were poorly organized and quickly fell prey to well-armed repression. People had learnt to be wary. Many Italian patriots were still in jail after their efforts of a decade before. Many were in exile. In 1857 Carlo Pisacane, who had fought beside Garibaldi in the Roman Republic, landed a small group of volunteers on the Tyrrhenian coast a hundred miles south of Naples in an attempt to provoke an uprising in the Bourbon kingdom. One hundred and thirty-six of his two hundred soldiers were killed, Pisacane among them; the others were rounded up and jailed for life. Rosolino Pilo, the Sicilian patriot who had let Pisacane down by failing to deliver promised support, was the man now organizing the revolution in Sicily and urging Garibaldi to go. It was hardly reassuring.

Basically, everyone was urging Garibaldi to go. Or not to go. It was widely believed, by both friends and enemies, that he was the only person who might transform fleeting popular unrest into lasting change. As a young man, enlightened by the socialist teachings of

Saint-Simon, Garibaldi had dedicated his life to freeing people from oppression. Above all the Italian people. Condemned to death in Piedmont, he had fought for many years and with remarkable success in Brazil and Uruguay. In 1848 he had taken advantage of an amnesty to return to Italy, and in 1849 led volunteers to victories over both French and Neapolitan armies outside Rome. In 1859 he had beaten the Austrians at Varese and San Fermo. An aura of destiny hung about him. So people felt. But he was growing old.

Day by day, at Villa Spinola, a stream of visitors filed in and out of these same doors that we watch as we eat our gnocchetti. The wild Nino Bixio was the leading enthusiast, a ship's captain with more adventures behind him at thirty-eight than most of us would experience were we to live to a thousand. The Sicilian lawyer Francesco Crispi, who had played a leading role in the 1848 revolutions, was liaising with Rosolino Pino in Palermo to organize the uprising and pleading with Garibaldi to commit to the venture. Inevitably, these men talked up the chances of success and glory. Sicily was definitely the weak point of the Bourbon kingdom. The Sicilians were so hostile to government from Naples that they had long since been exempted from conscription to the kingdom's army.

Other friends were sceptical. Giacomo Medici, hero of the siege of Rome in 1849, felt there was no chance of success. Medici had distinguished himself in the recent battles of Varese and San Fermo. He had fought with Garibaldi in South America. His loyalty was absolute, and his opinion carried weight. The young Giuseppe Bandi, a Piedmontese soldier who had recently become Garibaldi's close assistant, watched the older men disagree. "These idiots will sacrifice Garibaldi's life for nothing," Medici told him. When Bandi referred this remark to Bixio, "he shot fire from his eyes and cursed".

But disagreements between friends were minor complications. As patriotic young men flocked to Genoa and Quarto to volunteer, there were more serious arguments between the followers of the revered ideologue Giuseppe Mazzini, who was a diehard republican, and the majority who were ready to accept a united Italy under the Piedmontese monarchy. Garibaldi, himself a republican, insisted they must fight under the banner of Vittorio Emanuele, king of Piedmont: a united Italy was not going to happen if the conservative Italian bourgeoisie feared their privileges would be lost overnight. This was the lesson of the failed revolutions of 1848: Republicanism must wait. The Mazzinians said they would never follow a royal flag.

Spies were everywhere: Bourbon, Piedmontese, French, Austrian. It is hard to assemble large numbers of fighting men in secret. Friends insisted that Garibaldi stay inside the villa's grounds to avoid assassination attempts. He was notoriously careless about his personal safety. Still, what most gave him pause was the attitude of the Piedmontese government. Did they or did they not support him? It seemed impossible to know.

A word of explanation. One says Piedmont or the Piedmontese government, but in fact the state was officially known as the Kingdom of Sardinia. It had been ruled since 1700 by the Royal House of Savoy, and included the island of Sardinia, the tiny French-speaking duchy of Savoy (now part of the Auvergne-Rhône-Alpes region), the far larger Piedmont and, following the 1815 Congress of Vienna, the hitherto proudly independent Genoa, together with the surrounding region of Liguria. Initially a loose federation, these disparate territories had only been yoked together as a single kingdom in 1847. Many feared it would fall apart – it wasn't sufficiently homogeneous. But precisely this fragility had obliged Piedmont to become more dynamic than its older, well-defined Italian neighbours. It had introduced a liberal constitution and then begun to seek, in the idea of a united Italy, an expansionist raison d'être that might neutralize its internal contradictions. Rather than remaining an anomalous, higgledy-piggledy little state, it would provide the core of a single, all-inclusive Italian state. Hence the decision, taken by its brilliant prime minister, Camillo Benso, count of Cavour, to offer Napoleon III the French fringe of the kingdom's territories – Nice and Savoy – in return for the rich and wholly Italian Lombardy and Veneto, assuming they could be won from the Austrians. It made sense. Nevertheless, when Nice and Savoy were actually handed over to the French, in the spring of 1860, there was huge resentment in Piedmont, both on the royalist right and the democratic left. The king in particular was upset; Savoy was the home of his royal dynasty. Garibaldi was furious, Nice being his birthplace. Very soon the revolutionary hero came to be seen as the de facto leader of the "democrats" opposing Cavour and his "moderates". Since it was in Cavour's power to assist or prevent the military mission to Sicily, this antagonism was not helpful.

But Cavour didn't declare himself. He feared Garibaldi had made a secret pact with the king. He feared the man's popularity and energy. If the mission to Sicily went ahead and Garibaldi fought in the name of Victor Emmanuel, this could provoke hostile reaction from France and Austria. If it didn't go ahead, Garibaldi was perfectly capable of causing havoc nearer home. Or even attacking the Papal States, which would be worse.

As the days went by and everyone waited for news of the on-off revolution in Sicily, Cavour neither helped nor hindered. He could have had Garibaldi and his volunteers arrested, but did not. The king was sympathetic to Garibaldi's adventure, but warned him not to recruit men from Piedmont's regular army. "I have asked Cavour," Garibaldi told his young assistant Bandi in mid-April, "for a thousand rifles so that we can cheerfully go and get ourselves killed in Sicily." This time the rifles were delivered, but not the ones that had been newly bought. The weapons that actually arrived were old and, aside from their bayonets, hopelessly ineffective. Did Cavour want the garibaldini to be massacred?

On 27th April a telegram arrived at Villa Spinola announcing the collapse of the Sicilian revolt. Thirteen leaders had been executed in public. Garibaldi called off the mission, provoking angry scenes among the volunteers, many of whom accused him of cowardice. But just ten days later Cavour would send this message to his personal envoy in Paris, Costantino Nigra:

> Having promised to give up his mission, Garibaldi, on the basis of false reports from Sicily, set off at 3 a.m. this morning. I have telegraphed Cagliari and Sassari to stop him.

After lunch, we walked down from Villa Spinola through narrow winding lanes to the bay. Every street and alley is named after the men who went, but the signs are old and shabby. They blend nicely with high stone walls and dusty maritime pines, while all around the modern city demands attention. Quarto has been absorbed into Genoa now. High-rise blocks huddle together on the steep slopes. A 1960s school building is covered in graffiti. At the bottom of the hill you have to find a place to cross the railway line that runs parallel to the coastal road. Quarto dei Mille, the station is called. The town's name was changed in 1911 in honour of the adventure that so irritated Cavour. The big monument to the Mille, the Thousand, on the far side of the busy road was erected in 1915, a bronze monstrosity showing the Risorgimento heroes rising from their graves. It was inspired by the so-called 'Hymn' to Garibaldi written in 1858:

> Si scopron le tombe,
> si levano i morti,
> i martiri nostri
> son tutti risorti...[1]

Below, on a terrace closer to the sea, a thirty-metre-long metal plaque, placed in 2011, has the names of the 1,089 men who actually set sail that night recorded in bas-relief. "Is it possible," complained a recent newspaper article, "that the authorities didn't use a rust-proof metal?" Many names are illegible.

The bay itself offers a wonderful sweep of rugged coast, perhaps a mile in all, with little patches of sand and much bathing-station paraphernalia dating back to the early twentieth century. Today, in warm sunshine freshened by a stiff breeze, rocky reefs gleam black against the foam of the breakers and the intense azure of the sea. Beyond the promontory to the west lies the great port of Genoa. The plan was that the volunteers with all their gear would put out in small fishing boats, at night, and meet two paddle steamers, stolen from their berths in Genoa under cover of dark. But the ships were delayed by an engine failure, and the men kept waiting in a heavy sea till almost dawn.

The coastal road along the bay is called Via 5 Maggio – the date they left. A slender white stone column supposedly marks the rock from where they actually set out, though they surely couldn't all have scrambled down these same slippery boulders together: it would have taken too long. A little digging in early accounts and diaries tells us that in fact boats put out from various points along the coast east of Genoa. With its change of name and some astute storytelling, Quarto dei Mille has cornered the commemoration market. People always speak of the Mille as setting out from Quarto. Ironically, such opportunism goes hand in hand with a deeper process of forgetting.

---

[1] "The tombs open, / The dead step forth, / All our martyrs / Have risen again."

A historical event is simplified and neatly packaged for occasional commercialized remembrance. It can be pulled out and put away like an old medal. The dusty display cases at Villa Spinola featured scores of postage stamps recalling the departure of the Mille. None of them recent. The same three or four period paintings, where Garibaldi looks like Jesus on the Sea of Galilee and the garibaldini like the Mayflower pilgrims, are endlessly recycled. So genuine admiration decays into institutional kitsch. Often it seems the whole extraordinary enterprise has been deliberately caricatured so that the cynical can more easily dismiss it altogether.

Is this inevitable? Very soon I am going to head for Sicily, to see how close one can get, physically, mentally, to what happened there in 1860, but also to try to understand why, of all the moments of the Risorgimento, and indeed of Italy's modern history, this is the one most subject to sceptical revisionism. Was it a noble enterprise? Did it change the world? Or at least Italy? What does its progressive repression in recent years tell us about the Italian psyche? Or the modern psyche *tout court*?

Talamone

He was a simpleton.

He was uncouth, uneducated and violent.

He was a pirate and a smuggler.

He stole from churches and tortured priests.

He was a fool manipulated by powers he didn't understand.

He was a freemason, and the Risorgimento in general a masonic conspiracy.

He was in the pay of the British.

He was in the pay of the Piedmontese.

He didn't defeat the Bourbons: he bought them off, with British/Piedmontese money, sent to him via the masons.

He was just plain lucky.

He killed Anita's husband in order to have her, then strangled Anita when she became too ill to follow him.

He betrayed the peasants to have the support of the nobility.

He was a terrorist.

He was a brigand.

He was the prototype fascist.

Over the last few years, thinking, writing and talking about Garibaldi, I have heard all of these opinions, not just from ideologues invested in revisionist views of history, but even from the cream of Milanese society, people enviably cultured and generally well read, though they have never opened a biography of the man they dismiss, let alone a seriously documented account of the Risorgimento. All this at a time when the idea of Italian nationhood is under intense scrutiny, when many hope that the country might once again be split into smaller states and others wish it could be absorbed into the technocratic embrace of that larger, amorphous entity that is the European Union.

The Thousand were pampered young intellectuals with more ideas than sense.
The Thousand were a rabble of cut-throats, brigands and rapists.
The Thousand were deserters from the Piedmontese army.
The Thousand were Piedmontese soldiers masquerading as volunteers.
The Thousand were northerners bent on exploiting the south.
The Thousand were foreign mercenaries with a licence to plunder.

Why is it so important today that instances of collective idealism and heroism be denied? Is it because they were directed towards the creation of something we have fallen out of love with, the nation state? Is it because they used violence rather than passive protest? Here, as published in the *Official Gazette of the Kingdom of Italy* in 1878, is the breakdown, by origin and profession, of the 1,089 men who eventually made the trip with Garibaldi to Sicily.

441	Lombardy
164	Liguria
156	Veneto
81	Tuscany
47	Sicily
41	Emilia
32	Piedmont
24	Friuli
21	Calabria
18	Campania

That makes 1,025. The others were indeed foreigners – Frenchmen, Hungarians and Poles for the most part, all with a history of involvement in liberal causes, some already naturalized Italians. But the most surprising statistic here is that there were actually more Sicilians in the group than Piedmontese, though when they arrived in Sicily the locals would always refer to the Mille as "the Piedmontese".

Otherwise, the Thousand included:

76	landowners
27	clerks
24	doctors

22	cobblers
19	lawyers
18	engineers
12	carpenters
11	labourers
11	tailors
9	bakers
8	pharmacists
8	notaries
8	waiters
7	barbers
5	hairdressers

That accounts for only 265. Around a hundred were bricklayers, mechanics, caretakers, errand boys, saddle makers, dyers, boatmen, servants, shop assistants and porters. Many, being still in their teens, were too young to have a profession. Many were students. Many were disbanded soldiers. Five were officers deserting the Piedmontese army. Fifty-nine were members of a pre-existing volunteer force, the Genoese Carabinieri, so called because of the type of modern *carabina* that a generous benefactor had bought for them. They had fought with Garibaldi in the 1859 campaign.

There was one woman, Francesco Crispi's thirty-seven-year-old wife Rose Montmasson. And one priest, the fifty-eight-year-old Luigi Gusmaroli. During the voyage the lady and the priest played cards together to pass the time.

The average age was twenty-five. The youngest was a boy of twelve, brought along by his widower father who had no family to leave him with.

I am eager to arrive in Sicily as they did, by boat from Genoa. Unfortunately there is no such service. One cruise company offers trips from Toulon with a stopover in Cagliari, but when I tried to book I was told the service had been suspended. Studying a map, you see how absurd it was for Cavour to say he had told the governors of Cagliari and Sassari, in Sardinia, to stop the garibaldini. All the more so because he specified that they must do so only if Garibaldi put into harbour. There was no reason why he should do that. Admiral

Persano, commander of the Piedmontese fleet, then based in Cagliari, observed in a letter written on 8th May,

> It seems unlikely that the government wasn't informed of Garibaldi's mission. And if they decided not to stop him in Genoa, why would they want to arrest him in Sardinia? I can only suppose that these orders were sent to us as a diplomatic cover and that the coded message behind them is to leave him alone on the high sea.

The only sea trip to Sicily that I could find was from Naples to Palermo, the same that D.H. Lawrence describes at the end of his travelogue, *Sea and Sardinia*. But it hardly made much sense to set out from the wrong place and arrive in the wrong place. In short, without buying or renting a yacht of one's own, it was impossible to follow the route the Thousand took.

No sooner had the men climbed aboard at dawn on 6th May, scrambling up rope ladders from their small boats in the dark, than almost all were seasick. The rifles still had to be loaded. In packing cases. And the general supplies. It took time. The sea was heavy and the rain persistent. A miserable day, by all accounts. Food was scarce, and the men packed so tight on deck that some had to stand throughout the journey. No one was sure exactly where they were headed, whether to Sicily or Calabria, Naples or Rome. Towards midnight, unable to sleep, Giuseppe Bandi went up on the bridge, where Garibaldi told him they had no ammunition for their ancient rifles. Bandi, who was still officially a serving officer in the Piedmontese army, was stunned. "Garibaldi was a bad organizer," wrote the historian Trevelyan, who worshipped the man. They were also short of coal for the voyage.

But is it true that Garibaldi was a bad organizer? Munitions had been bought, on the black market, but the smugglers who were supposed to rendezvous with the ships off Quarto hadn't showed. Garibaldi imagined they must have sold the munitions to a higher bidder – in fact, anxious when the ships were late out of Genoa, the men had gone looking for the paddle steamers and missed them in the dark. These were old, barely serviceable vessels – a mail packet and a cargo ship – that Bixio and Crispi had commandeered in great secrecy. There could have been no question of taking coal on board prior to departure, since the crew themselves were to know nothing before being roused from their bunks.

In any event, Garibaldi remarked to Bandi, there was no point in whining about it: they had to find a solution. And while the two men considered coastal locations where ammunition might be bought or seized, the general solved another problem. He went to the bow of the ship, pulled down his trousers and hung his backside over the rail, hooking his feet under a rope. Bandi was aghast. What if their charismatic leader were to be lost overboard? Garibaldi "did his business as if he were in the most comfortable room in the house". There are some things that can't be organized in advance. "Don't fuss," Garibaldi told his young assistant, "I'm used to this."

The issue of Garibaldi's organizational skills and indeed the reasons behind his sudden decision to go to Sicily – despite much uncertainty as to what was actually happening there – are central to the question we've set ourselves: how to change the world? Or rather: how is it that some people manage to change it? And as so often with stories, above all true stories, your conclusions will likely depend on the level of detail you're willing to go into. With limited space at one's disposal, there is a tendency to simplify. So I haven't told you, for example, of the last-minute arrival of the mission's money, 90,000 lire (to buy food and supplies), which turned up from the Million Rifles Fund late in the evening of 5th May, only hours before departure, and in the form of a bank draft, which would be of no use in Sicily. Bankers had to be woken in the night to turn the paper into coin. Nor have I mentioned the collusion between Bixio and the agent who worked for the owner of the steamers. Nor about the decision to cut the telegraph wires at Quarto to delay news of the men's departure. In particular, I glossed over Garibaldi's experiences in the Tuscan army in the months between the war of 1859 and this new adventure. But it is the nature of experience that it is densely tangled. Nor is it always clear which strand counts most when the crucial decisions are taken. Those experiences in Tuscany, I suspect, weighed heavily on Garibaldi's mind as he considered his options in Villa Spinola.

He tells the story in his autobiography. After the disappointment of the 1859 armistice, which left the Veneto in Austrian hands, he had resigned his commission in the Piedmontese army and disbanded his volunteer brigade. He had never wanted to be a regular soldier.

Certainly not a peacetime soldier. But now, as Tuscany voted for annexation to Piedmont, he was invited to take over the Tuscan army with a view to moving the revolution south into the Papal States. Hoping to involve his volunteers of some months before, who he felt had been treated shabbily, and to complete the process of Italian unification while circumstances were favourable, he agreed. But on arrival in Tuscany he found he was not made commander in chief, as promised, but second in command. His volunteers were rejected by the Tuscan army. After which he was sent back and forth across the newly annexed territories on all kinds of minor administrative missions. Soon enough he came to the conclusion that the real purpose behind his appointment was to keep him out of trouble and sap his energies. "So I spent several months doing little or nothing when so much could and should have been achieved."

Surely this experience weighed on Garibaldi as he struggled to decide whether to go to Sicily or not. Was the same trick being played on him again? Cavour didn't want to lose popularity by arresting the charismatic hero, but was finding all kinds of ways to discourage the Sicilian mission. This was a powerful reason to go. Then there were the volunteers, old and new, who had flocked to join him. Garibaldi had seen their disappointment when the trip was called off. They wanted to go whatever the risks. Paradoxically, each time the trip was delayed, the numbers of volunteers increased – doubled, even. A tide was rising. The day – 30th April 1860 – that Crispi brought telegrams and letters to Villa Spinola claiming that the Sicilian rebellion was far from dead was the anniversary of the battle, eleven years before, when Garibaldi had defeated the French outside the walls of Rome. Those present in the room as Garibaldi read the reports waited anxiously for his reaction. Everybody knew how suspicious this sudden turnaround was. To many it seemed obvious that Crispi had forged the letters. "Garibaldi thought it over for some time," Bandi remembered, "then got up briskly from his seat, exclaiming in a loud, joyful voice, 'Get ready everybody, we're heading for Sicily.'" He had decided to go with the flow. Five days later, as they clambered into the boats in Quarto, he asked, "How many are we?" And, when informed "A thousand", sighed "So many!"

With this kind of attitude, a lack of ammunition was not going to prove an insuperable obstacle. On the morning of 7th May, the general issued a proclamation that was read aloud to the men: "The mission of this corps will be based on the most complete self-denial before the regeneration of the Homeland." On the morning of 8th May, the *Piemonte* and the *Lombardo*, for so the two ships were called, dropped anchor in the bay of Talamone on the Tuscan coast, two hundred miles south of Quarto ("Desolate, solemn landscape of the Tuscan Maremma," observed Ippolito Nievo in his diary). And it now turned out that Garibaldi had brought along his Piedmontese general's uniform from the war of the year before. He put it on to greet the commander of the local garrison, who boarded the ship to make the regulation sanitary checks. He also hoisted the Piedmontese flag and managed to find half a dozen other men who had Piedmontese army uniforms. He was on a mission, he told the commander, that was dear to the heart of King Vittorio Emanuele – who, however, could not appear to be involved and hence hadn't signed any written orders.

An envoy was then sent to the larger, better-equipped garrison of Orbetello, fifteen miles to the south, to spin the same story, which was true in its way, or not entirely false. The commander from Orbetello came to Talamone to talk to Garibaldi. Finding himself in a difficult position – an illegal request from the best-loved man in the realm – the commander dithered. Garibaldi schmoozed, complimenting everyone he spoke to, including the women who rustled up lunch in the village's only trattoria. The Tuscans were such wonderful people, he enthused, and the following morning was rewarded with the delivery of two old cannons and a quantity of empty cartridges, together with the gunpowder and iron shot with which to fill them. It wasn't enough. Bandi was dispatched to Orbetello to persuade the commander to give them more. You may as well be hung for a sheep as a lamb, the man was told. More rusty rifles were found. The cannons were brought up to five. One, a culverin, remembered Crispi, bore the inscription "*Opus Joannis Mariæ...* 1570."

Other events during the Thousand's brief stay in Talamone suggest how pointless it is to talk about organization in the way one might in a professional army. The men were disembarked in the early afternoon of 8th May, split into companies, assigned commanders and taken through some basic military drills. Then they began to look around the small fishing village for something to eat and drink. Some sat in churches and felt homesick, some wrote to their mothers to confess that they had volunteered for a mad adventure. Others swam in the bay. One man offered entertainment trying to ride a mule up the main street – was thrown, injured and sent to hospital, his mad adventure already over. A much larger number set about chasing the local women. "Although the Thousand included some of the cream of Italy's youth," Bandi observed, "there was also a generous sprinkling of wild and wayward types." Soon enough the bedlam was such that Garibaldi had to be called upon to intervene. Furious, he ordered everyone back on board. The general was so impatient, Nievo noted, "he grabbed the oars himself to row out to the ships."

But Garibaldi also took advantage of the stopover in Talamone to send off sixty men under the command of Callimaco Zambianchi on a mission to stir up a revolution in the Papal States immediately to the south, thus hopefully discouraging the pope from sending military aid to the Bourbons in Sicily. It was the move Cavour most feared, since it would upset the French. Watching this sideshow unfold, however, Bandi wondered whether Garibaldi hadn't simply found an excuse to be rid of a man he disliked: Zambianchi was vainglorious, disruptive and violent. When a handful of Mazzini supporters objected to Garibaldi's flying the royal flag and wearing his Piedmontese uniform, he warned them to take it or leave it: there was no room for dissenters. Half a dozen "puritans", as Bandi calls the Mazzinians, chose to stay behind. At the same time, it emerged that scores of soldiers from the Orbetello garrison had sneaked on board the ships: they wanted to fight for Italy. But Garibaldi had given the king his word of honour that he wouldn't steal his officers. Or not too many. Hours were lost finding these men and convincing them to return to their posts. "They clung to the ropes, climbed the masts, hid under covers," Bandi wrote. When the ships finally weighed anchor, four were still aboard.

As I mull over all this material – so many diaries and memoirs – I'm struck by the tumultuous vitality of these men born two centuries ago: how quickly and resolutely they took decisions that would compromise their careers and put their lives at risk, but also how implacably they tied their willingness to accept discipline to the pursuit of their shared cause. They were ready to die to make Italy, but never to "behave" merely for the sake of it.

Garibaldi knew this. He was riding a wave that must be harnessed and directed before its energy was lost or things got out of hand. But this was what he was good at, unlike Prime Minister Cavour, who always yearned for more time to weave his intricate webs of diplomacy. So the one took the initiative while the other tried to tie him in knots. On Cavour's orders, Zambianchi was soon arrested and his men dispersed. Very likely Garibaldi had expected this.

Departing Talamone on 10th May at 4 a.m., the ships stopped just hours later at the small port of Santo Stefano, where there was a government coal depot. And while the day before Garibaldi had sent his most diplomatic and gracious collaborator, István Türr, a Hungarian who had fought in the Piedmontese army, to speak to the military commander at Orbetello, now, to procure coal for their journey as rapidly as possible, he sent Nino Bixio. So here we must pause our story for a moment to introduce this extraordinary man. But do not imagine that we are going to reach any settled opinion about him. Bixio was off the scale.

Named Gerolamo, but never baptized, Bixio was born in Genoa, the last of eight siblings, in 1821. One brother died in infancy, one joined the British navy and disappeared, believed thrown overboard. A third was given in infancy to a French family and became a doctor in Paris. A fourth followed his father's profession as a goldsmith. A fifth would join the Jesuits in New York. The two sisters married into well-to-do families when Girolamo was still a child.

Having bequeathed him the cute pet name Nino, the boy's iron-handed mother died when he was eight. To the dismay of the children, the milder father remarried. Nino was utterly neglected. The house was a free-for-all. Combining a readiness for violence with an instinct to side with underdogs, Nino was expelled from school for hurling an inkwell at his teacher. Any perceived injustice was an excuse for a fight. When he was thirteen, his family, unable to cope, sent him to sea as a ship's boy. Like Dickens in his blacking factory, what most infuriated Nino was his demotion to the lowest of the low. He had been excluded from his own middle-class sort, reduced to cleaning latrines. The sailors mocked his well-to-do manners. Off the Argentine coast he jumped ship twice and was twice recaptured. Back in Genoa his parents now tried to force him into the navy in place of his elder brother, the future Jesuit, who had been conscripted. Nino refused. He was thrown out of the house, but granted a bowl of food, once a day, at a door or window. Aged sixteen, he slept on the street, never far from the next fight. After some months, when the police were sent to arrest him, he fled across roofs, leaping over the narrow alleys of the old port.

Finally captured and forcibly enrolled in the navy, Nino settled down to study, and over five years became an expert seaman. Among the young officers there were many Mazzinians. Bixio read their publications and was converted to the cause of that larger family, Italy, which hopefully would treat him better than his father and stepmother had. However, returning to Genoa, now a handsome man in his early twenties, he thrust himself back into his own close family in a quite unorthodox manner, falling in love with Adelaide, the daughter of his much older sister. "It was his account of all he had been through," his niece would one day explain, "that induced me to love him." For a decade and more the two carried on a romance, mainly epistolary, that was fiercely opposed by more or less everyone.

Unexpectedly bought out of the navy by the Parisian brother, whom he had never met, Nino went to sea again, this time on commercial vessels. In Brazil he was offered the captaincy of a ship trading slaves, but refused. Slavery was a disgrace, he said. Freedom was everything. In the South Pacific, oppressed by a Quaker captain who forbade all forms of merriment, he and two companions jumped overboard to swim to the coast which they supposed was nearby. It wasn't. There were sharks. One man died. Collapsing on the beach after many hours in the water, Nino found himself imprisoned by Malays, who threatened forced circumcision and conversion to Islam. Fortunately, the Quaker captain turned up to ransom him. Returning to Genoa via New York in 1847, he was soon prominent in the liberal movements that preceded the 1848 revolution. He became a close friend of poet and patriot Goffredo Mameli, who wrote Italy's national anthem, *Fratelli d'Italia*. Mameli encouraged *fratello* Nino to keep a diary, thanks to which we can read his account of the disastrous military campaign that Piedmont fought against Austria that year. Bixio had volunteered. His prose is terse and lucid, with none of the flowery rhetoric of the time. Surprisingly, this wild man seems closer to us today than his more conventional contemporaries.

Disgusted by the capitulation of the Piedmontese, in 1849 Bixio moved south to the Roman Republic and served under Garibaldi. It was the meeting he had been waiting for. Here was a commander he respected utterly, a man who could channel his manic energy towards some useful achievement. In the battle of 30th April, as the French began to retreat under the pressure of Garibaldi's counter-attack,

Bixio galloped wildly after a French major, grabbed him by the collar and ordered him to have his men lay down their arms. Three hundred French cavalrymen were captured. On 3rd June, during the disastrous attempt to retake Villa Corsini on the Gianicolo Hill, Bixio had two horses shot under him. Then was shot himself. The bullet sank deep into his groin. In hospital he lay beside his friend Mameli, whose apparently innocuous leg wound would lead to gangrene and death. Bixio was with him to the end. A month later, after the city capitulated, and still with the French bullet in his body, he returned to Genoa, where, to everyone's amazement, his stepmother took him in and nursed him back to health.

Now Bixio raised the money to build his own ship, named the *Mameli*. In 1855, after years of frustrating ecclesiastic vetoes, he won the right to scandalize polite society and marry his beloved niece, Adelaide. Shortly after the wedding he left her, pregnant, to set sail for Australia. The voyage was a disaster. Returning from Melbourne, the *Mameli* was severely battered off the Cape of Good Hope, its cargo lost. In 1858, after two years away, Bixio returned home to wife, child and bankruptcy just as the political scene was hotting up again. Undeterred, he started a newspaper, *La Nazione*, which every day exhorted Piedmont to free northern Italy from Austrian occupation. Again Bixio's writing style was plain, hardly brilliant, but effective. A meeting with Cavour ensued. When war broke out in 1859, Bixio joined Garibaldi's volunteers. "Always first, always in the thick of it," wrote his friend Giuseppe Guerzoni, "tireless on long marches, unflagging in all camp duties, tempestuous, ever impatient, occasionally violent, constantly showing what he might do but never getting the opportunity to do it… That, in a nutshell, is the story of Bixio during that brief campaign."

A year later Garibaldi gave this impatient man his chance. When the Thousand set sail from Quarto, Bixio was placed in charge of the *Lombardo*, the larger of the two ships, and thus became, we might say, the second most important man in the Thousand. "But please," Bandi begged Garibaldi after taking part in the expedition to requisition coal, "please, never put me under Bixio's command." Their orders that morning had been to persuade the soldiers guarding the depot to hand over the coal willingly, peacefully. However, as soon as one officer began to speak of requiring permission from his superiors,

Bixio grabbed the man by the scruff of his neck and started yelling orders. "The devil," Garibaldi shook his head. "He never changes." But he was pleased to have his coal without delay.

On the open sea again, the men spent their time cleaning rusty rifles, packing cartridges with gunpowder (there would be twenty each) and trying to find a tune for the patriotic hymn that Garibaldi had written – to no avail. Nobody liked the words, which were plodding and pompous ("The Foreigner tramples my land / Slaughters my flock"). Eventually, they fell back on a raucous song that mixed patriotism and bawdy. Garibaldi withdrew to his cabin.

All this on the smaller ship, the mail packet *Piemonte*, carrying just 300 men. Behind, on the larger, slower *Lombardo*, hatless, dishevelled and dangerously tense, Bixio paced the bridge looking daggers at his 800 tightly packed volunteers. "His profile cuts like a sabre," wrote Cesare Abba. "When he frowns, we all try to look small." Bixio was worried that some men were wearing red shirts on deck. An enemy might see. He was worried about the din they were making. It might drown out some important command, or a cry from the lookouts on the masts. Bixio, as his diary shows, was always worried. He noted that there were 340 men sleeping on the starboard side and 370 on the port side. The ship must stay trim. When someone complained about the food at table, Bixio hurled a plate in his face. He called the men together for an important announcement.

"I'm young! I'm thirty-seven and I've been round the world! I've been shipwrecked, I've been jailed. But now here I am, and I'm in command! On this ship I'm everything – I'm the tsar, I'm the sultan, I'm the pope. I'm Nino Bixio! You all have to obey me. Woe betide anyone who thinks they can turn their back or plot against me: I'll be on to you with my uniform, my medals, my sabre, and kill you all. The general has put me in charge with the order to get you to Sicily. And I'm going to get you there. Then you can hang me from the first tree. But before you do, by God, I'll get you to Sicily."

The men applauded. "We would have given our lives for him," Abba says.

On the *Piemonte*, Garibaldi was also concerned about the noise. His speech was shorter and quieter, but essentially the same: "The only voice to be heard on board must be mine. The first hothead who disobeys can expect to be thrown overboard."

With all this talk of killing and dying, it was probably inevitable that someone would try to beat the others to it. Leaving Quarto the first night, the *Piemonte* had had to stop to recover a man overboard. In Talamone this rescued man switched to the *Lombardo*. Now, on 10th May, with everything at last proceeding smoothly and the ships steaming west between Sardinia and Sicily, the man plunged into the sea again. The *Lombardo* stopped its engines. Again a boat was launched, and the flailing man pulled out of the water. Typically, Bixio switched from fury over the wasted time to compassion for a disturbed companion. The would-be suicide was given dry clothes and a cabin to himself, under guard.

Sea and Islands

We flew over the sea they sailed. Out of the windows, we caught glimpses of blue through billowing cloud. Sardinia was to our right; a black freighter trailed a white wake beneath us. Gazing down at that slow, steady ship, I was aware of envying the garibaldini. I envied them their contact with wind and water. And with each other. Of course they faced hardships, but they enjoyed a collective purpose that convinced them their sufferings were worthwhile. They were in life up to the eyeballs. Bandi talks of the men's pleasure when a school of dolphins passed by, leaping from wave to wave, and of Garibaldi's pleasure watching their pleasure. What would one not give to have been there? On the other hand, in our comfortable seats, we didn't have to worry about being blown out of the water by an enemy ship. The Neapolitan navy counted twenty-two well-armed steamships and ten sailing frigates. One diarist, Ippolito Nievo, was convinced they would die at sea. If a ship should intercept you, Garibaldi told Bixio, don't wait to be fired on: head straight for it, ram it side on, grapple and board. Which was exactly what Bixio did, or tried to do, when, during the night of 10th May, a ship ghosted into view, close by, showing no lights.

A little geography is useful. The more or less rectangular island of Sardinia lies on a north–south meridian that runs straight down to the Tunisian coast some 120 miles away. From that coast, Sicily is about 100 miles due east. So we have a triangle: Sardinia, Tunisia, Sicily. Or, more precisely, Cagliari, Tunis, Trapani. Had Garibaldi been planning to head straight for Palermo, on Sicily's north coast, where the Bourbon army was 20,000 strong, he would have kept well away from Sardinia and not even entered this triangle. Instead, he told his helmsmen to set a course that would take them between Sardinia and Sicily towards Tunis. Only when they were well beyond the western tip of Sicily did the order come to turn south, then east. It was important to keep the Neapolitans guessing.

But the night of 10th May was dark. The *Piemonte* was three knots faster than the *Lombardo*. The two lost sight of each other. Garibaldi cursed himself and turned back. Bixio saw a ship looming and manoeuvred to ram. Garibaldi counter-manoeuvred. The big paddles thrashed. On the decks of both ships men prepared for action. Rifles were loaded, cannons primed. Only when the two hulls were perilously close did Bixio's helmsman recognize the bell that Garibaldi used to give his helmsman orders.

Would Italian unity have been delayed a decade had the ships collided? Or a hundred years? Or for ever? So much can go awry when you're trying to change the world on a shoestring.

Disaster averted, the next question was where to land. Aware that if you plan meticulously beforehand it may be hard to adapt to circumstance, Garibaldi kept things flexible and told no one his intentions. That way he wouldn't seem to be changing his mind. On the morning of 11th May his lookouts sighted the Egadi, three small islands some miles off the west coast of Sicily: Marettimo, Levanzo and the larger Favignana. "It's as if they had just risen from the waves," wrote Cesare Abba. "Greens of every shade, shining rock in the blue air and a line of silver all around." Garibaldi took his ships between Marettimo and Favignana, then, once south of the islands, turned towards Sicily as if approaching from Africa.

There had been talk of proceeding south and west along the Sicilian coast to Mazara del Vallo or Sciacca. But it was already late in the morning. Garibaldi took advice from the Sicilians on board and chose the nearest port, Marsala. He wanted all men and gear offloaded before evening. No sooner was the decision made than three ships were spotted to the south-east, moving rapidly towards them along the coast from Mazara – Neapolitan warships: two steam-powered, one sail. A race was on. Since the wind was behind them, the *Piemonte* and the *Lombardo* raised their sails to gain speed.

I had been hoping to approach Marsala from the sea as the garibaldini had, with the sun in my eyes and the breeze on my face – to see what they had seen, more or less, and be, however superficially, *in their position*. My grandfather was a ship's captain, sunk and killed in the Atlantic by a German submarine. My father, who worked in a Liverpool shipyard through the war, yearned for the sea and missed no chance to take us out in boats. I learned to love the sting of salt, the slap of a wave. Even today, the faintest sniff of the sea is a thrill.

My wife Eleonora grew up in the ancient port of Taranto. She has the sea in her blood. So although it had proved impossible to book a long sea voyage, we thought we might at least approach Marsala from the nearby island of Favignana. There were ferries from Trapani to Favignana, then from Favignana to Marsala. We had set a day aside.

But just as the Thousand found Sicily quite different from their imaginings, so nothing went as we had planned. We had seen there were regular departures from Trapani. We had not realized that the vessels were hydrofoils, where one sits enclosed, as in an aeroplane, peering through grubby windows. There were, it's true, one or two more traditional ferries, carrying cars, but they were few, and all booked up. Even the hydrofoils, leaving hourly, were mostly booked. We would be travelling on Sunday. Favignana is a day-trip destination. Since 1860 the population of Sicily has doubled from two and a half million to five. People like to get away at the weekend. On Saturday evening, the ticket office on the seafront was doing brisk business. We settled for leaving Trapani at 9 a.m. and getting the boat from Favignana to Marsala at 2 p.m. the same day. There was very little choice.

Landing at Palermo airport, at Punta Raisi, you see a rugged mountainous coast, of grey brown rocks in a haze of heat. On the bus heading west to Trapani you move through a parched rolling landscape of dusty yellows and dark greens. To the south of Trapani, along the coast, there are extensive salt flats, the land being divided up much as the rice fields in Lombardy, but white, as if under a crust of snow. There are also any number of old windmills. Who would have thought? The historic centre of Trapani clusters on a small promontory at the north-western tip of Sicily with the busy port to one side and beaches to the other. It is at once a very Italian town – the monuments, street signs, restaurants, churches – yet a different Italy from the one I know. There is something Arabic about the squat white buildings along the seafront. There are no terracotta roofs. The people are darker, either lean and lithe or thick and chubby. There seems to be no body shape in between. In the Jesuit church of the Immaculate Conception, where a woman with a primitive prosthetic hand enthuses about rococo as she sells us our tickets, the cherubs are all gorgeously chubby and the saints austerely lean. Hundreds of cherubs, scores of saints. An aesthetic of overkill. And the woman's fake hand – it looks like it might have been borrowed from a plaster Madonna – starts me thinking of all the wounds and amputations the garibaldini were headed for. The pain and gangrene and death. How can I be enthusiastic?

But in Piazza Garibaldi, the General still stands whole and marble-white, his noble statue recently cleaned.

> A HUNDRED YEARS FROM THE REVOLUTION
> WHICH MADE ITALY ON THESE SHORES,
> UNITED ROUND THE HERO
> WITH SUBLIME MEMORIES
> AND IDEALS FOREVER FRESH,
> THE PEOPLE OF TRAPANI,
> THEIR GENEROUS SPIRIT
> BRIMMING WITH CIVIL JOYS AND FEARS,
> REVERENT AND STIRRED,
> REMEMBER PAST GREATNESS,
> NOBLE THOUGHTS AND DEEDS
> THAT SHOW PROMISE FOR THE FUTURE.

"Always and ever," a plaque on the town hall reminds us, "it is with the blood of the people that history's great epics are written."

Located in a narrow alley, the B&B Terrazza sul Porto duly provides breakfast on its rooftop terrace, from where, between pink-stuccoed palazzi, you can indeed glimpse the sea. At 8 a.m., after a rough night, everything is already blindingly bright, ominously warm. When our landlady, bringing abundant quantities of pastries and fruit, enquires about our plans, we are bound to mention Garibaldi. She's impressed. "Though now they tell us," she sighs, "that actually we were better off under the Bourbons."

"Fact is," announces a man who is rocking himself on a swing sofa by a pot of oleander, "historians always say whatever suits their agenda. You can't get to the truth."

I'm eating a peach, enjoying the bright morning. But this is a bait I always rise to.

"It's hard to deny," I tell him, "agenda or no agenda, that shortly after midday on 11th May 1860 about a thousand men landed at Marsala. Led by Giuseppe Garibaldi. There are so many documents. And that by the end of the year the Bourbon kingdom had collapsed and Italy was made."

"Right," my man says, "but what were the English warships doing in Marsala harbour when Garibaldi arrived? It was an international conspiracy!"

It is true that as the *Piemonte* raced towards Marsala with Bixio's *Lombardo* wallowing behind and the Neapolitan warships closing in, two more ships were sighted – not in the harbour, but anchored a half-mile or so to the south. Far from being part of a conspiracy, this was cause for further anxiety. Soon one could be identified, simply by its distinctive shape, as a British sloop. But the other? Neither was flying a flag. Garibaldi wasted precious time intercepting a fishing boat, partly to get news and partly to commandeer a means for a rapid disembarkation. The terrified fishermen could only confirm that the Bourbon navy had left Marsala the previous day. They didn't know what these other ships were. Only as the *Piemonte* drew between the ships and the harbour did they raise their flags – the White Ensign. For upwards of fifty years Marsala had been home to the companies first of John Woodhouse, then Benjamin Ingham, both producing Marsala fortified wine in quantities for the British market, and in particular for the Royal Navy. So there was a considerable British community in the town. Indeed, the harbour had been built specifically to service this trade with the United Kingdom. When the liberal revolution had begun in April, there had been demonstrations in Marsala, and the Italian tricolour had been flown. In early May Bourbon soldiers arrived, made arrests and ordered all weapons to be handed over. The Brits were not exempt. As a result, the British community had requested the presence of Royal Navy warships, then based in Palermo, to protect their considerable assets. Garibaldi knew nothing of this. Nor did he expect help from the warships as the *Piemonte* entered harbour and the men began to disembark, in great haste, opposite Ingham's bottling factory.

We also made haste to climb on our hydrofoil for our less eventful trip to Favignana. It's a short cruise. After twenty minutes the boat stops at the tiny island of Levanzo, where the harbour contrives to be both quaint and squalid: small white, flat-roofed houses with blue shutters are dwarfed by the barren rock face behind. But the sea is splendidly transparent, and each big yacht moored in the bay looks like it carries a price tag that could buy the whole island twice over.

From here it was just ten minutes to Favignana, where everyone disembarked and hurried to the main piazza for coffee or granitas. The port is a charming old place, once poverty-stricken, now spruced up for tourism. Given the fierce glare of the sunshine, you're inevitably drawn to the shade under white awnings where Sicilian specialities are on offer – at Milan prices. The attempt to create an atmosphere of hedonistic ease doesn't quite come off, which confers a curious poignancy on the bare piazzas and narrow streets. It's as if the town were trying too hard to deny centuries of privation. Above and behind, always visible at the top of a steep, conical hill, is the glum old fortress of Santa Caterina, which in 1860 was a prison. "Up there," observed Garibaldi as the *Piemonte* steamed past, punishing its engines for maximum speed, "is poor Nicotera."

Giovanni Nicotera had fought in Rome in 1849, and was one of the leaders of Pisacane's disastrous Calabrian adventure. He was serving a life sentence. The Bourbon prisons were notorious. "The negation of God erected into a system of government," Gladstone wrote after visiting the kingdom in 1850. Whatever the revisionists say now about life before Italian unification, all the evidence is that the Sicilians loathed rule from Naples. There was no freedom of press and no freedom of movement, even within the island. Permission was required to travel from town to town. Since very few Sicilians served in the Neapolitan army, it was inevitably seen as an army of occupation. Without this hostility, the mission of the Thousand would have been impossible. Nicotera later claimed that he had glimpsed the two ships from his cell window and wondered what was up. Days later he would be free.

The port of Favignana lies on the north side of the island. With a couple of hours at our disposal we walked along the coast east to see where the *Piemonte* and the *Lombardo* passed. But our path soon petered out. Broad shoals of low lava rocks stretch out into the sea. Inland, the country is a flat expanse of parched grass and crumbling walls. Palms, prickly pears, cactuses.

Returning to the port to make our connection to Marsala, we noticed a side street, with the name Via Pilota di Garibaldi. None of the sources I have read mentions a pilot, though Bixio would have done well to use one. While the *Piemonte* slipped easily into Marsala's small harbour and anchored close by the wharf, the heavier *Lombardo* ran aground just outside. The Neapolitan ships were approaching fast.

Marsala

"There lies Marsala, with its walls, its white houses and green gardens, its pretty slope down to the sea." So wrote Cesare Abba, while still on the deck of the *Lombardo*. And this description, together with a sketch map in Trevelyan's version of the story, showing a square of walled town to the top left, half a mile from the shore, and then the large English factories along the coast to the bottom right, was the simple image I had made for myself of Marsala. But through the murky windows of the Liberty Lines hydrofoil, what we actually saw was miles and miles of seafront apartment blocks. The area between the sea and the walls of the old town had long since been built up. This shouldn't have come as a surprise, of course, but it did. My head was stuck in 1860. Fortunately nothing is easier, once you have landed in Marsala, than to ignore these modern buildings. They are perfectly anonymous. As so often in Italy, only the old town matters: the rest exists merely because there is no longer room for everyone to live in the old centre – a suburban embarrassment that no one talks about, no one describes, as if nothing could ever be added to the things that count, built centuries ago.

"At 1.15 p.m. we arrive in Marsala," noted Francesco Crispi, who was travelling on the *Piemonte*. "At 2.15 the landing was completed in perfect order."

"One of the Neapolitan steamships arrives," jotted Nievo, "but doesn't open fire. Perhaps it's waiting for the frigate, which is being towed by the other steamship. The general is the last to leave the *Piemonte*."

No one could understand why the Neapolitans weren't firing at the grounded *Lombardo*, which was still spilling its men into the boats that raced out towards them from the harbour – a sitting target.

"The landing was effected in gallant style, and with the most extraordinary celerity and order," wrote an English eyewitness in a letter to *The Times*.

"On the shore our legs wobbled, still at sea," remembers Abba.

The Neapolitans continued to hold their fire.

"You would think they were short of powder," Giuseppe Bandi observed. He and the general were standing on the drum that covered the *Piemonte*'s port paddle, taking turns to gaze through Garibaldi's telescope. With the aid of its powerful lens they could see the English sailors, far away to the left, lined up on their decks to watch the scene. They could also see the Bourbon cannons trained on Bixio's ship and on the harbour wall, where the garibaldini were disembarking their equipment. "You should get out of sight, general," Bandi warned.

From the hydrofoil we disembarked, not on the harbour wall, but directly onto the land, where a line of taxis were waiting. Out of habit, we walked. At the point where the old harbour wall meets the land there is a roundabout, its grass withered brown by the sun. In the middle, a large stone plinth, seemingly the base for a statue that isn't there, bears this inscription:

> MARSALA
> MINDFUL AND PROUD
> IN ETERNAL MEMORY
> OF THE PLACE WHERE
> THE THOUSAND
> AND THEIR LEADER GARIBALDI
> DISEMBARKED.
> IN ANTICIPATION OF A MORE WORTHY MONUMENT.
> 11TH MAY 1893

From this roundabout a narrow street – Via dei Mille – leads diagonally inland towards the old city gate, now Porta Garibaldi. This must have been the way – only a path at the time – that István Türr took, leading the first fifty men, mostly Sicilians, off the ship and into the town. Their orders were to check that the situation was safe and to cut any telegraph wires. The locals, who had come out to watch, fled. They had no idea who these armed men were. There was no sign of any revolutionaries, nor of Bourbon soldiers.

"Lifting my eyes, the arch of the gate seemed the entrance to an Arab city," wrote Abba. "Yet at the same time it felt like the gate of my own village [in Liguria], which also has an arch like this."

It's a curious observation. The truth is that Marsala, like Trapani, feels foreign to me too, despite my forty years in Italy. Perhaps it has to do with a certain Sicilian style of neglect, such that anything new or orderly seems fragile and superficial. At any moment it will be swept away, and the world returned to its natural state of calamity and decay.

"The streets were all but deserted," wrote Bandi, who was sent on a mission to find the Piedmontese consul. "Doors and windows were hastily shut... Three or four beggars came with hands held out, calling me 'Your Excellency'."

But now, after an hour's delay, the Bourbon cannons at last began to fire. Why had they waited so long? Published in 1888 in *The Illustrated Naval and Military Magazine*, the journal of Commander Herbert Frederick Winnington-Ingram, captain of HMS *Argus*, solves the mystery of that precious reprieve that allowed the men of the *Lombardo* to land safely. Since March 1860, the *Argus* had been stationed in Palermo, where its captain, Winnington-Ingram, had been in a position to observe the disturbances of the April revolution. The dockside execution, by firing squad, of its thirteen ringleaders, had been visible and audible from the bridge of his ship. Many local British residents, but Sicilians too, had brought their valuables on board the *Argus* for safekeeping. In Palermo Winnington-Ingram met the wealthy Ingham family of Marsala, who eventually fled the island on 4th May. Many other foreign residents also left as sporadic fighting continued. Constantly sharing information with the British consul in the town, the captain visited the main city cemetery and saw the bodies of five soldiers being tossed into a lime pit. Otherwise he spent his time shooting quail and arranging for amateur dramatics to amuse the local Brits and anglophiles. "Our principal actor," he writes in his journal, "an ordinary seaman, excelled himself in the 'Thumping Legacy' [otherwise known as 'A Cockney in Corsica', by John Maddison Morton]. A grand supper finished the evening entertainment."

That was 9th May. On 10th May, the *Argus* received orders to accompany HMS *Intrepid* to Marsala. On the morning of 11th May, the two ships dropped anchor at a safe distance from the coast and the harbour entrance; throughout the brief voyage, Winnington-Ingram had been worried about narrow channels and shallow water. Both he and Commander Marryat, captain of the *Intrepid*, went ashore at once to speak to the British consul and the managers of the Woodhouse and

Ingham wine companies, whose property they had been instructed to protect. It was at this point, shortly after midday, that the *Piemonte* and the *Lombardo* steamed towards the harbour, closely followed by the first of the Neapolitan warships, the *Stromboli*. "It was a critical moment, and we asked each other's opinion as to whether she [the *Stromboli*] would open fire upon that vessel [the *Lombardo*] before the men were clear of her, for if so, we might witness a fearful slaughter under our very eyes, and at the same time stand a good chance of being ourselves struck by a ricochet shot."

However, rather than firing, the *Stromboli* changed direction to approach the *Intrepid*, which was the closer of the British ships. Some time later, a boat arrived on shore from the *Intrepid* to inform Marryat and Winnington-Ingram that the Neapolitan captain had wanted to know whether the men wearing red shirts on the *Lombardo* were British troops, since that was the traditional colour of their uniform. Receiving a response to the negative, but being told nevertheless that there were British officers on shore, the Neapolitan captain had asked that they be warned to get out of the way, since he was about to start firing – which, shortly afterwards, he did.

Alarmed, the British captains had themselves rowed out to the *Stromboli* to ask that the Neapolitans take great care not to hit the British properties which were in the line of fire. However, very soon afterwards, the Neapolitan frigate arrived and began "a veritable storm of shot and missiles of all kinds". Thanks to a rough sea, most of these managed to miss the harbour wall along which the garibaldini were unloading the last of their gear, so that in the event, despite the noise and the terrifying whistle of cannon balls and grapeshot, only two garibaldini were wounded. "One shot, however, entered Mr Woodhouse's wine establishment and nearly killed Mrs Harvey, the manager's wife."

The Neapolitans now sent a messenger to HMS *Intrepid* asking Captain Marryat to contact the commanders of the two rebel ships and induce them to surrender. Marryat refused. His instructions were to remain strictly neutral. In any event, Augusto Elia, Bixio's helmsman on the *Lombardo*, had scuttled the ship, which would soon be lying on its side. The *Piemonte*, on the other hand, was towed away by the Neapolitan ships, which were not carrying sufficient troops to contemplate a land assault. As Garibaldi summed up in his memoirs,

"The formidable colours of Great Britain flying on two warships of the country's powerful navy, as well as on the factories along the seafront, made the Neapolitans hesitate." In short, he had been lucky. "On the harbour wall the patriots stood fire splendidly," concluded Winnington-Ingram. "Hostilities ceased at sunset."

The sun sets late in Sicily at this time of the year. We took a walk through the town, which seemed dazed and deserted in the early evening heat. A grizzled old man selling souvenirs kept moving his barrow to keep it in the shade. No one was buying.

With time on our hands, we walked to the coast north of the harbour, then turned back towards it. In Piazza della Vittoria another monument marks the spot where Garibaldi landed, this time with a bust of the hero. It is about half a mile from the other monument, purporting to mark the same event. In between, by the seafront, in a huge empty plaza of white cement, is the extraordinary "Monumento ai Mille", completed in 2016. Were those words not written on it, however, you would have no idea what the monstrous structure was – nor is it easy to describe, since one cannot appeal to anything the reader already knows. Essentially, two parallel shapes, vaguely recalling the hulls of ships, have been sunk into the ground and surrounded by an oval of white wall and railings. Inside the wall, in a kind of semi-basement below the concrete hulls, is a small museum and conference centre, while above, on deck, as it were, the names of the Thousand are inscribed in copper plate. However, when we visited, the monument was closed. It was also cluttered with litter and defaced with graffiti. "A Tourist Attraction" is Trip Advisor's classification. Apparently it cost 600 million euros. "CITY OF MARSALA, GOLD MEDAL FOR CIVIC MERIT" announces a plaque. Of the three monuments, one has to prefer the earliest, the empty plinth near the old harbour wall with its poignant combination of pride and inadequacy.

Where the harbour wall begins, you move from seafront gardens to a neglected area of derelict warehouses, broken glass and rotting scaffolding. Unkempt men in shirtsleeves lounge about camper vans beside a melancholy merry-go-round. No children are about. We walked out along the harbour wall, where fishermen were preparing their nets and boats for the night ahead. This was more cheerful. The boats are tiny ramshackle craft, their hulls invariably painted white and blue. There are no expensive yachts here, no modern marina, and no evening strollers beside ourselves. Just as in Trevelyan's diagram, the harbour wall projects a couple of hundred yards from the land, then bends left to form an arm about a quarter of a mile long protecting the seafront where the Woodhouse and Ingham factories once stood. At the end of the wall is a white lighthouse, and, moored alongside it, an abandoned cable ship, orange with rust. Over the sea to the west, the sun is sinking so that the light gleams on the ruffled water where Bixio ran aground. We are standing where the grapeshot flew. And a sudden wind rises – a warm, damp, strange wind. The notorious sirocco.

Returning to our bedsit, we notice these words inscribed in stone:

> AT DAWN OF 12TH MAY 1860
> GASPARE COLICCHIA
> A HUMBLE COTTON WORKER
> LEFT WIFE AND DAUGHTER
> IN THIS HOUSE
> TO FOLLOW
> GIUSEPPE GARIBALDI'S THOUSAND
> AND DIE A HERO
> FOR A FREE AND JUST ITALY
> AT CALATAFIMI
> 15TH MAY 1860

The words seem more a warning than a commemoration.

Towards Salemi

"I'm sitting on a stone, by my company's arms pile, in this small, squalid, fearful piazza."

Cesare Abba always tells us where he is writing his notes. He was twenty-one, had studied classics and philosophy, and trained for the Piedmontese military. More than other diarists, he is curious about his fellow volunteers, eager to make friends, open to the Sicilians: "Monks of every colour were shouting at the tops of their voices. Women and girls admiring from balconies. I drank from the amphora of a young peasant girl coming back from the well. Rebecca!"

You feel he always wants to see things positively, poetically even, and is distressed when the world won't let him: "We passed by some hovels where people were waking up to their poverty, half open, filthy."

Above all, he expresses the common soldier's anxiety of not knowing what is going on or why: "Cannons firing furiously at the town. Many houses flying flags of other nations. Mainly English. What is that about?"

Published in 1880, his book seems authentically based on jottings made on the run.

"Entry in Marsala. Terrified look of the town."

Ippolito Nievo was twenty-eight and had already published collections of poetry and short stories. For the moment his great novel, *The Confessions of an Italian*, was still an unedited manuscript packed away in a trunk. His diary would be published posthumously, and is no more than the telegraphic notes he scribbled day by day with no later elaboration. Even the spelling is sometimes wrong.

"Seizure of public coffers, full of miserable copper coins. The gold coin from the Million Rifles Fund is used for all purchases, but first we have to issue a proclamation to make it legal tender."

Nievo had studied law and had an administrator's eye for the legal and financial side of the expedition, something Garibaldi would later reward. But he was unsettled by the realities of Sicily.

"African aspect of the country. Women veiled like Saracens."

"Approaching the town we saw one of the cannons still on the beach, and sent for a cart and quadruped."

A seaman by trade, helmsman of the *Lombardo*, Augusto Elia was thirty years old, but would not publish this memoir until his late sixties.

"Since the cannon had no carriage, we decided to tie it under the axle of the cart – and, being the strongest, I crawled under. But whether because the horse was skittish or perhaps I had upset it, it gave me such a kick in the back I thought I was done for."

Elia's patriotic father had been executed in 1849 for his part in the liberal revolution in Ancona. Passionately devoted to the cause, Elia himself proved woefully accident-prone on this trip. Nevertheless, he was determined to keep going: "At the house where General Garibaldi slept, I was able to get myself rubbed with alcohol and bandaged, and with a night's rest was well enough to march beside my companions in the morning."

"Marsala was all but deserted."

Giuseppe Bandi was twenty-five, son of a top-flight civil servant in the erstwhile Grand Duchy of Tuscany.

"However, as we were walking towards the castle, a hundred people crowded round asking us to point out Garibaldi. I did so, but when he turned and greeted them, they shook their heads and said in their very African way of speaking: 'What? Is that Garibaldi? Are you joking? It can't be.' Without a fancy uniform the general didn't look the part."

In 1858 Bandi had been jailed for helping three Mazzinians on the run. Released in 1859, he had joined the Piedmontese army, but not in time to fight in the war of that year. As Garibaldi's personal assistant, he was as proud and jealous of his master as ever a young man can be. In particular, he admired his modesty.

"I asked where the general was, and they led me to a humble-looking house... Soon I was helping to lay the table, on which there was sheep's cheese, some bread rolls, a basket of broad beans and two jugs of white wine. It was a meagre supper, and no one was satisfied, except the general, who declared it sumptuous, praising the beans to high heaven."

You never feel, though, that Bandi has any plans to emulate Garibaldi's frugality.

"In our hearts, the rest of us cursed our first Sicilian meal, saddened to think that the people of Marsala had welcomed us more or less the way you welcome a dog in church."

Serialized in 1886, after he had authored a string of historical novels, Bandi's account of events is the most detailed and liveliest of the garibaldini memoirs. Being close to the general, he was also the most in the know. "My aim," he tells us, "is never to write anything except what I saw and heard."

"Surprised by our sudden arrival, appalled by the thunder of the cannons, the people received us coldly. A few did come to speak to us, but there was no way of understanding their dialect."

Thirty-four years old and already an experienced journalist, Giuseppe Capuzzi managed to publish his short account of the mission towards the end of that same year, 1860, in Palermo.

"I was sent to guard the beach in case the enemy showed. The place was dark; silence of the grave, just the wind whistling in the grass."

Perhaps because he was writing so soon after the events, or simply because it was his nature, Capuzzi is the most attentive to the moment-by-moment experience of the volunteers: the boredom at sea, the hardships on land.

"Scanning the shore on an empty stomach, exhausted from the day's efforts, I thought of the lazy pleasures of home and prayed God to give me the strength for the tough life that was beginning."

Unfortunately, I hadn't discovered Capuzzi's diary before my own attempt to follow in the garibaldini's footsteps in June 2021. Otherwise I might have been warned by his account of the march, on 12th May 1860, from Marsala to Salemi.

"The walking got worse and worse, partly because we were tired, partly because of the rough terrain. We were tormented by thirst. Wells were few and far between, and anyway we were told not to drink from them for fear the water was bad."

In this regard, a hundred and sixty years haven't changed very much.

In Marsala the garibaldini were disappointed to see no sign of a revolution, no welcoming rebels. "Our illusions were blown away in an instant," writes Bandi. But with their ships lost, there was no turning back. Most of the men now expected that Garibaldi would take to the hills and begin a guerrilla campaign. Instead, on the morning of 12th May, the general announced – and this openness was rare – that they would be marching straight to Palermo, seventy miles away.

How galvanizing that news must have been. Perhaps Garibaldi remembered how many volunteers had deserted in his long retreat from Rome towards Venice in 1849, an interminable four-hundred-mile march during which he systematically avoided a showdown with the enemy. He had begun with almost five thousand men and ended, a month later, with two thousand. Only a clear and immediate goal can sustain the enthusiasm of the volunteer. And then, the general told Bandi, if the Sicilians were going to rise up and support them, they would "need to see we can fight and win. The world sides with the bold and the fortunate."

In any event, the first town on their route would be Salemi, an ancient hilltop borgo, easily defendable, twenty-six miles from Marsala.

Determined to walk the whole route, as they had done, we searched the map for a place to break the hike, which amounted to a straight line running due east inland from the coast. However, it seemed there wasn't a single hostelry or café or even shop before the village of San Ciro, just three miles from Salemi.

"We've done long walks before," I said.

Garibaldi was worried about the distance too, all the more so because he had been unable to pick up food supplies in Marsala. The shopkeepers had barred their doors. He did not order them to be broken down. We had been lucky to find a supermarket open on the Sunday afternoon and had stocked up on bread, cheese, fruit and water. Three litres each.

We left as dawn broke. Packs on our backs, poles in our hands. "The first ray of sunshine tinged the surrounding hills with gold," wrote Capuzzi, "and as if reborn to new life the whole of nature dressed itself in marvellous colours. The birds greeted the light, church bells called people to prayer, and the country folk left their cottages to lead their flocks to pasture." We found the suburbs of Marsala to be more extensive than we had expected: arrow-straight roads of low nondescript buildings in various states of disrepair. A minivan parked in a makeshift garage bore the legend "Garibaldini in Tour". Fortunately, the first rays of sunshine were veiled behind thin cloud. Perhaps we would be spared the heat.

"I get the impression," Bandi complained to Garibaldi, "that as soon as people see us, they hurry off." We had the same feeling. As town gradually gave way to country, we were struck by the piles of rubbish at the side of the road: bulging plastic bags, abandoned appliances, old clothes. "There was a delicious perfume in the air," writes Abba, describing fields of yellow flowers. "Intoxicating," enthuses Bandi. What we smelt was toxic. At a corner where we finally left the road for a path, a woman we had greeted with the customary *buongiorno* hurried to get her dog inside the white wall of her villa and shut the gate.

These are moments one would prefer not to write about. Away from the asphalt, we walked through fields of rubbish. This is uncultivated land of sparse dry grass, thistles and stones. Here and there someone had attempted to burn what others had tossed away, achieving little but ugly patches of charring. At one point I struggled to find a way through rusty tins and blanched animal bones. There was about half a mile of this. Broken sofa springs. Bicycle wheels. A microwave. Then, at last, the country proper: palm hedges, olive trees, miles upon miles of low vineyards. Relieved, we stopped for a first snack, more careful than ever to stow away our empty juice cartons and wrapping paper.

We took stock. On the low hill behind us a dozen wind turbines stood motionless. Otherwise the whole landscape, vast and open in all directions, was at once intensely cultivated and utterly empty. Traditionally, it seems, the peasants would walk tens of miles to work from the safety of walled towns. They did not possess the land and could not live on it. As far as the eye can see, there are neither towers nor campanili. No clusters of cedar or cypress. Nothing to draw the world into focus around some manifestation of human artifice. And no striking natural features either. The resulting impression is one of endless flow, softly sloping ocean of grasses and vines. Often you're not really sure whether you're walking uphill or down, so subtly do the huge fields tip this way and that. A distant stand of bamboo might be a fishing boat. The tall stem of a lone agave pricks the horizon like a mast. There are no birds. No wildlife. Strange as it may seem, I was reminded of the American Mid-West. But when I crossed Kansas I had been behind the wheel of a car. For the walker, this landscape is at once superb and daunting. And now the cloud cover was breaking up.

"A liquid sun poured down on this interminable rolling wasteland, where the grass sprouts and dies as though in graveyards." This is Abba. "And never a trace of water, not so much as a trickle, never a village to cheer the horizon: 'Is this the Pampas or what?' someone asked."

"Solitude and vastness," jotted Nievo. "True country of Theocritus."

We had been five hours on the road when the land began to climb. Far in the distance, as if on another planet, the grey shadows of mountains beckoned.

"A clammy heat," Bandi remembered, "that had us drenched in sweat and took our breath away."

That was exactly the sensation I had as the morning drew on. My chest was tight. I was having to draw deep for each breath.

"Sirocco weather," Eleonora said.

"Towards midday" – Capuzzi – "we left the road. At a farmhouse there was a huge bowl of wine mixed with water. They gave us a pot to drink with as we filed by. Champagne, Bordeaux... nothing was ever as fine to the palate as that mix of wine and water."

Towards eleven we too saw a farm, or at least a group of low stone buildings. They stood near a crossroads, abandoned. Broken walls and a rusty iron gate, but offering the miracle of a ribbon of shade tucked in among the weeds. No wine for us, but we gulped down tepid water and munched our bread and peaches.

"I'm in trouble," I said.

"All idle chat ended" – Capuzzi again. "No one wanted to talk; we all moved along in gloomy silence, hoping our destination wasn't far. The only question people would ask from time to time was: how many miles have we walked?"

We had fallen silent too. And stopped taking photos. There is a five-hour gap in my phone gallery. We checked our position and realized we were just halfway. Our water was more than half finished.

"Why do I do this to myself?" I wondered, plodding on. Why not phone Garibaldini in Tour and book a seat in their minivan? And I wondered if they had felt the same, the men from middle-class lives in Milan and Bergamo and Genoa, still wearing their middle-class clothes? Why are we exposing ourselves to danger like this? But I couldn't pursue these thoughts, because my head was swimming.

"Every time we stopped" – Bandi – "the men crouched under hedges and bushes along the road, or wandered here and there looking for water."

Of the landscape during this stretch of the walk I remember nothing but the desperate search for a scrap of shade. We too dived down into low bushes, collecting burs and prickles. Hornets buzzed. Beetles burrowed. With the sun vertical you had to get right inside the plants for any relief. There were no trees. Eleonora began to sneeze, her nose red and itchy. For twenty minutes we sat on a pile of round grey stones beneath a monstrous agave. The water was finished. Five hours to drink the first two litres. Half an hour to gulp the third.

We were climbing steadily, and I remember seeing, far ahead, a tiny red dot. Gradually it morphed into a freight container, perhaps used as a hut or tool shed. When we reached it, there were just six inches of shade. To enjoy them you had to press yourself against burning steel.

All our diarists speak of seeing shepherds and peasants along the way. "Half wild men dressed in goatskins," marvels Nievo. From time to time we saw two or three workers among the vines, wearing big straw hats. It was telling that no one was alone. Unless in a car...

Our path was a dirt track, the earth red brown. Reversing out of a field, an old Fiat appeared. The first vehicle we had seen in some time. Unaware of our approach, the driver stopped, lifted a big plastic canteen from the seat beside him and upended it into his mouth. He drank long.

I stumbled forward. "*Mi scusi!*"

He at once assumed that blank look of detachment we had noticed on so many Sicilian faces. As if he'd prefer to be in a position to say he'd never seen us.

"Do you have any spare water? We've run out."

We were looking at each other through the window of his car, two bald men in sweat-stained shirts. At least he didn't drive off. He sat and thought a moment, his lips still wet.

"No," he said.

Eleonora had caught up. "And you don't know where we can find any?"

Again he thought. "There's a drinking fountain."

"Where?"

"Along the road."

"How far?"

He shrugged. "A few kilometres."

There was nothing more to say. We let him drive off, but after a dozen yards he stopped. He leant out of the window to look back at us. Perhaps more at Eleonora than me. In the end he must have known what it is like to be out in this country without water.

"*Vi faccio una gentilezza,*" he announced. "I'm going to be kind." As if this were a major departure from standard behaviour. "If you walk up that hill" – he gestured to field he had just come out of. "See the first tree? At the base, there's a tap."

He drove away. We hurried up the hill. "Tree" was stretching it to describe a crooked stick with a bedraggled umbrella of leaves. It stood at the corner of a vineyard, and, sure enough, at its base, a black tube pushed out of the soil. There was a plastic tap. We got to our knees, twisted it, and the water gushed.

Capuzzi: "I asked a peasant for something to drink, and he told me he had no wine and to get water I'd have to go to the fountain nearby. It was down a steep slope; slithering and stumbling, I was soon there, and cupping my hands drank avidly."

We directed the water into our water bottles and drank from there. Eagerly at first, then less so.

"It's brown," Eleonora observed.

It tasted rusty. As soon as our immediate thirst was slaked, the question arose: was this wise?

"One of our group who managed to drink" – Abba – "despite orders not to, fell to the ground. We saw him writhing in pain… A doctor checked his pulse and shook his head. Let's hope he hasn't died."

"Surely the guy wouldn't have meant us harm," I said.

Eleonora was unhappy. We didn't want to have our stomachs wrung with dysentery. We poured the water on our heads and returned to the road, which climbed on and on, the air occasionally stirred by a hot damp breeze.

"My thirst" – Capuzzi – "mitigated for a moment, soon reared up again, more burning than before."

What I felt was a sour gumminess in the mouth and an urge to drink that outweighed every other consideration.

"I'm going to pass out," I said. We lay in a shallow ditch beside the track and covered ourselves with our groundsheet. It was oven-hot. As my head cleared a little – from lying down, I presume – I became aware of the hum and whine of insects: a fierce intensity of damp air and dry soil. Eleonora couldn't get comfortable.

"We came across Bixio," – this is another diarist, Emilio Zasio – "stretched out on the ground. Fainted from exhaustion."

What emerges again and again in the garibaldini diaries is the importance of companionship. A common soldier like Abba looks for a reliable companion to walk beside, fight beside. "I marched the entire way with Telesforo Cattoni," he says, "who I had wanted for my friend since Marsala." An officer looks for a loyal servant: "Remember you must never lose sight of me," Bandi tells a new recruit, and gives him his dagger, as a pledge. "I walk beside you not as a captain," Capuzzi's company commander tells his men, "but as a companion in arms. A friend. A brother."

There could be no more reliable companion than Eleonora. Now we were hiding under a bush. My ears were singing. "Something has to give," I said. But she had already understood and taken charge. "The nearest taxi service," she said, consulting her phone, "is thirty miles away. Otherwise we could call an ambulance."

The garibaldini moved with their own *ambulanza*: a few stretchers and medications, a cart, a doctor. Bandi's new servant was on the cart that day, suffering from a fever.

I felt feverish myself. I couldn't think – only longed for water. But now Eleonora was making a phone call.

Expanding the map, she had found an "*azienda agricola*" about half a mile off the road. Probably a wine press or crop-storage point. The phone number didn't answer. Since it was a mobile number, she sent a WhatsApp message. "Can we stop by for some water?" At once there was a reply. "Are you the two we saw walking on the road from Marsala?"

"Yes."

They must have passed us in a car.

"There's no one at the depot right now," came the next message. "It's locked up." But then came two location pins. "You'll find water fountains at these positions." One was a mile and more behind us. One rather further ahead.

"I'm not going back," I said.

Google Maps thought we could walk the distance in forty minutes. Eleonora thanked our anonymous helper.

The garibaldini did not enjoy such precise information. "Our steps slowed down" – Capuzzi. "Tiredness got the better even of the toughest of us, but we consoled ourselves with the thought that the general surely wouldn't keep us marching much longer. Vain hope. A rumour spread that there were eight miles still to walk, and now our despondency was complete."

It took us an hour and twenty to reach the fountain. We were on a single carriage road with wind turbines on the slopes to the left, telegraph poles every fifty yards to the right. I had the impression my legs must buckle at any moment. The trekking poles trailed limp in my hands. Until – joy! – there it was. A low stone pillar to the side of the road, almost overgrown with thistles. And a tap protruding. We turned it. Nothing.

All around the ground was muddy. But nothing came out of the tap. Sitting among the thistles, we texted our contact. "What?" He had drunk from there earlier in the day, he wrote. It must have run dry. He sent us another location pin. Miles away. Eleonora sneezed for the hundredth time, eyes streaming.

"Tell him," I said "that we're desperate."

The minutes passed. No response. Which was fair enough, I thought. A man busy at his job, far away, receives WhatsApp messages from two idiots who have set out on an improbable trek across a scorching empty landscape. He tries to help them in the only way he can. If they can't make it to the next fountain, it's up to them, surely, to call the emergency services.

"There's a café" – Eleonora was considering the map again – "in San Ciro." Three and a half miles.

It was two thirty. Where had the time gone? The silent landscape simmered. No birds, no cicadas even. The occasional buzz of a beetle. We got to our feet. Keep going, I decided, whatever the distance. But now came the ding of a message.

"A friend in the area will bring you a bottle of water."

Not ten minutes later a small black car appeared. It stopped. The window rolled down. A hand reached out with a two-litre bottle of ice-cold water. I confess I was the first to drink.

He was in his forties, bare-chested, glistening. He had thick black glossy hair and a wry smile.

"Walking?" he enquired as I passed the bottle to Eleonora. "How come?"

"We do a lot of walking," I said ruefully.
"You realize the temperature is up in the forties?"
"I can't thank you enough," I told him.
He shrugged and asked where we were going. Eleonora mentioned the café in San Ciro.
"You think you can make it?"
Was it an offer of a lift? We looked at each other.
"We'll be OK," I said.
All the garibaldini agree that to drink fresh water when you're desperately thirsty is the most voluptuous experience imaginable. And they didn't have the advantage of a bottle straight from the fridge. But where was that fridge? Where had this driver come from? All around, in every direction, we could see nothing but an oceanic flow of dark vines, feathery grasses, motionless wind turbines. The car was soon over the brow of a hill and gone. Had we thanked him enough?
"Exhausted as we were" – Capuzzi – "we weren't able to welcome those good local men as we would have wished."
The garibaldini too had visitors. They had been resting a moment when "some Sicilians armed with muskets appeared". Abba has them carrying "strange pikes. Several were wearing sheepskins." "Eighty or so," says Elia, "on horseback, carrying flintlocks." "Like so many Bedouins," says Bandi. And if the men were too tired to show much enthusiasm, then "Garibaldi paid for us all. After a few words, we saw him hug them to his chest and kiss them with indescribable effusion. We envied the luck of those men who set their lips on the hero's face."
Describing Garibaldi, contemplating Garibaldi, is a constant obsession of all the diarists. "Walking at the head of the column with his leading officers, he looks like one of the first conquistadors of America," says Nievo. "Always smiling," says Abba, "with good news written all over his face." And the good news now was that the exhausted army would not be pushing as far as Salemi that day. "Up and down through that rolling country," says Zasio, "towards seven we came to Rampingallo." It was an old isolated estate, a mix of farm and fortress, "where the rich, liberal owner gave us food, good wine and lodging." Fourteen sheep had been bought from a shepherd in the fields. "They passed bleating ahead of us, on their way to the slaughter," says Bandi. Though Nievo remembers goats. "Cool of the evening," he writes, "miserable meal of stale bread and

goat's meat." But whatever they ate, all the diarists felt they were re-enacting a heroic past. "The general sits at the foot of an olive tree," Abba tells us, "eating bread and cheese, slicing it with his knife and chatting with the men around him. I look at him, and have a feeling of antique glory."

Our feelings, stretched out on a bed in the half-dark of an antique palazzo in the centre of Salemi, were of relief. We had eked out those two litres of water until about a mile before San Ciro. The sight of the first modest houses was immensely cheering. The Aurora Gelateria and Tea Room even more so. Filled with liquids and sugars, the remaining two miles to Salemi – a steep climb, a plunge, another climb – seemed the easiest of strolls. We arrived at our B&B towards seven in the evening, after fourteen hours on the road. Then, showered and safe, we collapsed at once. In deliciously cool sheets, my whole body throbbed and ached and itched and glowed. It seemed sun and thistles and burs and beetles were all there with me under the covers.

"I can't walk tomorrow," I said.

"I don't want to walk tomorrow," Eleonora replied.

We had touched our limit. On day one.

Salemi

"They perched it up here," writes Abba, "one house on top of another, and the whole pile ready to come tumbling down any moment... Huge, crowded and filthy, the streets are like lava flows. It's hard not to slip; you look for a tavern and find a den."

We looked for a tavern and found nothing at all. Salemi is a snakes-and-ladders labyrinth of alleys and stairways built vertiginously upward towards a castle and cathedral at the top – except that the cathedral was destroyed in the earthquake of 1968, leaving only a few walls and columns.

"A real Saracen town," Nievo notes. "Or rat's nest, rather."

Still, this time the garibaldini were given a rapturous welcome. Salemi had a tradition of liberalism and anti-Bourbon revolution. Local notables rode out to meet the volunteers, who were marching in damp clothes after a night under heavy rain.

"Arriving, we were met by a throng of men, women and screaming children. You could hardly hear the band for the din." This is Abba. "When the general reached the gates, everyone went wild. All you could see were raised arms waving guns and swords."

"This was when we began to realize we hadn't come to a land of ingrates and cowards," remembers Bandi, who had found himself surrounded by men and boys wishing to examine his sabre and above all his revolver. "They were amazed that a single barrel could fire six shots without being reloaded." A "warrior monk on horseback with a crucifix in one hand and a sword in the other" had Nievo reflecting that "we really are back in the Middle Ages." Many of the locals, he discovered, confused Salemi with Jerusalem and believed that Christ had been crucified on this hill. Abba, true to form, was muddling poverty and eroticism: "A pale, sickly girl with big soft eyes offered me a citron with her right hand, then stretched out her left, imploring 'Signorino!' A rag of a skirt hung high on her shins, and her feet were bare. I put two *prubbiche*¹ in her hand, little coins that look like butterflies. She took them and ran off. I can still see her – her short, filthy dress flapping round skinny legs as she fled, whether in joy or shame I've no idea."

Many of the men broke ranks to buy food. "Our first thought was to slake our thirst" – Capuzzi – "and some unwisely started drinking wine and got drunk, while others ate oranges and lemons that people brought us in baskets and quickly sold." In Marsala the men had received their first pay. A lira each. Regardless of rank. At the time, the Piedmontese lira was pegged to the French franc. "We bought eggs, artichokes and bread." The better-off men were always happy to pay for the poorer, Capuzzi remembers.

The thing that strikes you most about Salemi today is the uneasy marriage of those same ancient streets and contemporary high-tech. Emerging from a narrow flight of stone steps, we are almost bowled over by a SUV, tires squealing on smooth stone. A tiny, ivy-hung piazza throbs with loud music. But it's not the local band welcoming their liberators: the presence of Englishness has morphed from warships in the bay to punk blasting from the window of a jeep. An only slightly larger space outside the town hall serves as a car park and is called Piazza Dittatura, Dictatorship Square.

GIUSEPPE GARIBALDI,
COMMANDER IN CHIEF OF NATIONAL FORCES IN SICILY,
ON THE INVITATION OF THE LEADING CITIZENS
AND FOLLOWING THE DECISION OF THE FREE
TOWNS OF THE ISLAND,
CONSIDERING THAT IN TIME OF WAR IT IS ESSENTIAL THAT
CIVIL POWER BE CONCENTRATED
IN A SINGLE MAN,
DECREES
HIS ACCEPTANCE, IN THE NAME OF VICTOR EMMANUEL, OF
THE DICTATORSHIP OF SICILY.
SALEMI 14TH MAY 1860

---

1   *prubbiche*: Sicilian dialect for *pubbliche* (from the words "*Publica commoditas*", "public commodity", written on one of its sides), coins used at one time in the Kingdom of the Two Sicilies and here used for an unspecified low-denomination currency.

Garibaldi dictator. And on another plaque: Garibaldi Duce. After the experience of Fascism, these terms ring alarm bells; but not at the time. What was happening was momentous. Garibaldi had arrived in Marsala on 11th May to find the people fearful and hesitant. But three days later the councillors of a large town were inviting him to assume control of their lives, and with them the entire island. Two developments help to explain. Throughout 13th May bands of rebels – *picciotti* they were called, which is to say "lively young men" – began to converge on Salemi. It's impossible to know how many, but Bixio thought there were more than two thousand. These men were not individual volunteers, in the manner of the Mille. They were in the service of nobles and landowners who were eager to kick out the Bourbon administration. Risorgimento critics speak of Garibaldi's dealings with these local figures as a pact with the Mafia, and in fact the word *picciotti* is now used almost exclusively to refer to young Mafiosi. But the Mafia as it was to become at the end of the century hardly had the same form in 1860. Ruled for many centuries from abroad, with no representation in the distant capitals where their destiny was decided, Sicilians had long learnt to run parallel and subversive forms of self-government at local level. "Mafia at the time," wrote Giacomo Fazio, a young Sicilian who would soon be joining the garibaldini, "meant an excess of deep hatred for Bourbons, expanded and sustained by the proud and stubborn character of the Sicilians." In any event, the *picciotti* were offering to fight for the cause and needed to be organized and armed. Quickly. "Word got around," says Capuzzi, "that a corps of Neapolitan soldiers was nearby and that we would be fighting them next day." In fact, the Bourbons were already in the town of Calatafimi, just twelve miles north-east of Salemi, blocking the road to Palermo. "The men reacted with joy, each of us eager to measure ourselves against the enemy."

Garibaldi thus found himself riding a mounting wave of enthusiasm rolling towards a sobering encounter with a well-equipped professional army. Having spent the afternoon of 13th May securing his position in Salemi, he had his men and the *picciotti* turned out for review in Largo San Nicola (now renamed Piazza Libertà) early the following morning. This is just outside the old town, where the road leaves for Calatafimi. It was raining heavily. "We were preparing for a miserable march," recalled Capuzzi, "when the captain sent us back to our quarters." Carriages had to be made for the army's cannons, rifles cleaned and mended, pikes and lances fashioned for those who had no guns. In Bandi's description these pikes were no more than "long sticks with a big nail in the end". The *picciotti* were given basic instructions on how to use them.

Salemi's Risorgimento Museum offers a floor-to-ceiling chart showing how the Thousand had now organized their chain of command. Garibaldi is at the top, of course. *Comandante in capo*. Then Giuseppe Sirtori, chief of staff. Gloomy and conceited, Sirtori was in his late forties. Photos show a hawkish nose under a high forehead, over which he regularly wore a black top hat. As a young man Sirtori had abandoned the priesthood, failed to complete his studies first in philosophy, then medicine, mathematics, biology and chemistry, before finally finding his vocation at the barricades of the 1848 revolution in Paris. He went on to join the revolutions in Milan, then Venice, where he fought and organized the defence of the city with great tenacity and skill. His job throughout the present mission was to keep the Thousand fed and clothed. "14th May," notes Nievo. "First makeshift supplies for the troops; water jugs for hip flasks, blankets for coats. Bizarre look of our men after this transformation."

Assisting Sirtori were Francesco Crispi, whose task as foremost Sicilian was to liaise with the locals and advise accordingly, and Giorgio Manin, a trained engineer and son of Daniele Manin, political leader of the 1848 Venice revolution. Beneath these two came the mild-mannered István, or Stefano, Türr, the general's aide-de-camp. Türr had fighting experience in the Hungarian army in 1848, the Piedmontese army in 1849, the British army in the Crimea in 1854 and again the Piedmontese army in 1859. Entering the fortress of Rampingallo, remembered Bandi, "we found Türr lying on a bunk pressing his lips to a bloodstained handkerchief. I asked him what was up, and he answered that he often spat blood, but didn't give it any mind. I touched his forehead, which was burning like a hot iron, but when I offered to get a doctor he said no: 'This is no time for doctors or medicine.'"

Other key names are the commanders of the two brigades into which the Thousand were now split. Bixio was one, Giacinto Carini the other. Carini had fought in the 1848 revolution in his native Palermo, and, after a long period of exile, with Garibaldi in the Piedmontese army in 1859. But many of these men had experienced long years of exile, hardship and poverty. They knew the world. They had fought in battles of all kinds, both as revolutionaries and in regular armies. So that while Garibaldi's Thousand might have been largely made up of uninitiated youngsters, his top staff, the historian Alfonso Sirocco calculates, had collectively more experience of war than that of any European army at the time. Casting your eyes down the names of the company captains, you can see that Garibaldi was choosing as many southerners and Sicilians as possible. Carini was made brigade commander because he was good, but also because he was from Palermo. It made sense politically.

In general the museum in Salemi stresses Sicilian participation in the Risorgimento and the island's long yearning for political freedom. Showcase after showcase features newspapers from the earlier revolution of 1848, when a free press briefly flourished. One paper is called *The Whip*. Another *The Hammer*. Others again *The Barber*, *The Truncheon*. The articles on display are hymns to liberalism. "Our undertaking," announced *The Hammer* on 3rd July 1848, "shall be to investigate the truth, so far as we are able, and to declare it openly... we shall not bow to threats of whatever kind, be they legal or physical... every patriot should take pleasure in seeing the iniquities of evildoers exposed and the good of his country advanced."

The museum also displays the proclamation that Garibaldi had printed and fixed on every rainy corner of Salemi the day he was pronounced dictator.

IN ANSWER TO SICILY'S HEROIC PLEA, I have brought with me here a band of brave men, remnants of the wars in Lombardy. We are on your side! We ask nothing but the liberation of your country. United, the task will be easy and brief. To arms then! Anyone who does not fight is a coward or a traitor to his country. Let the lack of weapons be no excuse. Soon enough we will have rifles. For the moment, in the hands of a brave man, anything will do. The town councils will provide for the women and children, the old and infirm. Every man to arms! Once again Sicily will show the world how to free a country from its oppressors, through the powerful determination of a united people.

A high alcove in the museum houses a single surviving rifle – or fails to house it. Four feet long, with another eighteen inches of lethal bayonet, it protrudes diagonally from the alcove, supported by a cradle of wires. The bayonet, Garibaldi thought, was the only really useful part of these antiquated weapons. Given the short range at which they were moderately accurate and the time required to reload, a soldier would very likely have only one shot to spend before the enemy was upon him – or, better still, before he launched himself at the enemy. "As we were going to bed," Capuzzi recalled, "the order came to be ready to march, and our rifles were checked to make sure they were properly loaded." Wait until the last possible moment before firing, the general told his men, and shoot to kill.

"From the balcony of a monastery in the glory of bright sunshine," Cesare Abba prefaces his notes on the afternoon of 13th May.

"We're billeted," writes Nievo, "in the college of the Jesuits, who've taken off to the country so that we can be more comfortable. 'They've taken off because they're rats,' a street urchin tells me. Which sounds more like it."

"The city may be filthy, Abba reflects, but "the monks do have lovely monasteries, and this one is even clean".

"When it comes to personal hygiene here," echoes Nievo, "the priests have an exclusive monopoly."

Curiously, there is nothing in Salemi's Museo del Risorgimento to tell you that this was in fact the very same Jesuit college where the garibaldini slept. Cesare Abba and Ippolito Nievo wrote their diaries right here, where now there are portraits of Garibaldi looking more saintly than any Jesuit.

It is a commonplace that the Catholic Church vigorously resisted Italian unification and would not be reconciled to it until the Lateran Pacts, made with Mussolini in 1929. It was an opposition that set religious and patriotic loyalties against each other and sank a deep wound into the very notion of Italian national identity. Many of the garibaldini were ferociously anti-clerical, something that alienated the pious bourgeoisie. "DOGS AND PRIESTS FORBIDDEN," warned a sign on the gates of Villa Spinola in Quarto. But in Salemi, wrote Augusto Elia, who had now recovered from being kicked by that horse in Marsala, "we made the surprising discovery that [ultra-conservative Jesuits aside] the ordinary priests were actually on the side of the revolution, and in some cases even leading it." It was a turnaround that would take some getting used to. 'Now I will narrate," announces Bandi, "how I met Brother Pantaleo in Salemi, and how it happened that the said monk was introduced that very day to Giuseppe Garibaldi, and consequently came along with us, half soldier, half chaplain."

Fra Giovanni Pantaleo was the same "warrior monk on horseback" who had had Nievo thinking of the Middle Ages. "A lively young friar with fire in his eyes," Bandi narrates, buttonholed him in the street and would not be brushed aside. "'Don't you realize,' the cleric said, 'that among people as blind and superstitious as the Sicilians, the Cross and the word of a patriotic friar are worth a hundred of your sabres?'" Within twenty-four hours, Fra Pantaleo promised, he could bring thousands of men to the cause, if only Garibaldi would allow him to do so. The friar talked on and on, "with the insistence of a blade grinder", Bandi remembered, but also "with an inspiration and vehemence that had you thinking of Savonarola".

At the general's headquarters other officers weren't happy – "Priests! Always Priests!" They started to rough the man up. Fra Pantaleo shrieked. Garibaldi appeared. There could have been few men more anti-clerical than Garibaldi. But "fortunately the general was in a good mood" and "with marvellous intuition" understood what was on offer. "In truth," Bandi concludes, "Fra Pantaleo proved an immense asset to our campaign, especially in that first part of the war. When it came to stirring people up for the crusade against tyranny, he had no equal."

While the rain poured on the garibaldini as they made their preparations for battle, the sun powered down on us as we wondered, after yesterday's brush with catastrophe, whether it still made sense to follow them across the scorching landscape. On the steep cobbles climbing to the castle, two big white Labradors lay with tongues out and paws splayed, as if dead. Every flight of steps – and there were many – was littered with broken birds' eggs, upturned beetles and shrivelled worms, as if a column of fire had passed by, consuming every living creature. Taking refuge in the Jesuit church beside the museum – a wonderfully sober baroque with flaky helical columns framing the door – we found reliquaries galore. These included fragments of Thomas à Becket and St Francis of Assisi. There is also a charmingly carved and painted wooden organ. Everything is lofty, decorous, from the grey-and-white marble floor to the flesh-coloured domes of the various side chapels with their elegantly tormented martyrs, in oil or bas-relief. It would be hard to imagine a cooler or more comfortable place to hide from the heat, or indeed from life in general.

"Perhaps," I suggested, "instead of walking, we could spend a couple of weeks sitting in cool Sicilian churches, communing with the illustrious dead."

But searching on my phone for some history of the place, I stumbled on an article in a Trapani newspaper: "All Cleared of Corruption for the Restoration of the Church of the Jesuits." A month after disappearing, Maurizio Russo, co-owner of a building company in Taormina, was found hanging from a tree in open country. In his pocket was a letter explaining that his partner had cheated him of 800,000 euros and that substantial bribes had been paid in relation to the restoration of the church of the Jesuits in Salemi. However, while the judge found that there had indeed been "anomalies" in the financing of the project, no proof of illegal payments could be found. So no one was punished. Nor does any trace of this unhappy suicide transpire in the deep tranquillity of the beautifully restored nave where we enjoyed ten minutes' rest.

Nino Bixio's diary is full of notes recording how much he paid to whom and for what. Moral rectitude was part of a garibaldino's identikit. "For the services of 38 seamen, 4,200 L. For catering, 1,500 L. For 400 pairs of shoes at 6.40 L. a pair, 2,560 L. For the chief stoker of the *Lombardo*, 500 L." Bixio also obsessively counted and recounted how many men there were in each company of the Thousand, adding and subtracting in interminable jottings. But on 14th May, he wrote:

From Salemi to	Palermo,	miles	 50
" "	Vita,	"	 4
" "	Calatafimi,	"	 12
" "	Alcamo,	"	 18
Road from Salemi	to Partinico		 36
" "	to Borghetto		
"	Monreale to Palermo		

in giant strides...

While Bixio was counting and calculating, Bandi was instructing the local "Bedouins" in "the fine art of killing one's neighbour". Doing so he was drawn to "a handsome boy, white and pink, with two huge eyes and teeth that looked like beans". Since Bandi's first servant had now been ordered to work with the *ambulanza*, the officer took the seventeen-year-old Nino back to his quarters, put a red beret on his head and a dagger in his belt and gave him his instructions, the most important being: "Always stay close to me, because I may need you from one moment to the next." When Nino tried to kiss his new master's hand, Bandi slapped his face and told him such servility was the product of a foul civilization. All the same, Bandi felt sure he had found himself "a faithful, appreciative soul who would follow me eyes closed into the very mouth of hell". Back in the street, he had to run to the town hall to catch the last part of Garibaldi's speech accepting the dictatorship before an adoring crowd. "I don't remember what he said," Bandi tells us, "only that he was as eloquent as any tyrant-hater in love with death for the triumph of a just cause can ever be."

"I threw open the windows of this monk's cell," writes the more down-to-earth Abba, "and looked out over the countryside, sleepy under the smoke rising from the valleys." We leant on a parapet, walking down from the museum, and looked out over the same landscape. The steep hill on which the town sits falls away in fifty shades of green: the silvery olive, bluish prickly pear, pale lettuce patches, the emerald carpet of a bean field, a dark cedar silhouetted on a ridge. All fading and fusing into the intense heat haze that we had walked through yesterday. A steaming minestrone of a landscape.

"In giant strides," I repeated.

Capuzzi was delighted when he learnt that he and his friends were to have a day of reprieve before the battle. "We split up into small groups and went to this or that household, where we had ourselves served all kinds of food and enjoyed all the comforts and delicacies that our money and this particular place would allow. Thinking that this might be our last day of pleasure, our jokes were the sharper and our merriment the louder."

We struggled to find much merriment in Salemi. Or many people. In Piazza Libertà, where Garibaldi reviewed his troops, a few elderly men were sitting on benches in the deep shade of a circle of carob trees. Shopkeepers idled just inside their doorways, hardly expecting any custom. However, as evening drew on, a *birreria* at last opened in the piazza at the top of the town with the ruined Duomo to one side and the massive walls of the castle to the other. Young people roared up the steep approach road in jeeps and on motorbikes. We seemed to be the only creatures deprived of motorized transport. A poster announced a jazz festival. In July. The proprietor of the bar brought craft beer and *panelle*, which is to say chickpea fritters. Then he brought more beer and chips and olives and fried onion rings. They were excellent. We enjoyed watching everyone laugh and eat and drink and play cards together. But what remains now of that pleasant evening is a photo I took inside the bar while waiting for a credit-card reader to process my payment. It shows a fluorescent-lit fridge with a glass door. Rows of beer bottles inside. Across the top of the fridge, shining even more brightly, white on a green background, is the foreign name, HEINEKEN. And on the wall above, half obscured by the Heineken light, is one of those mirrors that bear a black-and-white image: Garibaldi, in his poncho and cap. But you can see that the idea for this image has come, anachronistically, from the famous poster of Che Guevara in his beret. Garibaldi's cap is worn at the same angle. The tilt of his face is the same. Our hero, it seems, is just one icon among others. And the more I looked at this image, while the card reader failed to register my payment, so that in the end I had to pull out cash, the further I felt I was from Garibaldi and Capuzzi and Bandi and Elia and Abba and Nievo, and from that culminating moment of the Italian Risorgimento when these oddly assorted men took on the Bourbon army in the hills south of Calatafimi. It seemed the only way you might get anywhere near them again was to walk the way they walked.

"In the end it's only twelve miles," I told Eleonora. "If we leave at five, we should be there before it gets too hot."

Pianto Romano

"The entire night of 14th May was spent watching and patrolling."

Twenty-nine years old, a failed law student from Lombardy who had fought in both the 1848 revolution and the 1859 war, Emilio Zasio was one of only eighteen mounted scouts available to Garibaldi. Based in a monastery on the road to Vita, a small village between Salemi and Calatafimi, he rode back and forth between the Bourbon camp and a house in Vita, where he would wake Nino Bixio with the latest news. In 1868 he published his memoirs. "When you touched Bixio to wake him, it was like releasing a spring. He jumped to his feet, fully dressed, mind sharp and clear." Towards midnight, taking his horse back to the monastery to be fed and watered, Zasio discovered some monks in the cellar "laying into ham and meat and boozing like the English". His night finished at dawn, when he saw the Thousand marching down the steep hill from Salemi "in good order, with Garibaldi at their head… I could barely stay on my feet for sleepiness, but made an effort and kept going… The only thing that mattered was to be worthy of our leader."

We were awake at five, our minds far from sharp or clear. For lack of coffee we drank juice and shared a peach. I told Eleonora the story of Garibaldi's coffee that crucial morning. He had asked Bandi to sleep outside his bedroom door, so as to be on hand. Before 3 a.m. he had already woken another assistant, Giovanni Fruscianti, who regularly prepared his coffee. "Are you going to give me that coffee or not?" the general asked when Bandi came in. Fruscianti had knocked over the pot and had to start again from scratch. Bandi told the general the rain had stopped, the sky was clearing, and helped him to dress. Garibaldi paced the room, his spurs tinkling. Finally the coffee was ready. The *comandante in capo* drank it in slow sips, fired off a series of orders, then, at 3.30 a.m., burst into song:

Questa soave immagine	This sweet image
placa i miei spirti e parmi	Calms my spirits and I seem
veder sereno splendere	To see the brightness
il tempo che verrà	Of our future.

It was Donizetti's opera, *Gemma di Vergy*. "He must know something I don't," Bandi thought, but the young officer didn't ask what, since he knew Garibaldi hated prying of any kind.

"I could use a coffee like that," Eleonora said.

"Maybe when we get to Vita."

An hour and a half's march.

"Our officers were more generous than usual," Capuzzi remembered, "advising us to be cheerful and sing our favourite songs, to put us in the mood for the fray."

When a trumpeter sounded the reveille, Garibaldi was struck by its calm melancholy. It wasn't the usual refrain, but he felt he had heard it before. On a whim he sent Bandi off to fetch the man. "I rushed out, taking my Nino to guide me in the dark down the steep slippery alleys, the stone still wet from yesterday's rain."

We left our B&B just as the light was coming up. The air was warm and brooding. The sleeping palazzi seemed to huddle closer together, bracing themselves for the torrid day ahead. Once again I noticed the broken shells of birds' eggs on the stairs down to the piazza. I can't remember ever seeing so many. "We set out knowing a stern test lay ahead," says Capuzzi.

The army's sole trumpeter was from Chiuduno, near Bergamo. He had learnt this particular reveille, he told Garibaldi, fighting with the Cacciatori delle Alpi the previous year. "So you played it the morning of the battle for Como?" the general asked.

"*Sissignore.*"

"Always play that tune," Garibaldi told him.

"It's a wonder," Eleonora said, "he had time for such pleasantries, just hours before a battle."

"In fact at this point he settled down to dictate three decrees before dawn, one announcing the formation of a National Guard and one abolishing certain religious orders, the Jesuits in particular."

"So he had even less time!"

"He'd had an idea."

"Which was?"

"We'll see."

"All Salemi turned out to see us off," remembered Abba. "I wished I could have hugged every last one of them." The only person we saw was a baker pulling loaves from an oven at the back of a tiny shop.

Like Capuzzi, Abba remembers singing and cheerfulness. Emotions were running high, and emotions were going to play a decisive part in the day's events. "The warm light," he says "and the fragrance of the valley had us feeling exhilarated." We followed them along a chalk track in veiled sunshine, past a derelict farmhouse lit up by a blaze of crimson oleanders. The country did indeed smell good. Rugged hills of scorched white grasses, cactus hedges, dark trees, occasional explosions of colour: roses, bougainvillea. "The road sloped steeply down," says Bandi, "towards a broad valley, green and flowering, closed at the end by a high barren mountain."

"We entered Vita," remembered Capuzzi, "and the people crowded the streets – children, women with their heads covered in white shawls, greeting us and shouting *urrah!*" "The people of Vita," says Abba, "fled, carrying their belongings with them, dragging their old folk and children… You poor things, they called to us, shaking their heads in compassion."

Can both versions be true? Did some people cheer and others flee? I have read at least a dozen eyewitness accounts of the battle of Calatafimi. No two are the same. Everyone was in an altered state of mind. Everyone had an agenda. And each person saw only a fragment of the whole. "Arrival 6.30 in Vita," recorded Francesco Crispi. "Enthusiasm of the locals." "In Vita the people were neither friendly nor hostile," says Bandi, "because we hardly saw any people at all, and those we did see were no more interested in us than they would have been in a group of commercial travellers heading for market." "After four miles we came to the village of Visa," says Nievo. He gets the name wrong and has nothing more to say about the place.

You can see why. "Rounding a hill the Thousand came suddenly into the bare and characterless streets of Vita," wrote Trevelyan. He was being generous. We rounded that hill shortly before seven and found ourselves between drab cement walls with rare patches of crumbling stucco. "For Sale" boards on broken brickwork were old and fading. There had been no takers. That said, the main square was cleanly swept, with Italian, Sicilian and EU flags flying outside the town hall and two handsome palm trees to frame this one small oasis of municipal pride. More importantly, towards the end of a main street that turned out much longer than we expected, a tiny café was open, its proprietor standing arms folded, legs akimbo, at the door. He made us an excellent coffee and brought oven-fresh brioches and ice-cold water. "But we only stopped here a few minutes," says Capuzzi, "then set off at once, to Calatafimi."

The road follows a broad valley climbing steadily northwards. Prickly pears, bean fields, blackberries. Leaving his five ancient cannons in the valley to discourage any attempt to outflank his men and occupy Vita behind their backs, Garibaldi had the main body of the army climb the hill to their right, Pietralunga. It's easy walking on reddish earth and grey rock, though your socks are soon prickly with grass seeds. We watched a few horses searching for something to eat among the thistles, others switching their tails in the shade of an ancient olive. "Barren, rugged, scorched by the sun," says Abba. From the top of the hill, through their telescopes, Garibaldi, Sirtori and Türr could see the high fortress town of Calatafimi, four miles to the north-east. It was surely impregnable. Due north and barely a mile away was the flat-topped hill known as Pianto Romano. It was seething with Bourbon soldiers. The general deployed the Thousand in a long semicircle across the facing slope of Pietralunga, one line some distance behind another, the men stretched on their stomachs in the grass and scrub. "From up here we could see the enemy camp and the formidable position they held," writes Capuzzi. The five hundred or so *picciotti* who had come along were arranged at each end of the line, to prevent encirclement. "A wait of two long hours" – Capuzzi again – "listening out for rifle fire."

We climbed a narrow path between thick bushes in sweltering stillness, the sun veiled behind hazy cloud. Then the foliage parted, and you could see Pianto Romano directly opposite. We knew it was the hill of the battle because there is a monument on top, an obelisk, visible for miles. Beyond it, towards Calatafimi, the slope is gradual, but, looking across from where the garibaldini lay hidden, the hill presents a steep scarp, which, at the time, was cut into three high terraces for cultivation. The valley between the hills is not wide, perhaps half a mile, but quite deep and completely exposed. "As a result," Garibaldi remembered, "both we and the enemy were holding extremely strong positions, one facing the other… It made sense for both sides to wait."

Waiting was the last thing we intended to do. The temperature was already in the thirties, though this time we did have abundant water. Cost what it might in terms of weight, we were determined never to be thirsty again. "Does anyone have any water?" asked Francesco Montanari, one of Bandi's close companions. All their flasks were empty. The May sunshine was hot. "I saw two bottles of cognac in one of the general's bags," Montanari insisted. "Or are we planning to drink them after we're dead?"

Bandi has all the good stories. How he was sent ahead to scout the enemy positions, narrowly escaping a fatal encounter, how he heard that the Bourbons were planning to take Garibaldi to Palermo bound hand and foot on a donkey, how one garibaldino tried to cross the lines and betray his comrades to the enemy, how Bixio's stallion, smelling a female, reared up and pranced about, the brigade commander beating the creature with the flat of his sabre until it set off at a gallop and took him all the way back to Vita before he could turn it round, how another garibaldino tried to give him, Bandi, all his money in safekeeping, convinced he would be killed in the battle, how Garibaldi said, "Let Montanari have the cognac, if it will cheer him up."

There are no paths across the battlefield. We circled north and joined a narrow lane (Strada dei Mille). Toiling up the slope towards the monument, we saw a blue Fiat Panda driving towards us with a horse trotting alongside. A boy in the passenger seat was holding a halter through the open window. The creature was a handsome chestnut with a white flash on its head, much taller than the Panda, full of flounce and energy. The driver, who was uncannily similar to the man who had brought us water on the road to Salemi, smiled as Eleonora took a photo. "It must have been quite a business," she reflected, "recovering horses after the battle." Studying the slopes of the two hills, there was no trace of urgency or carnage, nothing but parsley flowers and plough land. At the top, we found the monument complex closed. If the garibaldini were to attack this morning, they would have to scale a two-metre-high steel gate. The whole hilltop is fenced off. It was 8.30 a.m.

If you're planning to change the world, it's useful to know exactly what your goals are, step by step, and tackle them with ruthless resolve. "Garibaldi was determined to fight that morning whatever the risk," Bandi remembers, "rather than make a bad impression on the Sicilians." The Bourbons were not equally focused. Shortly before midday, drawn up in their ranks on the big flat top of Pianto

Romano, they began to march up and down "as if they were on a parade ground and thought they might frighten us with a show of strength and discipline".

The general was sitting on a mound among shrubs and prickly pears. "Well-drilled troops," he sighs appreciatively in Bandi's version, lighting a cigar. "Fine soldiers, for sure." He was aware, Garibaldi tells us in his memoirs, that while he had been able to identify all the Bourbon positions, they would barely be able to see the advanced line of his Genoese Carabinieri. All the others were hidden. "Garibaldi was watching," Elia speculates, "for that most fleeting of tactical moments that always decides the outcome of a battle."

At midday the Bourbons blew their trumpets and began to advance, thus abandoning their secure position. All their recent experience had been with putting down undisciplined rabble. They must have supposed it was going to be a stroll.

"They came in wonderful order," remembers Zasio, "moving nimbly, as if it were a drill, not the real thing." "Nino" – Bandi whispered to his young servant – "any minute now you're going to hear the bullets whistle. Keep still and watch me, and when you see me run down the hill, follow closely. Don't be afraid, and don't stop till I do."

The sign outside the Pianto Romano monument, which also houses a museum, said the site would open at 9.30. At once I was impatient about the delay. But there was a phone number, promising "Information". I phoned, and at once a female voice replied: "We'll get someone to come right away," she said. We were startled. I hadn't even had to ask.

One feature of this valley is that it is surrounded by other hills and ridges. Throughout that morning – 15th May, 1860 – crowds of local people gathered on those heights "to enjoy the battle", says Bandi, "and decide, depending on the outcome, whether to cry 'long live Garibaldi!' or 'long live King Francis!'" This seems unkind. Many of those onlookers were *picciotti*. The Bourbons feared these men would join the battle at some point. They had a certain influence.

Smartly dressed in black caps, blue jackets, grey trousers, the Neapolitans advanced up the Pietralunga hillside, firing as they came. In the front line of defence, halfway up the slope, a carabiniere was killed. Others were wounded. Garibaldi's captains urged their men to hold fire. To fire early is a sign of fear. To waste a bullet is to encourage the enemy. But now, disappointingly, the Bourbons slowed down. Had they smelt a rat? "Let them hear our trumpet," Garibaldi decided. To the incredulity of his staff officers, he had their one trumpeter sound the same melancholy reveille he had blown in the early hours.

All the garibaldini who recorded accounts of the battle offer the same key events, more or less, though in slightly different sequences. Was the trumpet played before the shooting started? Or afterwards? Did the garibaldini fire when ordered to fire, or out of impatience? But whatever the exact time it sounded, all our diarists agree that the plaintive call of that reveille – "all sweetness and calm" – drifting through the midday heat had an extraordinary effect. There was a moment of enchanted stillness. It was not what the Bourbons were expecting. "Now," said Garibaldi (in Bandi's version), "let's see if we can't give these gentlemen a good thrashing."

In a matter of minutes a car drew up at the Pianto Romano monument and a tall elderly gentleman stepped out, apparently baffled and delighted to find two enthusiasts to show around the battlefield museum at such an early hour.

On the morning of 15th May 1860, another elderly man had been similarly baffled, but far from delighted. Thanks to online archives, it is possible to consult all the communications in the days before the battle between General Francesco Landi, commander of the Bourbon army at Calatafimi, and the man officially running Sicily at the time, the king's lieutenant in Palermo, Paolo Ruffo, prince of Castelcicala. It doesn't take long to do this, because the missives were not many. This was largely because, as Landi repeatedly laments, the telegraph lines were constantly cut and his couriers regularly intercepted. News of Garibaldi's arrival had resuscitated the revolution.

Initial instructions to General Landi, outlining his expedition's objectives, are dated 5th May, the same day the garibaldini set sail from Quarto. He was to march from Palermo through the mountains towards the south-west of Sicily, via Partinico, Alcamo and Calatafimi, "the main aim being to prevent a landing of 'immigrants' expected between Mazara and Capo San Vito" – which was as much as to say "somewhere along the west coast". At the same time a certain Colonel Donati was to sail right round that coast from Palermo in the north to Mazara in the south, thus creating the possibility of a pincer movement wherever Garibaldi landed.

This was a prompt and logical response to the intelligence the Bourbons had received. However, a secondary objective was also imposed on both commanders: they were to disarm the populations of the towns and ports through which they passed. Inevitably this slowed them down, when for their primary objective speed was of the essence. Even more perplexing, another Bourbon force, based in Trapani and hence well placed to go after the Thousand, assuming they did land on the west coast, was recalled to Palermo. It's not clear why. In the event, Landi took several days to disarm the citizens of Partinico and Alcamo, while Donati, having sailed round the coast and arrived at Mazara on 7th May, was then diverted to Agrigento, sixty miles to the south-east, where reports of a rebel landing eventually proved to be false. On 12th May, when Landi received news of Garibaldi's landing in Marsala together with an order to intercept, confront and destroy his army, he was still in Alcamo, seven miles north-east of Calatafimi, nineteen from Salemi. Reinforcements were on the way, he was told. "I am confident," wrote Prince Castelcicala, "that your long experience will guarantee a positive outcome."

Experience of what, exactly? It is true that Landi had been admitted to the Royal Military Academy in 1806 – fifty-four years before – when he was just fourteen. He came from a Neapolitan family of proud military traditions. With the rank of captain, he had been involved in military action on three or four occasions in his thirties without distinguishing himself in any way. Expelled from the army along with many others following a change of regime, he had been unemployed between 1821 and 1837. Reinstated, but for the most part inactive, he had helped put down a revolt in Calabria in 1848. And that was it. It was only a few weeks before the Battle of Calatafimi, thanks to the part he had played in suppressing the April revolution in Palermo, that Landi was at last awarded the rank of general. This was his first solo mission, aged sixty-seven. Suffering from poor health, he found it painful to ride on horseback, and tended to follow his troops in a carriage, which was how he arrived in Calatafimi at dawn on 13th May. Hours later, reinforcements arrived from the northern port of Castellammare del Golfo.

At this point Landi had more than three thousand well-equipped soldiers under his command. He had cavalry. He had cannons. Nevertheless, his dispatches from start to finish are those of a man who sees only the downside of everything. The public mood, he complains, is fanatically anti-Neapolitan. He doesn't trust any of the local scouts, who constantly contradict each other: "Here one lives in the dark among an ambiguous people." His main request is for an *ambulanza*, a field hospital. He is expecting casualties. All the same, he promises to obey orders and approach Salemi, where the enemy is believed to be gathering: "I won't fail to adopt all necessary precautions to avoid surprises." In a message on 14th May labelled "Urgent and Secret", he worries that "the rebel hordes are growing all the time" and that, surrounded by olive groves, Salemi is the perfect place for an ambush. "To attack would be imprudent." He writes three versions of this dispatch, looking for more and more convincing reasons for staying put in the stronghold of Calatafimi. People have been leaving the town in droves, he says, no doubt because they are aware an attack is imminent. "I can't find a single faithful spy…"

On 15th May the anxious general orders a classic half-measure. Three columns of men will be sent out from the town – west, south and east – to put on a show of strength and to sound out the enemy. The same morning he receives an order to retreat, first to Partinico, then to Palermo, where Prince Castelcicala has now decided to concentrate the entire army in order to be absolutely sure that the capital city is safe. This U-turn throws Landi into confusion. He knows the order was sent two days before, by sea to Castellammare (35 miles west of Palermo) and then by land, this because lone couriers are unable to get through the mountains between Partinico and Palermo. So it was written before the Prince had seen his, Landi's, dispatch of 14th May. To withdraw from Calatafimi now would look like defeat, and offer a huge boost in morale to the enemy.

It was while Landi was pondering over this dilemma that Major Sforza, commanding the column sent south from Calatafimi, ran into Garibaldi's troops and called on the other exploratory columns to hurry to Pianto Romano to reinforce him. Sforza was altogether a more enterprising man than Landi. His soldiers were up for a fight. Some were reputedly indignant that "foreigners" were meddling in the Bourbon Kingdom's internal affairs. On the other hand, these men had not spent the last months preparing mentally for this battle. They did not believe their destinies depended on it. When the mournful trumpet sounded the last note of the reveille, Garibaldi ordered his men to attack.

"No," says our guide. "The undisciplined garibaldini started firing and attacked of their own accord."

Having unlocked various gates and doors, the generous old man led us into the small museum at the base of the obelisk. First a narrow corridor, no wider than our shoulders, adorned with lists of names, old photographs, handwritten dispatches. Then a room almost entirely occupied by a huge trestle table bearing a relief model of the battlefield. The guide picked up a pointing stick and launched into his spiel, indicating bands of painted soldiers, a little too large for the ground they trod, but wonderfully detailed with their feathered caps and white ammunition belts criss-crossing blue jackets. Drawn by six horses, a magnificent cannon is being manoeuvred into place. The hills come complete with clumps of yellowing grass, ferns, trees, cactuses and outcrops of greyish rock. Little signs on tall sticks give the names of the different bodies of troops: 2nd Battalion of the 10th Regiment: 8th Infantry; Battalion Bixio; Battalion Carini; *Picciotti*. It's the kind of thing my brother and I would have killed for as children. Garibaldi is noble on his horse at the very bottom of the valley, while above him on the terraced scarp of Pianto Romano a tremendous skirmish is underway as the garibaldini rush up after the Bourbon soldiers retreating to their hilltop stronghold. In the midst of the crush, a tricolour is held high. I felt an intense desire to get on my knees and play.

The guide was pleased at our level of interest, but became wary when I foolishly told him I had read a couple of books. He was used to people who thought they knew more than he did. Polite and teacherly, he pointed to a sign on a stick that said "9th Company, Commander Mosto". "The carabinieri lost patience, and when the Neapolitan soldiers hesitated, they started firing and rushed them."

"Their bullets flew over us with such a provocative wailing" – Abba – "that we couldn't stay still. First one shot, then another and another. Then the trumpet sounded the reveille, after that the charge. It was the general's trumpet."

"The first shots had barely reached our ears" – Capuzzi – "when we got the order to advance. We were arranged in groups of four, each ten paces from the next. We moved as fast as you can on stony ground thick with brambles… the Bourbons had set up two cannons that spewed iron balls and death… their rifles could strike at a thousand paces, ours at three hundred… they had three thousand six hundred men, we one thousand two hundred... and their position was all but unassailable."

"It's not true," our guide clarifies, "that the Bourbons had such an overwhelming numerical advantage. There were about two thousand four hundred soldiers, once the reinforcements arrived."

"At the sound of the reveille" – Elia – "spurred by youthful ardour, Menotti Garibaldi [the general's son], Schiaffino (with the flag in his hand) and I sprinted after their infantry, who were retreating before the Genoese Carabinieri. We rushed up Pianto hill, all three of us, clambering up the high terraces that formed the formidable enemy position. It wasn't long before the brave Schiaffino was wounded and fell, butchered with bayonets."

"Simone Schiaffino, aged twenty-five, was indeed killed," our guide confirmed, "but rather later in the battle."

"'Losers, bastards, brigands!' those poor Neapolitans were shouting as they advanced towards us." This is how Bandi remembers it. "I grabbed the trumpeter's rifle and leapt down the slope. Montanelli followed with his sabre in his fist. Garibaldi yelled, 'For God's sake! Can't you ever stay still for a moment?'"

"So Garibaldi actually lost control of the situation?" Eleonora asks, and the guide confirms. "The garibaldini sacrificed their advantage, chasing after the Bourbons, and then had to fight them climbing up the hill to the top here, where we stand."

In his memoir, Garibaldi suggests a more dynamic situation.

"The aim of the first charge was to chase off the enemy vanguard and get hold of their two cannons... certainly not to attack the formidable position they were defending on the hill in large numbers. But once these bold passionate volunteers had started after the enemy, who was going to stop them? Our trumpet sounded the halt... but they pretended not to hear and pressed on with their bayonets until they clashed with the main body of the enemy."

The guide points with his stick. For all his generosity turning out for us at 8.30 a.m., he manages to make his account of the battle rather dull. A retired schoolteacher, he has spent his life dotting i's and crossing t's in stuffy classrooms. Everything he says is guarded, hyper-aware of what a contentious subject this battle has become in Sicily, where many people now think of Italian unity as something imposed upon them by the north. In deference to these views, the elderly man downplays the heroism of the Thousand and the charisma of Garibaldi. But he also insists on the involvement of those Sicilians who fought with the garibaldini. And he has kind words for Landi. It's true that the Neapolitan general followed the battle at a distance, from Calatafimi, while Garibaldi threw himself directly into the fray – all the same, there were good reasons why he held back some eight hundred soldiers in the town rather than committing them to the battle.

The well-informed voice talks on and on, evenly, reasonably. He has said these things a thousand times before. And his aim, I realize, is to be beyond all childish side-taking, sensibly detached from this feverish, confused event of a now-distant past, and hence, in some benevolent way, superior – the way twenty-first-century man is of course superior (is he not?) to nineteenth-century man. We wouldn't stoop to this madness now, surely. He doesn't mention the bleeding or the pain. Or the fact that the men knew there would be bleeding and pain, and went towards it anyway, raced towards it, eagerly, vigorously. "These early losses," remembers Capuzzi, "fired us into a passion to fight for the freedom of our country and to avenge ourselves on the assassins who had killed our companions."

"Tell us about the flag," I suggest.

Everybody else talks about it, at length. All the garibaldini diarists. And Major Sforza in his report. And General Landi in his report. Only Garibaldi himself has nothing to say on the subject. "There was no time to lose," he wrote in his memoirs. His captains had managed to hold back most of the men, but the advance guard – the carabinieri and various other hotheads – were now climbing the first terrace, going hard after the enemy. They would be overwhelmed if not reinforced. It was not the first time Garibaldi had found himself in this situation; volunteers had their qualities, but discipline was not one of them. He ordered the entire corps to attack. "The situation was extreme: we had to win."

How? The many versions of the battle are as tangled and confused as the mass of plastic soldiers pressed together in a bristle of sabres and bayonets on the second of the steep hill's three terraces. "In seconds," remembered Bandi, "I was wrapped in smoke – then, through the smoke shifting in the breeze, I saw that we were all mixed together, garibaldini and Bourbons, fighting hand to hand, with any weapon you could grab, including knives, including rocks."

In the chaos, the flag stood out. "Nino Bixio was up front, on horseback, spurring us on to a third attempt, galloping around the terrace with Garibaldi's flag in his hands. In a hail of gunfire, he seemed magically immune, waving the flag in the very face of the enemy." That's Bandi again. "The final, almighty clash" – Abba – "came as the flag passed from hand to hand to Schiaffino – you saw it waved a few moments, here and there, in a packed and terrible mêlée."

"Every time you climbed from one terrace to the next" – Garibaldi – "you had to expose yourself to tremendous gunfire." On the other hand, under the bank, or wall, of each terrace there was an area of cover, and the terraces themselves were sufficiently narrow to privilege the bayonet over the return of fire, hence "well suited to those old crocks the government had given us, which almost always refused to shoot". Bandi described loading his rifle three times. To no avail. Twenty-one-year-old Luigi Cavalli claimed his rifle fired once in fifteen attempts.

The dead and wounded were mounting up. Both Nievo and Capuzzi describe their exhaustion after repeated attempts to take the second terrace were beaten back. "The enemy defended their position" – Garibaldi – "with a tenacity and valour worthy of a nobler cause." "Everyone was asking for a drop of water" – Capuzzi – "but no one had any. I found an orange in my bag, and, keeping one segment for myself, shared the rest with the officers; we even squeezed the peel, our lips were burning so badly."

In this desperate situation, the favoured method of attack was to have someone dash ahead with the flag; this spurred the others to follow through to defend it. The flag became the cause. The Neapolitans understood this, and did everything they could to capture it. Elia and Menotti Garibaldi climbed up the second bank together waving the big flag. Menotti was immediately wounded in the hand. The two men tumbled back down the bank among the others.

"It was not a simple tricolour," our guide explains, "but a flag made for Garibaldi in 1855 by the Italian women of Valparaíso. Garibaldi had passed through the Chilean port as a sea captain. Local Italians had spoken of their disappointment that they still didn't have a proper nation of origin, as the French, Spanish and British communities did. The flag was made in the hope that one day Garibaldi would rectify that."

In a later, more reflective account of the Thousand's campaign, Cesare Abba offers a detailed description: "On one side, amid the intense hues of the tricolour, were emblems of silver and gold showing broken chains and cannons and weapons of every kind, together with Italy, in the form of a beautiful woman in triumph, wearing a tall crown. On the other side, in letters embroidered in gold, were the words 'TO GIUSEPPE GARIBALDI, the Italian residents of Valparaíso, 1855'. Then on three ribbons hanging from the top, written with gold studs, were three words that in those days would have us sighing, as if over a dream that could never come true, three things that, now we do have them, seem always to have existed: Independence, Unity, Liberty."

"This is when Schiaffino died," explains our guide, "on the second terrace." His stick points to the throng of miniature warriors around the flag. Zasio's version of the story is the simplest, though his syntax reads like a schoolboy translation from the Latin, and he gets the flag's donors wrong: "Then Schiaffino, waving the Montevideo flag, which was given to Garibaldi for his services to that Republic, having boldly pushed forward among the Bourbons, was mistaken for the general, since he looked identical, and fell. The flag was torn away, and only the pole was left. His corpse was found twisted and broken in a thousand ways. In a space of twenty metres the dead and wounded lay huddled together. Blood soaked the contested soil."

I put it to our guide that this extreme attachment to a flag, a symbol – the idea that you might willingly die for it – seems strange to us today. In reply he tells me how Major Sforza's men boasted of their acquisition, though meantime they had been forced to retreat up the third and last bank, so that now there was only the hilltop to defend. "Our men," wrote Landi that evening to the king's lieutenant in Palermo, "killed one of their officials on horseback and captured their flag, which remains in our possession". "Unfortunately," the guide says, shaking his head, "it has never been found. It would be wonderful to have it here, in the museum."

But did Schiaffino really look like Garibaldi? Is that why the Neapolitans went for him with such determination? All the images we have suggest he did. He had the same beard, the same noble forehead and powerful torso, though he was a good twenty-five years younger. Certainly by 1860 Garibaldi had become as iconic as any flag. And he was aware of this. It's clear from all accounts of Calatafimi that Garibaldi used his body like a banner, pushing forward and exposing himself to the enemy so that in their anxiety to protect him his men would rush ahead. "He encouraged us with kind words" – Zasio – "but at all costs attack, at all costs victory." Shortly after tumbling down the second bank with the flag, Augusto Elia "turned and saw General Garibaldi, with no care for himself, exposed, alone... advancing with heroic sangfroid into withering enemy gunfire." Elia and others rushed to join him. "I was in unspeakable distress, keeping a constant eye on him, when I saw a Bourbon marksman step up to the top of the bank and take aim. I barely had time to step in front of Garibaldi when a terrible blow struck me in the mouth and threw me to the ground."

A second of our diarists also went down. In the aftermath of the big tussle for the flag, Bandi launched his bayonet, so he says, at the same red-haired sergeant who had shot Schiaffino at point blank range, but "a huge blow struck me above the right breast and I hit the ground, exactly as if I'd taken a violent punch".

How did Garibaldi respond to these losses? Under cover of the steep bank of the second terrace his men were regrouping. The Neapolitans had begun pushing rocks over the edge, where they couldn't see to fire. Someone spoke of Schiaffino and the flag. "You think this is the right moment to announce a public disaster?" Garibaldi demanded (Abba's version). This was around the time that Bixio approached the general and suggested they retreat, something he later confirms in a letter to his wife. They were now exposed to cannon fire from the right, and there was an imminent danger of being surrounded. They were exhausted. Between dead and wounded they had lost a hundred men and more. "Retreat where?" Garibaldi answers in one version. "Here we make Italy, or die," he says more colourfully in another. And in yet another, replying to the question "What should we do now?", he says, "Italians, here we have to die."

Our guide is now explaining that at this critical moment it was a young Sicilian, Simone Marino, who turned the tide by capturing one of the two Bourbon cannons. Other accounts give the honour to men from Treviso and Vicenza. "There was nothing tactically brilliant about the Battle of Calatafimi," our guide goes on. "Garibaldi was far from controlling events, and it could have gone either way." Fortunately, at the same time as the Neapolitan cannon was captured, the garibaldini finally got their own cannons to land a shot or two among the enemy on the hilltop. Morale lifted.

"'Rest, boys, rest a bit'" – Abba has the general say – "'one more push and we're done.'"

"Few but firm were the words he spoke" – Capuzzi – "and on hearing them we felt our courage rise again: we felt we were heroes."

In his later book, torn between the ugliness and glamour of war, Abba tries to put his finger on Garibaldi's role at Calatafimi: "In the three days before the battle he had managed to communicate to all of us a deep, steady, proud awareness of our situation; his art in that battle lay in his having gathered us all up in his hand, like so many thunderbolts, to the point that we were simply unable to abandon the field as losers; then he was free to release us, each to our own devices, sure that the deepest virtues, strengths and genius of each would shine out, from the liturgical calm of Sirtori to the fury of Bixio, from the brilliant impetus of Schiaffino to the boldness of Edoardo Herter, Achille Sacchi and a hundred others."

No sooner had Garibaldi told his men to take a breather before the final push than he was struck on the shoulder by a rock and fell. "He made nothing of it – just went on exuding the sort of confidence that creates confidence in others. All this in a fifteen minute lull," Abba concludes, "when, had the Bourbons dared to rush down on us with their bayonets, all two thousand of them, the battle was theirs."

The final assault was launched "towards three", says Nievo. "The sun was setting," says Capuzzi. "It was four o'clock," says Crispi. "Everything I've related in these last pages," says Bandi, "took place in just a few minutes, but they were minutes that seemed like centuries." "After eight hours of fighting, both sides sounded the retreat," wrote Landi in his report. In fact, it was only the Bourbons who retreated. Insisting, in his later book, that war is a terrible thing, Abba nevertheless concludes: "That last bayonet attack was truly marvellous. Even the dying got to their feet to play their part. The Neapolitans couldn't stand their ground; they turned and fled." "How we did it," Bixio wrote to his wife the following morning, "only Garibaldi could first have imagined, then made it happen."

"What were the casualties?" Eleonora asks our guide. The elderly man leads us back through reception, where a neat little woman is now sitting behind the ticket counter with nothing to do. We are taken round the building to a more noble entrance mimicking a Doric design. A fading red carpet leads up stone steps to a grand wrought-iron door. Inside is a small mausoleum, or ossuary – white walls, grey marble floor, plaques, photos, flags, memorabilia.

"The bones used to be on view, but people find that morbid these days, so they've been walled up."

All the same, there is a large black-and-white photograph of how it used it be before people learnt to be squeamish. Bones on shelves. Each man reduced to a skull resting on crossed femurs above a tidy heap of fingers and vertebrae. The skulls share a gaze of ghastly astonishment. "There were something over thirty dead on each side," our guide says. "And a hundred or so wounded, but many of the wounded would die days or weeks later." Captain Montanari, Bandi tells us, who hadn't wanted to wait till he was dead to drink the general's brandy, was shot in the knee as the two men fought side by side. Amputation could not save him from the gangrene that set in, and he died on 6th June.

Bandi had fought on after his first wound, even joining the final charge, during which he was hit again, this time above the left shoulder blade. He now had five bullet wounds. Young Nino was nowhere to be seen. Bandi rolled down the steep bank to escape the fighting and found himself next to a wounded Neapolitan infantryman whom he defended against a group of Sicilians looking for spoils and revenge. "Seeing the Bourbons flee, the Sicilians rushed down from the hilltops in long lines, like swarms of ants, and in no time were all over the battlefield." Hours later, when Bandi had at last been carried to the tiny church in Vita that was to serve as a hospital, he "realized that merciful hands had relieved me of my sabre, my revolver, my pack and my wallet."

Our guide crosses the floor of the ossuary to point out a photograph of Rose Montmasson, Crispi's wife, who did what she could to help the wounded. None of our diarists speak of her, yet she must have been there all along, marching with the men, eating with them, and now applying bandages, or speaking softly while bullets were gouged from bloody flesh. "Rosalina... did her duty with the wounded," wrote her husband to a friend. The photo shows a glum face, tightly curled hair, a hint of jowliness. The men lay on straw pallets, or directly on the floor. It was hard to sleep for the cries. "How long I was left on the battlefield for dead, I don't know," Augusto Elia writes, "but when

I opened my eyes it was night and I was surrounded by corpses that had been piled under a fig tree." He had been stripped of everything but his underwear. Taken on muleback to the church in Vita, his face was unrecognizable, and he couldn't speak. The bullet, fired from the hillside above, had passed downward through his mouth and lodged in his shoulder. But he recognized the garibaldini's doctor. Holding his shattered jawbone in place with one hand, with the other he wrote, "Dear Ripari, please look after me, Elia." Months of suffering had just begun.

"Picturesque aspect to our camp after the battle," noted Nievo. "Attending to wounded Neapolitans. Poverty of medical supplies born with cheerful resolve."

In the ossuary there are photos of the Sicilian dead, and a list of the Sicilian wounded. Our guide complains that the Sicilians' role in the victory is underplayed, both by fans of the garibaldini, who only have eyes for their heroes, and revisionists who don't want to acknowledge that the Sicilians played an important part in the Risorgimento. Capuzzi mentions a number of Sicilians joining the attack up the terraces – "in particular two friars armed with muskets who charged alongside us". One was killed. "Otherwise they hung back," he says, "waiting to see who would win." "The *picciotti*," writes Nievo "made their contribution by firing into the enemy's flanks, from a most prudent distance."

Our guide stopped at every photo, read every caption out loud and explained every object in the melancholy room. "Do you get many visitors?" Eleonora eventually interrupted. "Not as many as we should," he replied. And still the tour wasn't over. We were taken outside, where the day was now ninety minutes hotter. Along the flat ridge of the hilltop there was an avenue of cypresses – Viale della Rimembranza – with white-stone memorials between the trees bearing the names of Italian towns and lists of the garibaldini who came from them. The men fought together in their regional groups for the national cause. "Hurrah for Bergamo!" cried Bandi when he realized he and his comrades were being reinforced by a group of Bergamaschi.

"But no names for the Bourbons?"

Our guide shakes his head.

"The dead Neapolitans, how pitiful to see them," writes Abba. He describes wandering back over the battlefield, kissing the corpses of dead friends. Dusk came suddenly, and there was a chill wind. "To gather the wounded," says Crispi, "took from six in the evening till the following morning." "Kill the rat!" Bixio yelled when a peasant was seen venting his rage on the corpse of an enemy. After a night sleeping on the cold hilltop, Abba was up early the following morning, clambering back down the terraces again, turning over bodies. Finally he found his friend Eugenio Sartori. "Dead where he had fallen. No one had touched him, but he looked as though he had been dead three days." This time Abba couldn't muster the courage to bestow a last kiss. "The skin was so yellow you couldn't look."

At the end of the cypress avenue, fifty yards of coarse grass lead you to the edge of a steep downward slope. "This is where the garibaldini climbed up for the final attack," says the guide. Right on the spot is a concrete structure of four slender pillars about three metres high arranged in a curve and topped by an architrave that bears the words "QUI SI FA L'ITALIA O SI MUORE" – "Here we make Italy or die". Designed to look (vaguely) like the remains of an ancient temple, the monument lies exactly at the borderline where commemoration slides into kitsch. Beside it, on a high mast, the Italian flag flies in perpetuity.

"The garibaldini," the guide explains, believed the hill was called Pianto Romano ("Roman Lament") in memory of a battle that the Romans lost against the Carthaginians. In fact an earlier version of the name appears in seventeenth-century documents indicating a plantation – *pianto* – of vines cultivated by the Romano family."

"Still," I reflect, "the misunderstanding seemed to help the garibaldini to think of themselves in relation to classical history. So it was useful in its way."

Again the guide isn't interested in discussing things. He's been doing this job for years. Very likely he hadn't had his breakfast yet. Eventually he left us, and we scrambled a little way down the scarp that the garibaldini had stormed up. Prickly grass and loose white stones. Our feet slithered. All around, a patchwork of tawny stubble and dusty vineyards stretched away over shapeless hills, uncannily silent but for the whirr of the crickets. The only visible creatures were two black goats cropping weeds by the fence. We turned to leave and climbed back up towards the tricolour. Seen from below, high in a milky sky, it seemed to beg a thousand questions. Am I a flag of triumph or of mourning? Do I gather the landscape in celebration or am I utterly insignificant in the vast wash of hazy summer? You imagine Garibaldi's men, their bayonets lowered, racing towards it, the tricolour. As towards an enigma. Italy. The future. Our present.

In his memoir, Garibaldi summed up the day thus: "Although hardly important in terms of our acquisitions, having captured one cannon, a few rifles and a handful of prisoners, the victory at Calatafimi was immense for its effect on morale, encouraging the local people and demoralizing the enemy army."

On another occasion he wrote: "If, drawing my last breath, after all my battles, my friends see me smile, that will be for you, glorious fighters of Calatafimi."

PART TWO

SWIRL AND FLUX

Calatafimi Segesta

The past is a foreign country we cannot visit. It conditions our lives from afar, but issues no visas. We feel we need to know it, but the closer we come to its misty beaches, the more elusive it proves. What you supposed was the past, as in a historical novel, turns out to be only a fancy-dress version of the present. How to come to grips, then, with a world whose most distinctive feature is its absence? We can only examine the clues time has spared: the ruins, the artefacts, the texts. Contemplate them at length. Accept that any joining of the dots will never entirely convince.

Late in the same day that we visited Pianto Romano, we also managed to see the ancient temple of Segesta. It stands some four miles north-west of the town of Calatafimi, which is itself about three miles north-east of the battlefield. Our guide at the monument had told us that Garibaldi visited the temple the day after the battle. None of the written sources confirm this. Bandi says the temple was visible from the Pietralunga hilltop, but we didn't see it from there. We took a bus that leaves you at another fence, another gate. But while Pianto Romano had been forlorn and empty, the Segesta site was buzzing, and a café was doing a brisk trade in ice creams and cold drinks. Once you've queued for your admission, you follow a stony path lined by stunted olives and spiky agaves up a sharp slope. A uniformed woman sheltering from the sun in a wooden cubicle nods distractedly at your ticket. Then the path turns to the right, climbs a few more steps, and there it is – intact, magnificent, dominating range after range of hills, away to a hazy sea.

"The emotions of the day after," wrote Cesare Abba, "the tiredness and the need for reflection, didn't discourage those who had a strong feeling for places from doing a little sightseeing. Leaving the town to the west, they walked to the ruins of Segesta, growing more and more excited as they approached. The ancient columns seemed strangely recent, and inspired a lofty melancholy. Was it possible that this countryside had once been inhabited by men so rich and noble as to have built this temple, while now its people are almost all poverty-stricken?"

The hilltop is barren, the grass brownish. Arranged in the classic Doric rectangle, thirty-six grey columns are held together with a solid architrave, while the front of the building has the typical tympanum – alas, half hidden by scaffolding when we visited. The columns taper as they rise, but are not fluted as in most Greek temples. The stonework is rough, and the blocks at the base still have the protruding bosses that made them transportable. There is no sign there were ever decorations, or even a roof. Built in the 5th century BC by the Elymian people to a Greek design, the huge structure was never finished. The Elymians, who may or may not have been indigenous, were at war with the people of Selinunte, on the coast to the south. To defend their territorial sovereignty they made alliances with foreign powers. The Athenians. Then the Carthaginians. Finally the Romans. In the long run they became collateral damage in larger wars. Nearly two thousand years later, Machiavelli would lament the fact that the smaller Italian states were always willing to call foreigners into the peninsula to defend their independence, as a result of which the whole country was enslaved. Unity was the only solution, he thought.

"The columns seemed alive, thoughtful," wrote Abba, "and the temple appeared to have a soul, and to suffer at finding itself surrounded by careless goatherds in whom, nevertheless, ancient man surely lay sleeping. The visiting soldiers believed they had come here to awaken him."

Knowing almost nothing of the past – who were these Elymians? – we nevertheless draw it into our present. The garibaldini imagined they were enacting a political renaissance; they would rouse the local Sicilian peasantry and renew ancient glories. In Calatafimi a plaque reads: "Stifled by long tyranny, but cherished with religious love, the torch of liberty shone forth whenever hope breathed on its flame – in 1812, 1820, 1848 – until in 1860 the powerful spirit of Giuseppe Garibaldi blew it into a national conflagration that overwhelmed and destroyed the regional statelets, whence emerged, to new and beautiful life, the third Italy." The "third Italy" means a third avatar of Rome as the centre of world culture, after imperial Rome and papal Rome.

We walked round the temple and took photographs. There were no careless goatherds, but plenty of carefree tourists. A low wooden fence prevents you from entering. In the evening sun, the columns do indeed seem quietly alive, their porous stone soaked in heat and light. There is evidence that the temple was dedicated to Aphrodite, though historians have no idea what ceremonies were performed here. Animal sacrifices? Scapegoating? If you want to sit for a while, a solitary bench is available at the front of the building, looking away across the hills. It's a red bench – the only bright colour in sight – to remind us of the scandal of violence against women. I make an effort to connect this well-meaning contemporary campaign to the ancient temple. Iphigenia perhaps? The rape of the Sabine women? Europa carried off by the bull? Then it occurs to me that while the garibaldini were generally anti-Catholic, and certainly left no churches or shrines, they nevertheless expressed a religious fervour that drew everything ancient and noble into their narrative. The word "miracle" occurs over and over again in their diaries. In this they were quite unlike the Neapolitan generals, who often seemed more concerned with the terms of their contracts. "On the one side," observed nineteenth-century historian Raffaele de Cesare of the two armies facing each other at Calatafimi, "was a bravery blind to the point of folly and an apostolic faith in the cause to which they had sacrificed their lives. On the other was a much bigger army with no ideals, no leaders and no solid organization, destined to fight solely on behalf of the king."

Yet fight they did. "Last year's battles in Lombardy," Garibaldi wrote to a friend the morning after the clash at Pianto Romano, "were nowhere near as fierce as yesterday's." It was a "disaster", he reflected, that Italians had to fight other Italians, but also a promise of "what could be done with this family the day we see it united".

We left Segesta with a feeling of having seen something extraordinary but utterly enigmatic. And beyond any controversy or dispute. Who would take sides now between Segesta and Selinunte? Conversely, the history we're following on our walk through Sicily left nothing so grand architecturally, but is still fiercely disputed in scores of texts that contradict each other at every point. If the temple that the garibaldini were building was Italian national unity, it remains unfinished. The family Garibaldi yearned for is stubbornly dysfunctional.

Giuseppe Buttà was military chaplain of the 9th Infantry Battalion in the Bourbon army. In 1875 he gave his account of events in Sicily in 1860. Outside Salemi, he claimed, Garibaldi had actually sought to avoid contact with the Bourbons. He was hesitant and indecisive.

Major Sforza attacked with just five hundred men. The garibaldini took heavy casualties and fled. But at that very moment, General Landi ordered the retreat, betraying his own men and handing the field to Garibaldi. The explanation, Buttà reveals, is that Landi had been promised a letter of credit, delivered by Garibaldi to the Banco di Napoli, for the sum of 14,000 ducats. A year later, on retrieving the letter from the bank and finding that it was for only 14 ducats, the general had an apoplectic fit and fell down dead.

Giacinto de' Sivo, a Neapolitan playwright and administrator, published a similar account of events at Calatafimi in the second volume of his *History of the Two Sicilies*, in 1867. Again the battle was in reality won by Sforza's Neapolitans, who were then betrayed by General Landi. Neither writer witnessed the fighting. Buttà was stationed in Monreale, near Palermo, De' Sivo was in Naples. Landi did not die of an apoplectic fit, and bribes are hardly paid by regular letters of credit. Garibaldi had no history of paying off his enemies, nor would his men have wanted him to. Yet, after a long period of neglect, both these authors have recently been republished and much appreciated in Italy. In general, there is a desire to reimagine the Bourbon kingdom pre-1860 as a flourishing, benevolent state, tragically destroyed by the Risorgimento. The challenge, for those investing in this narrative, is to explain how a country with a population of around nine million and a capital city, Naples, that was the largest metropolis in Italy and the third largest in Europe after London and Paris, could have failed to halt the incursion of a thousand poorly armed men. Their response is to posit a combination of international conspiracy and internal betrayal: General Landi together with the commanders of the ships who failed to stop Garibaldi's landing at Marsala, and many others, are all to be accused of treachery. No evidence has ever been adduced.

Certainly the garibaldini didn't feel they had been gifted the victory as they settled down on the hillside at Pianto Romano to pass the night among their dead. Giuseppe Capuzzi was relieved to be sent off in an advance party to guard against a counter-attack in the night. The hillside, he feared, would soon begin to smell. After a dinner of bread, cheese and wine, he and his companions felt so sure they would fall asleep on duty that they sprawled across the road, reckoning the Bourbons wouldn't be able to get past without waking them. In any event, the battle, they thought, would surely resume the following morning. The enemy would be reinforced. High on its hilltop, Calatafimi seemed unassailable. Instead, shortly after midnight, two men approached. They had news: the Bourbons were retreating, in the direction of Palermo. When these visitors made to return to their homes, Garibaldi said no. They could sleep here beside him, "under a big olive tree", wrote Zasio. "And they didn't realize," remarks Abba, "that very likely Garibaldi didn't trust them, because the news they had brought was too good – unbelievable, in fact."

"Your Excellency, help. Help at once." Such are the opening words of General Landi's report to Prince Castelcicala, the king's lieutenant in Palermo, immediately after the battle at Pianto Romano. "Without reinforcements I will have to retreat... please understand that my column here is surrounded by countless enemies."

"The only thing populating the hills with countless enemies," wrote De Cesare, "was General Landi's imagination." The historian, De Cesare, it should be said, was born and bred in the Kingdom of the Two Sicilies, and often accused of being nostalgic for it.

Hours after writing his dispatch, to the dismay of Major Sforza and other senior officers, Landi had his army on the road, heading back to Palermo. "I fooled the enemy," he boasted, "by having campfires lit around Calatafimi, giving the impression we were still in the town."

"Landi's Shameful Retreat" is De' Sivo's chapter title.

"We climbed the road that leads to Calatafimi" – remembers Capuzzi – "gazing in amazement at the castle with its strong defensive position, astonished that the Bourbons hadn't chosen to hold it, if only to block our march to the capital."

"16th May. 6 a.m." – Nievo. "Arrival in Calatafimi. Medical assistance to the enemy wounded. Fanatical patriotism of the women. Garibaldi speaks to the crowd, brought together by the band from Alcamo. Exhortation to enlist en masse."

When we had left Pianto Romano that morning to follow in their footsteps, it was almost 11 a.m., with the temperature up in the high thirties. A black billy goat watched us depart, chewing dry grass between dark gums. The track winds down from the battle monument through vineyards, low scrub and outcropping rock. An old bridge crosses a marshy creek, then you climb steeply up three or four hairpins towards the castle above. The air hums with insects. To the left, a conical hill of inky pines and antique villas seems invented by a seventeenth-century landscape painter. We move slowly, breathing deeply, until at last the outlying streets funnel us into narrow canyons of shade. Via dei Mille, Via 15 Maggio.

We're beginning to understand what characterizes these small towns of western Sicily: long terraces of nondescript flat-roofed housing, only occasionally broken by side streets; no pavements, no vegetation. A space that contrives to be both bare and cluttered. Power cables swinging slack just below the roofs. Flaking stucco. Balconies shaded with curtains of bamboo, shutters closed against the heat. After the open countryside, the pressure of the built-up community is palpable. Here and there, suspended at about shoulder height, tightly stuffed plastic bags hang on long strings from upper windows. It was some time before we realized they were placed there for the dustman. Beyond the reach of cats or rats.

At midday the streets are empty. Steep alleyways link one long narrow street to others above and below. There are few piazzas as such, but occasional open spaces where roads drift together or divide. Our B&B is in Casa di Anita in Via Anita Garibaldi. A recent monument, no more than a block of grey volcanic rock, is dedicated to the Women of the Risorgimento on the 164th anniversary of the Battle of Calatafimi, which is to say 2014. Our landlady is welcoming and genuinely amazed that we should have walked from Salemi, but makes no connection with the name of her house.

For lunch, since all the shops are closed, she directs us to La Locanda di Nonna Ciccia, Granny Francesca's Tavern. The narrow window on a drab side street is hardly encouraging, but the promise of air-conditioning is irresistible. Inside, a spic-and-span retro decor cheers us up at once, and in very short order the proprietor, who appears to be acting as both chef and waiter, has brought us an abundant *tris* of the most exquisite pastas. Spinach-and-ricotta ravioli in cream of crab sauce is the one I recall. Giuseppe Capuzzi also remembers enjoying good food and wine in Calatafimi. "Living it up is so wonderful," he writes, "when you've done your duty and your conscience is clear." Afterwards there was no alternative but to take to our beds.

Giuseppe Bandi was to spend many hours and days in bed in Calatafimi. His accounts of the miseries of his wounded companions, of overdoses of laudanum to dispatch dying teenagers, of gangrene and haemorrhages and the rasp of the surgeon's saw removing infected limbs, dispel any notion that the garibaldini diaries are naively gung-ho. He also got used to being around priests for the first time in his life: "In the small monastery of San Michele... the friars watched over us day and night, and did everything possible to alleviate our pains." One day he was woken from feverish dreams by the sound of sobbing. His young assistant Nino was sitting at the foot of his straw mattress. "Excellency," he wept. "My poor Excellency." Bandi was furious, and called him a coward. "Where were you when I needed you?" Nino spun a story about having had a brother in the battle, wounded, whom he had carried back to Salemi. He'd brought a gift, he said, and "he laid beside me a bunch of wild asparagus". Bandi burst out laughing and told the boy to go to hell. "I never saw him again."

The wounded Elia meantime had been moved to a private house in Vita, where doctors inserted a feeding tube through his shattered jaw and ordered him to lie face down with his head over the side of the mattress so that the pus forming in his mouth wouldn't poison him. He was in that position when Major Montanari – the brandy drinker – died in the bed beside him.

Cesare Abba describes visiting wounded Neapolitans in Calatafimi. Sixty-two of the Bourbon soldiers had been left behind. "The victors went to see them in churches and monasteries," Abba writes. "We comforted them, caressed them." The hope was always to bring about a mass desertion in the Bourbon camp. In general, Abba remembers, the town was in a state of shock; the Bourbons had taken most of the food, the shops were empty and the people terrified that the war would soon be back.

One can't help feeling that Abba was in a state of shock too. Calatafimi had been his first experience of war. He decided to spend the day alone in his quarters above the town, another monastery, where he enjoyed a fine view north across the hills to the bay of Castellammare. He thought about his dead friends, picturing them as they had been just two days before: "daring, optimistic, cheerful". He worried about his wounded comrades in Vita. What would happen if Bourbon soldiers found them? He gazed towards the sea, whose "distant waters held a smile of promise where a soul might lose itself, as in the eyes of a sweet girl". Whenever Abba is melancholy, a sweet girl swims into vision. Perhaps he was helped on this occasion by the contents of Garibaldi's daily communication to his men, which Abba personally was to read out to his company that evening. "I had copied the words down," he tells us, "in the town hall, where Captain Cenni was in a furious mood. 'Soldiers of Italian freedom,' it began, 'with comrades like you there is nothing I will not dare... When they get news of the battle, your mothers and girlfriends will come out on the streets full of pride, heads held high, radiant.'"

Returning from our visit to the temple, we found ourselves in Via Cesare Abba, at the centre of Calatafimi. In the fullness of time, the soldier's diary would bring celebrity status. It's more a flight of steps than a street, leading into Piazza Plebiscito, which recalls the referendum held later that year to sanction unification with the Kingdom of Italy. At one end of the piazza, where pink azaleas glow in the twilight, Pippo's Chiosco is serving beers to a dozen tables arranged around a bust of Garibaldi. We sit down and order a local craft beer. Only as we're getting up to leave do I notice that there is actually another monument in the shadows behind our seats: *Ai Caduti*, the Fallen. Here a full-size Garibaldi clasps a wounded soldier to his breast. On the pedestal beneath, two boys in black T-shirts are sitting beside their scooters smoking.

Alcamo

Hindsight is a great simplifier. "The Bourbon state was rotten, and Garibaldi was always bound to win" is a typical modern summary of events. No heroism here. The Kingdom of the Two Sicilies was an admirable state, but hardly a match for a vast international conspiracy. In this version, the naive garibaldini are an instrument in evil hands. Their ideas and sacrifice count for nothing.

"From Calatafimi to Alcamo was a cheerful walk through green fields," writes Abba. "But everywhere there were signs of the defeat we had inflicted on the Bourbons: backpacks, berets, bloody bandages abandoned along the way.'

"Our retreat proceeded smoothly," General Landi reported. "We arrived in Alcamo at 2 a.m. and camped outside the town to give the troops some rest." However, leaving Alcamo at 5 a.m., the column, three thousand strong, ran into an ambush at Valguarnera, a village three miles from Partinico. Then, entering Partinico itself, Landi writes, "we met with stiffer resistance. The town was full of armed bands. A double ambush, to the right and left, met us with sustained rifle fire." It had taken just a few hours, in the dead of night, for a large body of Sicilians to organize an elaborate attack.

We also enjoyed the hush of dense vegetation outside Calatafimi in the half-hour before dawn. This really is the best moment of the day. Vineyards and cornfields breathe softly in the stillness. Trees are wrapped in balmy darkness. But when the cocks began to crow and the light stole up behind distant hills, we, like the garibaldini, noticed things abandoned beside the road. Not bandages and backpacks, but, once again, plastic bags and rubbish. And the question is, for both 1860 and the present day, how can you really sound out the collective state of mind behind this or that behaviour? Why do people do this?

When some pundits claim that the South was better off before the unification of Italy, you have to wonder which "before" exactly they mean. The Kingdom of the Two Sicilies, whose army Garibaldi was fighting, had only come into existence in 1816. In medieval times there had been one Sicily, which meant the whole of southern Italy, including the island of Trinacria, also known as Sicily. When the island rebelled against the mainland in the late twelve hundreds and a separate kingdom was established, people began to speak of the "Two Sicilies". In 1733 the Spanish Bourbons, who held the island, conquered the mainland Kingdom of Naples, and the "Two Sicilies" were henceforth ruled by the same king, but as separate kingdoms. It was important for the islanders that they not be a mere province of a Neapolitan state.

The French revolution and the Napoleonic era brought upheaval throughout Italy and initiated a struggle between liberal republicans and conservative monarchists. In Naples a republic was set up in alliance with French revolutionary troops in 1799, but soon overturned. The French were back in 1805, and Napoleon's brother Joseph was crowned king of Naples, though not of Sicily, where the Bourbon king had taken refuge, protected by the British Navy. The south of Italy was thus split in line with the great power struggle between France and Britain. France ruled the Continent, Britain the waves. In 1808 Joseph Napoleon left Naples to govern Spain and was replaced by Joaquim Murat. It was these French rulers who brought the Neapolitan kingdom into the modern age, curbing feudal and ecclesiastical privileges and introducing the *Code Napoléon*. Meantime in Sicily, in 1812, the British, represented by the hyperactive William Bentinck, pushed the Bourbon king to adopt a liberal constitution along British lines.

After the fall of Napoleon, both Sicilies were returned to the now ageing Bourbon king, Ferdinand, who in 1816 united the two territories in a single kingdom with Naples as its capital. This allowed him to ditch the generous constitution he had granted in Sicily, which he loathed. Nevertheless, it proved hard to turn the clock back; many of his Neapolitan administrators and army officers had served under the French. In Sicily many administrators had appreciated the British-inspired constitution, and in June 1820 the island rebelled, demanding that the constitution be reinstated and the two kingdoms once again separated. The following month liberal pro-French elements in Naples instigated a major uprising under General Guglielmo Pepe and forced the king to grant a new constitution. The Austrians, who had set themselves up as defenders of a pre-revolutionary, anti-democratic Europe, were alarmed. They summoned Ferdinand to Ljubljana and proposed an Austrian invasion of his territories that would return him to his throne as an absolute monarch with unlimited powers. He agreed. The arrangement set a pattern in Italy for the next forty years, with despotic dukes and princes increasingly relying on Austrian military support to prop up their ancient privileges. Once the Austrian army had occupied Naples, all officers and administrators who had previously served under Murat and Pepe were removed from their positions. These included the young General Landi, and indeed the kingdom's most decorated and successful general, Carlo Filangieri, who had fought with Napoleon at Austerlitz. The implication was that loyalty was inevitably ideological: you couldn't simply serve your country however it was ruled. Taking over the crown in 1825, Francis I managed to convince the Austrians at least to withdraw their unpopular troops, which they did in 1827. However, he then replaced them with four Swiss regiments, three in Naples, one in Palermo. The presence of these foreign soldiers, whose loyalty was strictly to king, not country, indicated the dynasty's intention to protect itself against internal unrest, rather than external threat.

So much for potted history. What's useful for our story is an awareness that both of the "Two Sicilies" had passed through many phases in recent years. Change was not unthinkable. Nor, whatever the Austrians might seek to impose, was it unimaginable to serve under different kinds of regime. In 1830 Ferdinand II came to the throne and reinstated the officers purged nine years before: they included some of the most experienced men in the realm. At an international level, Ferdinand sought complete neutrality, avoiding military alliances with Europe's major powers and asserting a dynastic rule based exclusively on loyalty to himself. There would be industrial innovation and educational reform, but no constitution and no power-sharing of any kind. This experiment was interrupted by the Sicilian revolution of January 1848, which forced the Bourbon army out of the island and reintroduced a modified version of the 1812 British-inspired constitution. In February 1848, when the Neapolitans threatened to follow suit, Ferdinand quickly granted them a constitution, only to revoke it after further unrest in May. Five hundred people were killed when the Swiss regiments broke down barricades and stormed the Parliament. Meanwhile, the veteran general Carlo Filangieri was put at the head of a 20,000-strong army to retake Sicily, something he did with systematic ruthlessness in a series of battles that involved thousands of deaths and unspeakable cruelty on both sides. The Swiss were in the forefront. Notoriously, Ferdinand agreed to the use of heavy cannon fire against the port of Messina, reducing whole areas of the town to rubble in five days of uninterrupted shelling. Having regained his kingdom, the king then battened down the hatches for what came to be known as the "Decade of Immobility". He would not contemplate a constitution. He would not consider a move towards a federal Italy. His administrators and generals were always the same administrators and the same generals, growing older and older.

This was the situation that Francis II inherited in May 1859 after his father had reigned for twenty-nine years. The new king was twenty-three, the only child of Ferdinand's first marriage; he was surrounded by the twelve half-brothers and sisters born to his father's second wife, Austrian princess Maria Theresa von Habsburg-Teschen. Having dominated the court in Ferdinand's last years, Maria Theresa was reputedly plotting to have Francis replaced by her own eldest son. In the north of Italy war had broken out between Piedmont and Austria, with the French fighting beside the Piedmontese. It was understood that Piedmont, which had maintained its liberal constitution of 1848 despite Austrian opposition, was fighting for Italian unity and attracting all the peninsula's liberal energies. Franco-Piedmontese victories at Magenta and Solferino in June 1859 were greeted with rejoicing on the streets of Naples and Palermo. In the same month, a rebellion of students at the Naples medical school was put down by the Swiss Guard. But in September, the Swiss troops themselves revolted. Under pressure internationally for hiring out its army to despotic regimes, Switzerland had chosen not to renew its arrangement with Naples; individual soldiers could stay in the kingdom, if they wished, but their regiments must no longer be officially known as "Swiss" and could no longer display Helvetian insignia. This was unacceptable to the soldiers, who felt strongly about their national identity. Twenty were killed when one group surrounded the royal palace. After this crisis, their regiments were dissolved, and a new foreign force was hurriedly formed with recruits from Austria and Bavaria. In short, the Kingdom of the Two Sicilies had become a turbulent place where change seemed inevitable, though no one was sure what form it should take. "The garibaldini," wrote De Cesare, "could fight with the certainty of having the sympathy of all the peoples of Italy, and Piedmont at their backs, not to speak of the enthusiasm of the free nations of the world. The Neapolitan soldiers were certain of the opposite."

Hardly taken seriously by his own family, let alone the citizens of Naples, weak, mystical and fatalistic, Francis II appointed the seventy-five-year-old General Filangieri as his first minister, then objected to his attempts to grant a constitution, form an alliance with France and Piedmont, and start discussions on the future of Italy. Filangieri resigned and retired to his home in Sorrento. That was March 1860. In May, immediately after Garibaldi landed in Marsala, Filangieri was recalled to Naples and invited to become the king's lieutenant in Sicily, replacing the prince of Castelcicala, who was widely believed to be incompetent and anyway in open conflict with the head of police in Palermo, Salvatore Maniscalco. The prince, who had grown up in England and was Eton-educated, believed in a softly-softly approach to liberal unrest, which in recent years, he observed, had always been quickly snuffed out. Maniscalco, on the other hand, was alarmist, repressive and ruthless.

Filangieri turned down the job: he was too old, he said, too tired and too sick. Pressed by the king, he proposed the prince of Ischitella, another ageing general who had fought with Murat. Ischitella refused; he had no desire, he explained, to play the cruel executioner in Sicily. So now Filangieri proposed General Ferdinando Lanza, yet another man born in the 1780s who had begun his career under the French. Lanza had been beside Filangieri in the battles for Messina and Catania in 1849, so he was no stranger to violent suppression. On the other hand, on 9th May 1849, in his first experience as commander-in-chief, he had confronted Garibaldi at Palestrina to the south of Rome and been soundly beaten. Accepting the offer of ruling Sicily, he was perhaps hoping for revenge. In any event, like General Landi (with whom we must be careful not to confuse him), Lanza at seventy-two was scarcely able to sit on a horse. He was obese.

The prince of Castelcicala was informed that the king was demanding his resignation on the evening of 15th May, exactly as General Landi began his retreat from Calatafimi. News of the defeat at Pianto Romano didn't reach Palermo till later that night. So the first thing General Lanza would hear on arrival in Sicily was that things were far worse than he had been told. Despite orders to go on the offensive and take the fight to the rebels, in the light of this new situation, he decided to gather all his forces in Palermo and wait for Garibaldi there. Meantime, the furious prince of Castelcicala returned to the mainland and devoted all his energies to putting the blame on the incompetence, cowardice and treachery of everyone else. The Bourbons were in disarray.

"Leaving Calatafimi at dawn, we were singing," wrote Abba. "Then, when the sun came up to crush us, everyone fell silent, and we marched on like wraiths."

"The road seemed longer than it was," remembered Capuzzi. "We were so eager to arrive, so excited by the thought of being welcomed, as elsewhere, by a cheering crowd. All these acclamations had begun to tickle our vanity."

Likewise oppressed by the sun but not expecting any acclaim on arrival, we sat and snacked in the shade of thick rushes near a swampy stream. It's a landscape of low hills, at once intensely cultivated – vineyard after vineyard – and uncannily empty. Not a soul in sight.

"I suppose if Garibaldi had retreated," I said, "when Bixio thought that was the only option... or if the Bourbons had reinforced their positions and attacked, as Abba feared, when the garibaldini were exhausted and exposed, things could well have turned out differently. Then hindsight would have reverted to the line that it's mad to take a thousand men to attack thirty thousand."

"We marched into Alcamo at eleven," says Abba. "It's a pretty town, albeit melancholy; in the shade of its streets you feel you're moving into a Moorish atmosphere. Palm trees lean evocatively from garden walls; every house looks like a monastery; a pair of bright eyes sparkle from a high balcony; you stop to look, but the vision is gone."

Maybe one could still offer this generous description of the very centre of Alcamo. But the 160 years that separate us from the Risorgimento have been the age of population explosion and urban sprawl. The countryside no longer rolls its lush carpet right up to noble city walls – rather it frays away in rubbish tips and prefab warehouses, cement depots surrounded by black railings. Lorries are parked with their engines running. Traffic races in narrow streets. Unlike Salemi and Calatafimi, Alcamo is more or less on the flat. In the Arab tradition, a long road – Corso 6 Aprile – runs arrow-straight to the centre. 6th April (1860) was the day local notables had started recruiting men for the uprising that preceded Garibaldi's arrival. Drivers fret behind double-parked cars. Hooters sound. As in Calatafimi, there are few breaks between the buildings, so that baroque façade and 1950s cinema, medieval brick and modern prefab, lean against each other in a crazy collage of styles, blended together by a patina of grey pollution.

Fortunately, Piazza Ciullo, right at the heart of the town, is as gracious as they come. Ciullo d'Alcamo was the first Italian poet to write in the vernacular, back in the early thirteenth century. Dante mentions him respectfully. A single surviving poem, 'Rosa fresca aulentissima' ("Fresh, most perfumed rose"), offers a witty back-and-forth between a would-be lover and a well-to-do damsel who plays hard to get. Invited to lunch with a local family, Cesare Abba remembers discussing the poem over wine, while highly conscious meantime of his host's two pretty daughters. "Couldn't Ciullo's charming exchange," he wonders, "have happened over one of these garden walls or hedges? Everything seems so antique."

The seeming antiquity is partly an illusion. The main piazza, named after the poet, was in fact restyled by the celebrity architect Gae Aulenti in 1996. A row of six marvellously tall palms leads up a gentle slope to the great baroque façade of the Chiesa del Collegio dei Gesuiti, whose pastel colours are picked up in a majestic flow of marble paving. Ancient ficus trees have been pruned into thick boxes of foliage offering the densest possible shade. All around, flowering shrubs and café tables animate the space beneath noble façades of one century or another. We settled on the Caffè Impero and ordered coffee.

It was Ascension Day, Capuzzi remembers, when the garibaldini arrived in the town, exactly as the local people were coming out of mass. This fits with Nievo's jottings: "17th May. Excitement in Alcamo. The friar marching beside us blessed Garibaldi at the church door and ended with the cry, 'Long live Garibaldi, long live Christ in the Blessed Sacrament.'" "Very simply and frankly," Abba confirms, "standing in the midst of the people, Garibaldi bowed before the cross that Fra Pantaleo placed on his shoulder as he declared him God's warrior." This was "a flash of real mysticism", Abba assures us. Others saw it as a canny playing to the crowd. Afterwards Garibaldi appointed Francesco Crispi secretary of state and set him to work issuing legislation to govern the provinces they had occupied, so to speak. It was important that the local people believe they were here to stay. Crispi, who had trained as lawyer and served in Sicily's revolutionary parliament in

1848, had brought plenty of ready-drafted material with him. One is struck, reading through all the decrees issued, printed and distributed to local administrators in these hectic days on finance, taxation, public security, military service and so on, by how organized the whole operation was, in its ramshackle way. Crispi had spent eleven years in exile preparing for this moment.

Meantime, having reached the centre of town, the soldiers gathered in the very space where we were now drinking our coffee. New officers and company commanders had to be chosen to replace those killed or wounded at Pianto Romano. Capuzzi's company accepted four Bourbon deserters, who asked if they could serve under the Italian flag. It was an encouraging sign. "And more than a hundred pairs of shoes were requisitioned... Except they were hardly suitable for long marches," says Capuzzi. "How many delicate feet accustomed to soft gentlemanly leather were chafed and tormented in those rigid boxes. Many men ended up sitting on the ambulance carts."

Abba wrote his diary perched on the steps of a church with the northern coast of Sicily spread out just five miles below. It was only ten or eleven days since they had left Genoa, he wrote, yet it seemed months or years, as if they'd "sailed a great distance, walked a great distance and been almost forgotten".

We too felt strangely detached in Piazza Ciullo, almost hallucinated. The heat was ferocious, the light too bright for comfort. In the afternoon we visited an exhibition of the so-called *pupi*, handsome marionettes used since medieval times to dramatize stories like the *Orlando Furioso*, or the *Song of Roland*. They are splendidly colourful, gloriously upright, their shields and armour bright silver, moustaches extravagantly wavy, helmets garishly plumed, eyes the brightest of blue. You can understand why the locals weren't impressed by the bedraggled, footsore garibaldini. One of the first things General Lanza did on arrival in Palermo was to promise that very soon the Sicilians would have a member of the royal family as the island's lieutenant. It was common knowledge, historian De Cesare remarks, that the Sicilians could be impressed with pomp and show. "But no one took the new lieutenant seriously, since this promise had been made many times before." None of the king's half-brothers were eager to live in Palermo.

Partinico

Walking in this heat is a spiritual exercise. Accept the discomfort, you repeat to yourself. Remember to drink every ten minutes. Keep your head covered – keep the sweat from your eyes. Don't scratch itches or insect bites: it only makes matters worse. Above all, beware of irritability, the temptation to bicker. For much of the time we walk in silence, or humming together, letting the heat soak in, drawing pleasure from the landscape, the scented air, the steady rhythm of our trekking poles. Fortunately, the ten miles from Alcamo to Partinico are hardly challenging. You're walking across grassy flatlands towards blue mountains, the bay of Castellammare a couple of misty miles to your left. From time to time you glimpse a sparkle of sea over hedges of prickly pear. Pines and cedars offer shade if you're desperate. The only real danger is the traffic; on a long stretch of busy road Eleonora stops to photograph an enormous toad flattened on the tarmac.

The garibaldini had other horrors to contemplate. "It was a happy day we spent in Alcamo," Abba remembered, "but what a different world awaited us on the morrow."

"18th May" – Nievo. "March to Partinico, where the dogs are still busy eating roasted Neapolitans. Not a mark of civilization."

"In a ditch" – Capuzzi – "beside a dead horse, lay a heap of charred corpses, already rotting."

"Waves of unbearable stench came to us on the breeze" – Abba. "Topping a hill, we saw that much of the town had been burnt. Smoke still rising from the rubble."

"The sight took our minds back to God knows what horrors in the past" – Zasio – "the Inquisition and worse."

"Chaos," fumed Bourbon chaplain Giuseppe Buttà, describing Landi's retreat, "infantry marching any old how, mixed up with carts and cannons and cavalry."

"Hands joined in a chain" – Abba – "a group of girls, hair loose, wild as the Furies, were singing and dancing round the corpses, the fires still burning behind them."

"Killing your enemy in battle is a right," reflects Capuzzi. "Venting your rage on a corpse is despicable."

"Shot at from windows and balconies" – Buttà – "the soldiers burned down the houses." Sixty buildings in all. But what were they to do, the priest asks, just accept being shot at?

"We found the corpses of Bourbons gnawed by dogs" – a rare detail from Garibaldi himself – "torn and mauled by their fellow Italians."

"The women pointed to their ruined houses and wept," remembers Capuzzi, "demanding we give them revenge."

"The bells were ringing wildly" – Abba. "Priests, friars, people of every kind cheered the soldiers marching behind Garibaldi, but he kept his hat pulled down over his eyes and crossed the city fast, gloomier than we had ever seen him."

"The people of Partinico," commented Salvatore Salomone-Marino, nineteenth-century expert in Sicilian folklore, "adore but one god: homicide."

It would be heartening to contrast this misery with a sumptuous account of what a wonderful place Partinico is today. We approached along narrow lanes offering the usual mix of the rickety and the picturesque. Everything seemed blanched in the summer light. Rough cement walls and flourishing vegetable gardens defended by yapping dogs. Once beyond the circular road, Corso dei Mille drives straight through sprawling outskirts to the great crossroad that always marks the centre of these once-Arab towns. The streets are wider and more breathable than those of Calatafimi and Alcamo, but uniformly drab. Only boxes of fruit and veg outside the greengrocers offer a splash of colour. To the south of the town, a reddish-brown rock face rises a thousand feet to loom over the cluttered housing. In Piazza Duomo, where Corso dei Mille meets Via Vittorio Emanuele Orlando, there is an ornate eighteenth-century fountain where old men gather to fill bottles of water from eight elaborately carved waterspouts. But you look in vain for the kind of gracious open space that makes most Italian towns so liveable, somewhere to lounge and eat and drink and soak up the scene.

There is a pleasant park, though, Villa Margherita, where amongst pines and magnolias and great banks of exotic dracaenas we almost stumble on the bust of a melancholy Garibaldi exchanging stony glances with an equally melancholy Victor Emmanuel a few yards away. Both men seem in danger of being overwhelmed by thick foliage. And while the busts themselves are quite small, the plinths they sit on are incongruously tall and large, perhaps to make room for the very long inscriptions on all sides. But the pale stone must be quite soft, because time has taken its toll: the letters are barely legible. I can just make out: "*Sacco e sangue vendicati con sangue.*" "Pillage and blood avenged with blood." And again: "*La stancata pazienza dei popoli si converte in furore.*" "The peoples' exhausted patience turns into rage."

We're feeling weary too. The landlady of our B&B shows us a pleasantly roomy apartment in a shabby street, musing aloud that there's no way she can make money if tourists stay for just one night. I don't tell her Garibaldi stayed only a few hours, the time needed to detail his men to bury the dead, take protection of the few Bourbon prisoners who hadn't been lynched and have Crispi draw up a decree promising compensation for war damage. "Then we were almost joyful," Abba remembers, "to leave that bloody place behind us."

Still, some of the garibaldini had fun. The local women were in a kind of frenzy, Capuzzi remembers. They wanted to drink together, dance together. Bixio had to break up the party. "Do you men want to go to Palermo?" he bellowed. The question was met with a great cheer. "Well, soon you'll be in Palermo, or in hell."

Perhaps to compensate for the disappointment of what must have looked like a promising situation, the garibaldini were given their second pay of the expedition, another lira. Capuzzi used it to buy a plate of macaroni with fresh tuna, cabbage and lettuce. And, for dessert, strawberries washed down with wine. "Then a swift coffee, a cigar, and we hurried back to our gear to be on our way."

Abba also mentions strawberries. One of the younger garibaldini brought a handful in a basket of leaves and offered them to the general where he was sitting under an olive tree. "What would your mother say," Garibaldi asked, "if she saw me taking your strawberries? Eat them yourself. You'll enjoy them more than I could."

Reading the diaries of the common soldiers, who had no direct contact with the general or his staff, one becomes aware of how many rumours were going around, how desperately uncertain everything felt. In Alcamo Abba heard a rumbling noise across the hills. Was it cannon fire? Had Palermo risen against the Bourbons? "Some of the men started hurrying down to the sea, thinking they might get news from a ship at Castellammare." In the event, it was only thunder.

"Then word got around, mysteriously" – Abba again – "that the general had lost hope of winning against the thirty thousand men the Bourbons had in the island. So our column was to be disbanded. We would all be left to our own devices. It was dismal news. But false. Maybe a trick the enemy was playing on us."

Capuzzi recalls similar stories. The victory at Pianto Romano had been a boost, but the men knew there were greater challenges ahead. In his sick bed in Calatafimi, Bandi was told that Garibaldi had been defeated and the mission was over. He fell into depression. If hindsight says triumph was inevitable, this wasn't the men's experience. Or the people's. It was because Garibaldi saw public morale so low, remembered Crispi, that he insisted on the decree on war damages.

"Wretches begging in the streets," remembered Zasio, "half naked, cursing."

We didn't see any begging in Partinico. But then, crossing the town in the evening, we didn't see much of anything at all. Nothing was open, nobody was out walking. Drinking fruit juice on the balcony of our B&B, we were able to listen to the conversations on all the other balconies stacked above, below and beside each other along the narrow street. And the televisions. A variegated buzz with shrill crescendos. Gunfire. Stadium sounds. Everybody seemed to be safely at home. Salvatore Maniscalco, who by 1860 had been head of police in Palermo for more than a decade, was convinced that, aside from "a few hotheads", the people of Sicily wanted nothing more than "safe streets, low taxes, religious festivals and cheap food". But isn't that the norm anywhere, any time? Perhaps the art of changing the world, we decided, involves recognizing those very few moments when this is not the case, and exploiting them to the full.

In the Mountains

From here on geography is everything. Topography, rather. Palermo is only twenty miles away. Marching without a break, Landi's battered column was already in the city before the garibaldini left Partinico. But these are complicated miles. And Garibaldi couldn't simply chase Landi into the city. Shortly before Palermo there is the fortress town of Monreale. It was defended by four thousand soldiers.

We departed before dawn, walking swiftly north-east, stopping only to photograph a road sign: Via Vittime del Dovere. "Victims of Duty." What a name for a street!

Turning a corner, we were witnesses to a crime. A man was unloading rubbish from his car and dumping it by the side of the road. A dozen fat blue bags. It was 5.15 a.m.

"Don't!" Eleonora muttered when she saw me pulling out my phone.

"What do you think he's going to do?"

"I don't want to find out."

Abba also worried about the possible violence of the locals on this stretch of the trip. The *picciotti* marching beside them, he reports, kept a man prisoner, tied hand and foot, a "*maffioso*" [sic] who had taken advantage of the revolution to kill and steal. Smartly dressed "but big and mean", at some point this man simply disappeared. It was hardly reassuring. A volunteer who had joined their company in Partinico "seemed born to kill". He wore two pistols in his belt. Instead, "when you spoke to him, he was generous and gracious... almost apologizing for the part he had played in the slaughter of the day before". These mountains, Abba concludes, "are notorious for their grim tales of brigands. A person travelling alone was at risk of never being seen again."

A couple of miles out of town we struck off to the right and began to climb. The narrow road twists and turns into dry hills. Not a car passes in either direction. Sun-bleached grass and clumps of cactus stretch away as far as the eye can see. Rugged cliffs of grey rock. You might be in a spaghetti Western. All the more so when a dozen horses appear trotting down the slope. Handsome creatures, black, white and brown. Foals and mares. No one is with them. Seeing us, they turn back, hooves clattering on the tarmac, before escaping into a scrub of eucalyptus and heather. To the front left of this bucolic scene someone has abandoned a tattered red sofa.

Above a hairpin we come across a man in shirtsleeves and braces carrying a bucket. Snails, he explains. A little later there's a whistle in the gulley to our right. Then a cry. Beside a trickle of a stream, a young cowherd is trying to gather his animals. They are huddled in a thicket of dry bushes. You can see tails switching, plants shaking.

"The heat really bothered us that day," says Capuzzi. "Fortunately, there was a brook with fresh water halfway up the valley." He describes using rifles and cloaks to make shelters from the sun. We just kept moving, eager to have our fifteen miles behind us before we shrivelled up. Even the air seemed burdened with an excess of brightness. At times the soil was streaked with red. There were strangely conical formations on the skyline. Ancient volcanoes, perhaps. Then we came across a wooded area, corralled off and alive with grunts and squeaks. Boars.

On a ridge at about 2,000 feet there's an ancient stone tomb with two cypress trees to each side. It's a massive thing, far bigger surely than any corpse could need. There is no plaque, no information, but it certainly looks like a tomb, and almost as out of place, in this wild landscape, as the red sofa. Consulting our phones, we discover it's called "La tomba del gigante". No one knows quite when it was put here or who, if anyone, is in it.

Our route zigzags south and west now, approaching the Renda Pass. What you need to bear in mind is that Palermo, on the north coast, is protected inland by a great semicircle of mountains embracing some forty square miles of low hills and plain known as the Conca d'Oro, the "Golden Bowl". In the past the area was entirely given over to orange groves; now there are second homes, olives, cornfields. The Renda Pass takes you into the Conca d'Oro from the west just above the mountain village of Pioppo. From there, nothing would be easier than to turn left along the flank of the mountain, inside the Conca, and walk four miles down to Monreale, then another five to Palermo.

The long hot day – 18th May 1860 – had given way to a chilly evening. The general stopped his soldiers here, in the mountains, before the pass. It's rough, empty terrain. "When we arrived, we were tired, dog-tired," Abba remembered. "The men threw themselves down where they stood, and for a while there was a deep silence." Between the lines one senses a note of despondency. "We'd come a long way from Alcamo, but before Partinico we hardly counted the miles. We were singing. After Partinico the singing stopped."

They had witnessed something uglier than a corpse-strewn battlefield. Leaving Partinico, Capuzzi mentions seeing more "bloodstained stumps, exposed to public scorn along the road". The savagery was disturbing. Now, at nightfall, they felt exposed, on an open plateau between high peaks, only a few miles from a Bourbon garrison. The enemy could easily manoeuvre to climb above them. Or they could send forces from Castellammare, the port near Partinico, to steal up behind them. Anxious, the men hunkered down, munching bread and cheese. "For eight days we'd eaten nothing but bread and cheese," Abba complains. Unlike Capuzzi, he wasn't spending his pay in taverns. But then Garibaldi had been eating nothing but bread and cheese either. "The general was a simple man who made us all become simple like him." Unable to settle, some of the garibaldini gathered, timidly, to watch their leader sleeping. "In a nook between two rusty rocks… his saddle for a pillow… sleeping calmly, with no guards. It felt like a dream."

Further down the mountain, Capuzzi's company had camped earlier. Worried that the grass was wet with dew, he and his friends fell asleep in the dust on the road, huddling together for warmth, but were woken by a clatter of hooves. A loose horse threatened to trample them. In the end Capuzzi hunkered down by a fire that some Sicilians were feeding with trunks of prickly pear. One was a solicitor, and the two men spent the night discussing "the state of Sicily, its education, agriculture and industry" until, "towards dawn", Capuzzi tells us, "I went off on my own to contemplate the rising sun." A nightingale sang. The soldier's heart "swelled with sweet melancholy". Then, "almost unconscious of being alive, I gazed at the bright coming of the light, adoring the works of the Supreme Maker".

This was a crucial difference, perhaps, between the garibaldini and their Bourbon enemies. The rebels were never simply in their barracks, keeping their ranks. They were on a wild adventure that they had sought out themselves, of which this immersion in nature was an important part. "Dear mother," wrote another garibaldino, Enrico Cairoli, "I assure you that this expedition is so poetic..."

Towards ten in the morning, after five hours' walking, we reached the end of the pass and found ourselves looking down into the Conca d'Oro, with Palermo spread out along the coast far away and the sea lost in haze beyond. It's a magnificent sight. "Palermo!" – Abba was here at dawn on 19th May. "Glimmering down there between the mist and the sea. You could see the ships along the waterfront – so many, as if all the fleets of Europe had gathered to see the day we storm the city."

But it wasn't to be. Or not that day. Garibaldi waited. "We knew," says Abba, "that behind those walls there were twenty thousand soldiers – but also, of course, two hundred thousand citizens."

This was the equation that mattered. There was no way that the garibaldini, now fewer than nine hundred, could beat such an army. The Sicilian bands offered vital support, but they were even more poorly armed than the garibaldini and lacked a core of experienced men to give them discipline. In these circumstances, the only hope was to get the people themselves to rise up. By all accounts Palermo was a powder keg of public rage. But someone would have to get past the city's defences and toss in a match if that keg was ever to explode. There wouldn't be much point in fighting a pitched battle, however valiant, outside the city, if the people didn't rise up. "Palermo or perish" was the formula on everyone's lips.

From Calatafimi Garibaldi had written to Rosolino Pilo, the Sicilian revolution's most charismatic figure. Since the collapse of the rebellion in Palermo, Pilo had been trying to keep the struggle alive in the mountains around the Conca d'Oro, using the promise of Garibaldi's arrival to encourage local men to join him. He now had something over a thousand volunteers. On 16th May he had repulsed a Bourbon attack at the mountain village of Piana dei Greci (now Piana degli Albanesi). It was a rare victory. Giuseppe La Masa, another Sicilian leader, who had sailed with the Thousand, had gone on ahead of the column and was recruiting men on the other side of the Conca d'Oro, to the east, around the town of Misilmeri. To link up with these forces would be strategically crucial. The Bourbons knew it.

"Wait for us," Garibaldi wrote to Pilo. "Harass the enemy... light fires, shoot at their sentries in the dark. Intercept their communications. Disturb them any way you can."

IN THE MOUNTAINS

With the garibaldini now camped at the Renda Pass, the two forces were just a few miles from each other – Pilo's Sicilians perched a thousand feet above Monreale, the garibaldini at the top of a road that cuts down towards Monreale along the flank of the mountain. On 19th May Garibaldi wrote again. "Stay on top of the enemy... without exposing yourselves too much. When we're ready for a direct attack, you launch a determined attack too."

Pilo was a few weeks short of his fortieth birthday. "Handsome," Garibaldi remembered, "chestnut hair... the sort of delicate features you find in aristocratic families." Fourth son of the count of Capaci (a district around ten miles north-west of Palermo), he had spent his life fighting for the cause of republicanism, democracy and a united Italy. His political positions had always been extreme and uncompromising, his behaviour unflaggingly bold. During the 1848 revolution, he had organized the rebels' artillery in the battles that chased the Bourbons from the island. And he was one of the few who opposed any surrender to the Bourbons when they returned later in the year with overwhelming force. As a result, he had spent the last twelve years in exile, living in poverty, conspiring. He had been in Genoa with Bixio, in London with Mazzini and Crispi, in Malta with La Masa and a whole community of Sicilians who had abandoned their homes after the Bourbon victory in '48. It must have seemed to him he was on the brink of realizing his life's dream.

Our route, climbing down from the heights towards the village of Pioppo, took us along chalky tracks through dark pines clinging to precipitous slopes. With the altitude, the temperature had eased a little, and the air was fresher and drier. For the first time in five days, the walking felt pleasant. It seemed a good moment to try and get our minds around the garibaldini's vicissitudes on these heights between 18th and 21st May.

At a vantage point we stop to survey the landscape. A great sweep of rugged mountains falls away in crumpled folds of green and gold down to the distant coast. Nothing is more difficult than understanding the manoeuvres of armed men in a wild landscape like this, which is why Garibaldi spent so much of his time on his horse, beside local scouts, exploring the slopes and peaks, stopping to gaze through his telescope. All his life he had believed that the key to military victory lay in understanding the terrain better than your enemy.

On 19th May, shortly after hundreds of men had stripped off to bathe and wash their clothes in a watering hole – "a Biblical scene," Abba thought – it came on to rain. Heavily. Persistently.

"19th May" – Nievo. "Rain. Fatigue and misery setting up camp. Sorties to local villages to find clothes to cover our backs. Coats and hoods. We look like an army of monks."

"Soaked to the marrow" – Capuzzi on 20th May. "It occurred to me we might find some small caves to hide in, so I set off with a couple of friends up the rocky slope... In vain. After that we tried cutting twigs from some wild cherry trees and making a shelter... The roof leaked, the water trickled onto our hats and down our necks."

"Pouring rain" – Bixio. "Miserable weather."

"Oh, for a place in the Ministry of War!" one wag cried, and Abba explains: "The Ministry of War was a half-wrecked carriage that travelled behind us carrying the expedition's documents and money... Nievo rode in the carriage," he adds. "A poet... and a fine soldier." Crispi was there too, writing letters and decrees. It was a government on wheels.

"Having no shelter and hardly any wood," Garibaldi remembered, "we were obliged to burn the telegraph poles to keep warm."

Abba and Capuzzi both describe cooking rice the evening of the 19th, in the rain, only to realize they had no bowls or spoons. They were at a loss until the Sicilians showed them how to eat off "paddles" of prickly pear.

But if all the diarists agree about the weather and the poor food, when it comes to military action their versions vary enormously. They were assigned to different companies, receiving different orders, hearing different rumours.

"In the morning" – 21st May, Capuzzi – "our battalion advanced [along the road] towards Monreale, while the Sicilians [on the slopes above] started to fire. Battle engaged, we waited for the order to advance further, and instead we were told to retreat to our position of the day before."

Garibaldi dismisses the day's events in a couple of lines: "In a skirmish during which the Thousand exchanged a few shots with the Bourbons below the Renda Pass, Rosolino Pilo, who had sat down to write a dispatch to me on the heights of San Martino, was struck by enemy fire and fell down dead."

We are well below the pass now, tackling the last drop into the village of Pioppo. To our left are a range of forbidding rocky cliffs, beyond which, about three kilometres away and directly above Monreale, is the monastery of San Martino delle Scale. The chief abbot was a relative of Pilo's. His men had gathered on the hillside above the monastery. But there was no way the garibaldini could have gone directly there to join up with their allies. The cliffs are impassable. We found ourselves being funnelled down into a narrow street, steep as a water chute, all balconies and brightly laden washing lines, that eventually spills you out onto Pioppo's main street, a busy thoroughfare carrying most of the traffic from Partinico to Monreale and then on to Palermo.

Abba has a much more elaborate version of the engagement. Or two versions, one in his earlier book, one in the later. In the first, the impression is all confusion and disappointment. The men had moved down to Pioppo the night of the 20th after two days in the rain. On the other side of the Conca, to the east of Palermo, the Sicilian bands under Giuseppe La Masa lit scores of bonfires on the peaks and beat drums late into the night in an attempt to create a diversion. The garibaldini slept in Pioppo and at daybreak on the 21st advanced towards Monreale. "A dawn so lovely you wanted to dissolve into the colours of the sky, the smells of the country." From above came the sound of gunfire. The Bourbons had climbed towards San Martino to attack the Sicilian rebels and outflank the garibaldini below. The Genoese Carabinieri were deployed in the scrub on the hillside to prevent this. "We saw the smoke of gunfire, and our men retreating across the rocky slopes." Then came a line of ponderous mules carrying stretchers for the wounded. "'Is today the day we get beaten?' the men began to ask." Garibaldi rode by with Sirtori and Türr. The rain had stopped, and the sun was hot. "We had no idea what was going on." After an hour they got the order to retreat.

But in Abba's later version, everything is explained. It was all an elaborate plan of Garibaldi's, he now believes, to trick the Bourbons into imagining he was going to fall into the trap of attacking Monreale. While in reality he was laying a trap for them: when they tried to outflank the column from above, they would be caught by the rebels shooting from higher up.

Abba's account sounds plausible – but other sources claim that the Sicilians were attacked first, and routed. One looks in vain for some sober work of history that might throw a little light on this. After all we're talking about a crucial moment in the events that led up to national unity. But the unresolved polemics surrounding the Thousand's adventure are such that there is no interest in sober accounts: the campaign has to be represented either as an unremitting triumph or as one long fraud. Only a reference in a footnote eventually led me to two articles published in the *Italian Military Review*, the oldest official publication of the Italian armed forces, in April and May 1911. The author, Colonel Casimiro Vagliasindi, quotes all the exchanges between Pilo and Garibaldi's staff, as well as details of the Bourbon troop movements, putting together the only coherent picture of what happened that I have found. Garibaldi, it emerges, had indeed prepared for a full-scale attack on Monreale. Over the last two days he had received ecstatic dispatches from La Masa suggesting that a general uprising was just hours away. But the Bourbons attacked first, well-organized and determined.

"6 a.m." – Pilo to Garibaldi. "Shooting has already begun. My men have only 4–5 bullets each. When our ammunition is finished, I fear they will disperse."

Garibaldi tried to help, pressing the Bourbons on the Pioppo–Monreale road below. But the professional army was too strong. "Long live the king!" they cried. They had mounted cannons on the slopes to fire down onto the rebels on the road. Rather than take casualties for nothing, Garibaldi chose to fall back. Pilo was killed that morning. But his men didn't disperse at once. They fought on, effectively preventing the Bourbons from encircling the garibaldini on the road below.

This account conclusively lays to rest the notion – recycled as recently as 2021 in Jamie Mackay's book *The Invention of Sicily* – that the garibaldini's victory was inevitable. Here were the Bourbons taking the initiative, not afraid of the locals nor harassed by them. The Sicilians lost their charismatic leader. Garibaldi was chastened, his men demoralized. Capuzzi says how reluctant he and his company were when the order came to retreat. The thought of more nights on chilly mountaintops was depressing.

But our problem now was heat, not cold. We needed to reach our B&B before the sun reached the zenith. The only room we had been able to find was in Caculla, a tiny settlement in the valley immediately below Pioppo. It was less than half a mile away as the crow flies, but the mountain below Pioppo is so steep that we first had to walk a mile on the road towards Monreale, then backtrack along a path that cuts sharply down beneath the road to the village.

The road was narrow and busy, on one side a high cement wall shoring the mountain against landslides, on the other a crash barrier beside a sheer drop. Walking in single file, with vans and trucks rumbling only inches away, I was struck by how unnerving this advance must have been for the garibaldini. But also for their enemies. On the slopes above and below the road, the vegetation is dense. There are shrubs and cactuses and great banks of purple bougainvillea. Prickly pears reach out their ungainly paddles over steep drops. Majestic agaves. It's very beautiful, but it would be so easy to find yourself caught in an ambush. Abba mentions his fear of being forced over the edge of the road into the orange groves below. It's not the kind of slope you would want to scramble down, though in his article in the *Military Review* Vagliasindi explains that at a critical moment of the battle Garibaldi did send a group of Sicilians down there with orders to circle around Monreale, then climb back up to the road and cut the telegraph wires between Monreale and Palermo. Very likely it was the news that they had lost communication with the capital, Vagliasindi speculates, that led the commander of Monreale's garrison, Colonel Von Mechel, to call off his attack.

Snaking round the flank of the mountain, the road winds between looming cliffs and sheer drops. When we reach the top of our path, there's a bus stop and an old stone shelter that seems part shrine and part post office. Inside are images of the Madonna and even a candle. Outside, twenty or so letterboxes have been haphazardly fixed to the wall. The name of the locality is written with small black tiles on a background of white: "PENSABENE" – "Think Well".

In the Golden Bowl

What we'd like to hear from Garibaldi is: how did you do it? How did you get these men to do things that – as we are about to see – appear well-nigh impossible? And to stick together when all seemed lost? Or, again, we'd like to know: how did you plan these campaigns? Militarily, strategically. Was there some formula? At the very least, you think, he could have given us an exhaustive account of what happened.

Instead, in his memoir, published twelve years on, Garibaldi offers only the barest storyline, as he remembers it, sometimes wrongly. And plenty of Risorgimento rhetoric, as if he were still at the hustings. Gratitude too. He tries to remember the names of the wounded and the dead. He wants us to share his awareness of the sacrifices they made. Their valour. But nothing about his techniques for motivating them, or what was going through his mind as he contemplated the conundrum: how do you get a thousand men inside a city defended by 20,000?

Nor did those beside him offer much in the way of enlightenment. "Garibaldi preferred to decide and command himself," said Crispi. "On the battlefield he was a clairvoyant." In later years his closest assistants, Sirtori and Türr, as well as the commander of the Sicilian bands, Giuseppe La Masa, would each insist that they personally had been responsible for the campaign's key strategic successes. No one was convinced. Garibaldi didn't bother replying. He makes no claims. And when things go wrong, he doesn't look for someone to blame. Nor does he blame himself. He moves on. Of the decisions he took on the afternoon after Pilo's death, having retreated in haste from Pioppo back to the heights of the Renda Pass, with the Bourbons now very much on the front foot, Garibaldi wrote:

> Our position [above the pass] was favourable, tactically, a good place to meet an enemy attack. But the road from Palermo to Corleone seemed better for our situation, in that it offered a far broader theatre of operation and brought us closer to the more numerous

Sicilian bands around Misilmeri, Mezzojuso and Corleone, where I had sent La Masa to gather them.

I thus decided to cross, by night, from the road we were occupying to Parco, on the Palermo–Corleone road.

How calm and reasonable it all seems. And what a miserable situation it implies. Garibaldi is expecting to be attacked, very likely the following morning, by an enemy who have their tails up. He had counted too much, perhaps, on the demoralization of Landi's army, only to find Von Mechel's foreign regiment in Monreale in fine form. Very soon he could be shut out of the Conca. He has lost Pilo and much of his band. He has lost any element of surprise. He is farther than ever from meeting up with La Masa's bands on the other side of the Conca. The road to Palermo is impassable.

So, despite the fact that his men have been awake since dawn and have spent the day fighting, or at least manoeuvring, not to mention the two previous days under heavy rain – their civilian clothes in rags, their shoes in tatters – despite having just marched them back up to Renda, a thousand feet above Pioppo, in their first experience of retreat, he now feels he has to move them, at once, in the night, down into the bowl again and across it to Parco (known today as Altofonte) on the first slopes at the far side of the Conca. That will put them just five miles from Palermo, on the Corleone road, which offers a line of escape, if need be, southwards into the centre of the island. The move has to be made at night, of course, because they mustn't be seen, mustn't be open to attack. Which means they mustn't be on the regular road either, but the remotest and most roundabout of paths.

No sooner was this decision taken than it began to rain again.

In blistering sunshine we rang a bell beside imposing iron gates. Our hostess, a florid woman in her fifties, was taken aback by our sweat-soaked state, our backpacks. Where was our car? They had never had guests without a car. From Partinico! *Santo cielo!* How long does that take?

In a flurry of welcoming gestures we were drawn onto a broad terrace and sat at a bright-white table, where bowls of fridge-cold fruit and chilled lemon tea quickly appeared. Then, as so often in Italy, the first real question was, "Where are you from?"

"Taranto." Eleonora announced.

"I knew it," she clapped her hands. "Your accent!"

It emerged the two had been born only streets apart.

"Of course you can use the pool!" she told us.

So the afternoon was spent on deckchairs beneath sunshades, gazing at the hills all around us, trying to get a sense of what the garibaldini went through that night.

"Returning to the Renda Pass," says Crispi, "the men were settling down to rest. Instead the order came to break camp at once."

"In haste," says Zasio, "for an unknown destination."

"Raining hard" – Bixio. "Horrible roads, had to carry the cannons on our shoulders."

"As dusk fell" – Abba – "the rain began to blow in our faces – big, stinging drops."

"We took a precipitous path" – Capuzzi. "At every step brambles, shrubs, plants in your way – streams full of water and rocks."

"Not a man" – Zasio – "whose foot didn't slip on that tortuous path."

From our position in Cacullo, we can see the saddle in the crest of the ridge where the road drops down from the pass. But they would have circled further to the south, out of sight of Monreale. No one has ever established exactly the route they took.

"Suddenly a torrent plunged across our path" – Capuzzi – "and trying to jump it we found ourselves deep in the water; it was so dark you couldn't see what you were doing."

"A rain so dense, in the darkness" – Abba – "you felt you were walking in the clouds."

"Prodding the ground in front of us with our rifles" – Capuzzi – "like blind men in procession."

"Faces like ghosts" – Abba – "muddy clothes in shreds; some men almost barefoot."

All this is hard to imagine today. There's a book, *A Vademecum to the Visitor of Those Locations where the Military Operations of Giuseppe Garibaldi Took Place, from Renda to Palermo*, published in 1910, that has photographs of all these hills. You're struck how empty the landscape was back then. Now it's all parcelled out, fenced in, cemented over.

High up at Renda a group of Sicilians kept campfires burning through the night. To deceive the enemy. "How we wished we were sitting beside them," Abba remembered. And for the first mile or so they themselves could see the Bourbon campfires beyond Pioppo, towards Monreale. Scores and scores of them. Then it was pitch-dark, and the rain lashed. Each man had been given three loaves of bread, which they kept on their bayonets to balance the rifles over their shoulders. The rain made the bread soggy. The loaves fell apart. They had dismantled the cannons from their carriages. Garibaldi himself bent to it. Six men to carry each cannon in the dark. Soldiers stumbling in single file. Others backed up behind when someone fell. Soaked to the skin. Getting to their feet, they found they had lost the man ahead and had to call, in the dark. "Silence!" Bixio snapped. When his horse started neighing and just wouldn't stop, he put a gun to its ear and blew the animal away. Another horse was wounded when a rifle went off by accident. You had to be so careful, Capuzzi remembered, not to fall on the bayonet of the man in front of you. A certain Giovanni Acerbi dropped the chest with the army's money; much time was lost scrabbling for silver coins in the mud and stones. "Worst march of my life," Garibaldi said.

Our hosts, a pleasant middle-aged couple, came to sit beside us at the pool with a bottle of wine. They wanted to know about our walk. At some point I just couldn't resist raising the subject of dumping. Why was there so much rubbish abandoned by the road? Our host hung his head. It was shameful, he said. And the problem was compounded by the Sicilians' famous *omertà*. "Nobody ever blabs on the people doing the dumping."

It is something all historians marvel at when telling the story of Garibaldi's night-time move from Renda to Altofonte. "Aside from their hospitality" – Abba – "the people are even more to be praised for the way they took us in and kept us hidden all that day and the following night, without the Bourbons hearing so much as a whisper." Considerable rewards were on offer in return for any information about the rebels, but no one betrayed them. *Omertà*. It can be negative, it can be positive. In the event it was not until 23rd May, a full twenty-four hours after their night-time ordeal, that Von Mechel realized where Garibaldi had got to.

La Portella

Today we're following the king's men, not the garibaldini. What shape were they in? What were they fighting for? "Ferdinand II," writes De Cesare in the 1890s, "had spent the last years of his reign building up and consolidating the army." Between 1848 and his early death in 1859, the number of men under arms increased from 40,000 to 90,000, absorbing more than half the kingdom's revenues – this in a country of which one third was an island and two thirds a peninsula sharing a single land border of 150 miles with the Papal State, which was also the Kingdom's closest ally: "We're caught between excommunication and salty water," Ferdinand liked to say.

The king was the supreme commander and wore his uniform every day. The army's one achievement during his reign was to suppress the revolutions of 1848, maintaining Ferdinand's position as supreme monarch with absolute power. The kingdom had no foreign enemies and no foreign ambitions. All military equipment was produced inside the kingdom to avoid reliance on other states. Ferdinand himself chose the colour of the uniforms, which were splendid. The first regiment was called the King's Regiment, the second the Queen's, the third the Prince's, the fourth the Princess's, the fifth the Bourbon, and so on. In short, it was a dynastic army – "or rather," as De Cesare thought, "Ferdinand's own personal army, whose officers feared the king, despised their country and hated liberty."

Bereft of national sentiment, soldiers made up for it with an excess of religious zeal. Men would wear amulets and carry sacred images in their packs; military exercises were interrupted for the clang of the Angelus bell, when soldiers would kneel wherever they found themselves; mass was heard every Sunday and feast day, and the royal anthem always played at the Elevation of the Host. Promotion came with length of service. Discipline was enforced with brutal cruelty. Faced with conscription, the kingdom's young men would resort to every form of subterfuge to avoid the four years' active service – "despite the fact," De Cesare remarks, "that conscripts were not being sent off to war, but to laze in the garrisons of Naples." Pay was lower than in any other Italian army, except for the foreign regiments, whose soldiers received three times what the native Neapolitans were given. It is a foreign regiment we will be following this morning. Having searched for Garibaldi on the Renda Pass on 22nd May, Colonel Von Mechel's men occupied Pioppo on the 23rd, and, having been reinforced with 5,000 more troops from Palermo, at dawn of the 24th they set out across the Conca, heading south-east.

An hour before dawn, we left our bedroom, then the house, moving with stealth so as not to wake anyone. The moon was full, sailing in an indigo sky just above the distant crag we were headed for. It was a narrow road with sagging cables strung up each side, climbing through a scatter of rural housing and luxury villas. At 5.40 exactly we took a photo of a long unfinished house whose gate had been draped, time ago, with the ragged sign "Project by NO PROBLEM." Looking at the sad house, it was hard to say whether this was more irony or denial.

One man not in denial, back in 1859, was the unusually young (forty-one-year-old) Palermo-born General Pianell. "Everything is rotten," he wrote to his wife of the situation in the army. "Let's hope the moment to act never comes, because it will be the moment of disaster." There were, concedes De Cesare, some excellent young officers in the Neapolitan army; they had come up through the Nunziatella Military College, which could boast talented and committed instructors – just that there weren't enough of them. This goes some way to confirming the version that our Bourbon chaplain, Giuseppe Buttà, offers of 23rd May after it finally became clear where the garibaldini had got to.

"Monreale was full of soldiers doing nothing, waiting for orders from Palermo... condemned to watching the garibaldini across the valley in Parco calmly performing military manoeuvres. The men's grumbling was starting to concern us, and if they didn't rebel it was only because neither Von Mechel nor Bosco could be suspected of treachery."

The day dawned a hazy pink, and as our road climbed higher towards the mountains on the south-east side of the Conca you could look left over dark stands of pine and dry white grass to the village of Altofonte, once called Parco, tucked at the bottom of the steep slopes that form the eastern wall of the bowl. Beyond, on the shimmering coast, Palermo seemed a mere stroll away. "We gazed at the city," remembered Capuzzi, "the way the Bedouin, after a long, tiring trek across burning desert sands, must gaze at the oasis he yearns to reach."

Despite this proximity and eagerness to arrive, there was no question of advancing at once. Arriving in Parco at around 4 a.m. on 22nd May, the garibaldini were utterly exhausted after their hazardous march under heavy rain. And then there was the enemy.

"We placed our forward positions" – Bixio – "and heard heavy cannon fire from the direction of Bagheria; if the rumours going around are right, we are about to be attacked."

In fact it wasn't until the afternoon of 23rd May, thirty-six hours later, that three thousand soldiers advanced on them – not from Monreale, but directly from Palermo. Garibaldi was ready for them. The "military manoeuvres" that Buttà reported seeing from Monreale involved splitting the garibaldini into two groups, one at the bottom of the hill in Parco itself, one five hundred feet above on the so-called Cozzo di Castro, where, with much help from the local peasantry, earthworks were thrown up and a platform built to place their five cannons pointing north along the road to Palermo.

"An almost impregnable position," Capuzzi thought. To Giuseppe La Masa, whose rapidly growing rebel bands were now just a four-hour march away across the mountains further east, Garibaldi wrote: "I like this position, and we will make sure to defend it until we're ready to attack. We'll harass the enemy as best we can." He asked La Masa to send him as many men as possible. Six hundred arrived on the 23rd and were deployed in frontline positions beneath Parco. But Garibaldi now insisted that La Masa bring all his forces, some three thousand, to protect the right flank of the garibaldini. "We're going to have a major battle here," he told Bixio. "La Masa has received the order to approach," records Bixio, "but he's playing deaf."

In the late afternoon of the 23rd, Bixio was sent to meet the advancing Bourbons below Parco. His instructions were to retreat slowly uphill, making the enemy pay for every yard gained, and then defend the fortified position at Cozzo di Castro. In the event, the Bourbons withdrew shortly after engaging with his advance guard. This was only a preliminary reconnaissance.

That night the men slept in the cemetery halfway up the hill. "You could see camp fires" – Bixio – "on all the surrounding heights." La Masa's men. "Looking forward to tomorrow's battle" – Capuzzi remembered – "stretched on earth that contained the bones of the deceased, we slept the placid sleep of men with happiness in their grasp... Victory, defeat or death, we wanted a rapid resolution." "When everyone got up in the grey light of morning" – Abba – "it was like the resurrection of the dead."

It was also the moment when Garibaldi realized they were on the brink of catastrophe.

One says the Conca d'Oro, the Golden Bowl, but this is not a simple semicircle of mountains surrounding a well-defined plain. Rather, a number of mountain ridges converge from east, south and west, falling into low hills with no obvious orientation shortly before the coast. There is no really flat land. If you're in a position to see the sea, then, you have a fairly good idea of where you are. Otherwise, the landscape could hardly be more disorienting as mountain piles on mountain, ridge runs into ridge.

Leaving Caculla, we were climbing along a line that leads from Pioppo, where the Conca narrows to the south-west, to a high crag something over four thousand feet on the other side. We passed under the elevated highway which now crosses this part of the Conca – a Madonna presides beside a concrete pillar – then climbed up lanes and tracks through dense vegetation opening out in great slabs of balmy upland – pastures, gorges, pine thickets – as the civilized world slipped away behind. Without a map you would be in serious difficulty here. But the Bourbon troops knew the territory well.

"Then as now," wrote Colonel Vagliasindi in 1911, "the army carried out annual exercises in these hills. They knew every path and vantage point." In particular, they knew that from the top of the ridge we're now headed for – Serre della Pizzuta – they could command a position above Parco to the north and, crucially, they could cut off Garibaldi's line of retreat along the Palermo–Corleone road, which runs through the valley the other side of this ridge. In short, they would have the garibaldini trapped between themselves and the battalions approaching Parco from Palermo.

"As the mist dispersed," Abba remembered of dawn 24th May, "we saw a column of soldiers leaving Monreale. They advanced determinedly in close ranks along the road to Pioppo until the whole road was packed. There was no end to them, though the head of the column had long since entered the woods, to come to Parco."

And not only to Parco. Dawn almost always found Garibaldi on his horse, telescope in hand, on some high vantage point. He saw thousands of men approaching directly from Palermo, as on the previous afternoon. He saw the enormous column occupying all four miles of the road from Monreale to Fioppo before descending into the orange groves. "The whole valley sparkling with weapons," Abba said. It was a daunting show of force. And the intent was clear. "I wasn't afraid of a frontal attack" – Garibaldi's memoir – "however superior the enemy forces, but this movement behind our backs, up in the mountains, overlooking our position…"

It was one of those moments that require an instant decision. Stay or go. Just to reach Parco had cost the garibaldini an enormous effort. They had sacrificed the line of retreat to Partinico. Then a considerable investment had been made in preparing to defend this position and stay close to Palermo, their ultimate goal. The men knew that. They were primed. Morale was high again. And of course La Masa's men were arriving from the east. Albeit poorly armed. A matter of an hour or two. Garibaldi watched the Bourbon forces spreading out, grey and blue, from Pioppo "Moving in force" – Bixio – "to occupy the heights to the side of our positions." How long would it take them to cut off the road to Corleone? There was no time to consult his staff, no time to exchange messages with La Masa. Perhaps it was already too late. "I ordered an immediate march, cannons and baggage first."

We passed a lonely house – Rocca dell'Aquila, "Eagle's Rock". This is high, open pastureland with rusty wire fences whose makeshift gates are no more than strands of barbed wire that you drag aside and hook up again. There were no animals about, perhaps because the grass was so prickly and dry, the air so close and warm. In an empty field a man was drawing buckets of water from a watering hole to clean his red Panda. But that was the last car we saw. Towards seven we passed the narrow lane that much of the Bourbon army would have taken, turning left along the flank of the ridge to attack Parco below. One wonders at the complexities of dividing, moving and deploying thousands of armed men in this rough terrain, making sure they arrive at the point of conflict in some kind of useful formation. But we were already climbing again, more and more steeply now, up a dusty grey track through rough rock and gorse. It was 7.30. We had been walking two and a half hours and were still about an hour from the top. Those were the kind of times Garibaldi was looking at.

The Palermo–Corleone road zigzags up the hillside above Parco and Cozzo di Castro, heading south-east, then turns sharply south-west and drops down under Serre del Pizzuto, the other side of our ridge, towards the small town of Piana dei Greci (now Piana degli Albanesi). Google maps gives the walking time from Parco (Altofonte) to Piana, following the road that the garibaldini took, as two hours and forty-four minutes.

"There was some initial rifle fire down below, under Parco," remembers Abba. "The Genoese Carabinieri were soaking up the first Bourbon attack – but just as everything seemed ready for us to hold firm where we were, the general rode by, with his staff and his scouts, at a gallop, a whirlwind, and us right after him, at a run."

"We were waiting to join the battle" – Capuzzi – "when the order came to climb further up the hill. But as soon as we were on the road, we were led towards the rising sun, away from the battle... it felt like we were fleeing from Parco, from Palermo."

"We despaired," wrote Nievo to his beloved cousin Bice.

"We marched at top speed" – Abba – "then slowed a bit, then speeded up again. I saw men panting hard, desperate, throwing themselves on the ground, others in tears from the disappointment: some said the Bourbons had broken through the carabinieri, set Parco on fire and were coming right after us with their cavalry. Drunken Bavarian mercenaries, they wanted us dead. The retreat brought a dreadful sense of loss, like we were running away."

That was certainly how it looked to chaplain Buttà, from the Bourbon side: "The garibaldini offered almost no resistance and were chased up the mountainside, where they suffered a great deal in the rugged terrain." It was proof, if any were needed, how easily these bandits could be beaten if only the army's generals would show some loyalty and mettle.

For us it was our most beautiful walk so far. The altitude brought a little freshness. The morning sun sucked up, then slowly dispersed a thin haze. The high slopes, folding this way and that, burnt and barren above, dark green in gorges and valleys, were a constant tease for the eye. It seemed impossible to gauge distances, or see where the top was, or which way exactly you were supposed to go. The path came and went in tall feathery grass, parsley and bramble, white flowers and pink. We studied our navigation app, cast about this way and that.

Nor was it possible of course to know exactly the route they had taken – the Bourbon soldiers – whether or how they spread out across the mountainside. Or what frame of mind they were in, what precise orders they had. But there was a point – finally it became clear – where the rocky crest of the skyline was broken. That was where we were being drawn. The high pass, from inside the Golden Bowl, out towards Piana.

Just below the pass, on a steep slope of stunted gauze and coarse grass was a shepherd's hut. A dry-stone building. Inside, a fireplace; the only furniture a log raised on two stones. We were sitting outside, eating cherries and generally congratulating ourselves on having completed the climb so early – it was only eight thirty – when we were startled by a movement right at our backs. A man had appeared from nowhere, or from behind a clump of pine, or a rocky outcrop; he was just four or five yards away, with his Rottweiler dog. At which you were bound to realize how easily you could be ambushed in this territory. And how hard it would be to know how many men you were facing.

"The king's men" – Bixio – "begin to appear on the crests of the heights, firing down at us from long range to disconcert our column."

"With a handful of *picciotti* and Cairoli's company" – Garibaldi – "I set off up the mountain towards the *portella*, where the second Bourbon column was trying to cut off our retreat."

A *portella* is a little door, the name they give here to the mountain passes. We reached the place about five minutes after being surprised by the man with the dog. I have a photo of Eleonora, in profile, pack on her back, poles in hand, standing in a narrow passage with slabs of grey rock rising to the left and a tumble of boulders to the right, the bright glare beyond turning her to silhouette. Peaked cap on her head, she looks surprisingly soldierly.

"Panting, hungry, scorched by the sun" – Abba – "we relaxed a little at the sight of the town nestling in the valley."

The other side of the passage we found ourselves looking straight down on Pian dei Greci. First a wild, pine-strewn drop of a thousand feet or more, then the town, or village, strung along the bottom of the slope, with a broad golden plain beyond, complete with an extensive lake, surrounded by dark mountains. Watching over the scene, just to the right of our pass is a concrete gun emplacement, no doubt from the Second World War. It would certainly be the right place for a cannon.

"All at once" – Abba again – "three scouts on horseback were barring the road, telling us to climb to the right, straight up the grey, dismal mountainside. Other scouts at rocky vantage points were shouting, urging us on – "The general is in danger!" – and us clambering up towards the ridge, whence we heard a trumpet sound an anguished reveille."

This would certainly be an arduous climb if you had to rush straight up the slope. Looking down from where the Bourbons were, the ground seems to disappear, and you have that feeling that the only way to get to the bottom will be to jump, or fly. We began a cautious zigzag through tangled pine roots, prodding the ground with our poles.

"We reached the top" – Capuzzi – "as the *picciotti* were fighting with the Neapolitans."

"The general had been up there a while" – Abba. "The bullets hissed by like snakes."

Crispi, who had been at the head of the retreating column in the "Ministry of War", remembers waiting on the road shortly before Piana while the cannons were turned round to confront any Bourbons in direct pursuit and his fellow garibaldini scrambled up the mountain to meet the threat on the ridge above. Back in Parco the carabinieri, together with La Masa's six hundred *picciotti*, had been fighting a rearguard action. "For a while we feared they were lost," says Crispi. La Masa's men had fled. "Then they began to arrive in threes and fours."

"The carabinieri joined us after a while" – Bixio – "but Mosto's younger brother is missing." Antonio Mosto was the commander of the carabinieri; Carlo, aged twenty-four, his younger brother. "We don't know whether wounded or simply exhausted."

Up on the ridge "the shooting lasted maybe an hour" – Abba – "then the Neapolitans began to withdraw."

"The king's men thought we were marching to Corleone" – Capuzzi – "and that the only reason we had appeared on the ridge was to keep the road open."

"Garibaldi withdrew too and occupied Piana" – Abba – "which nestles in a grey stretch of country, grey itself with its walls and roofs and everything else. At least that's how it looked that day, seen through the burning air of midday that trembled like a fine web of silver thread."

"So we entered Piana dei Greci" – Crispi. "And left again at 6 p.m."

We entered Piana around 10 a.m. After a five-hour hike. The descent from the pass is a knee-challenging plunge through warm resiny vegetation with eagle-eye views over the roofs of the village, which are no longer grey but a shimmering terracotta. Finally you dive down steep steps, into a cobbled alley – via Discesa dei Mille. Window boxes, a wheelbarrow full of weeds, a shadowy arch where a house is built over the street. The walls are indeed a rough grey stone. Then the main street – Transito Giuseppe Garibaldi – and just a few minutes later we were peeking into the Cathedral of San Demetrio Megalomartire. It's a sixteenth-century building brightly frescoed with the high cheekbones and stern gazes of Greek saints. It was because of the particular religious rite the people here observed, arriving in the island four centuries ago, that the Sicilians called them *greci*, "Greeks". Only in 1941 was the village's name changed to Piana degli Albanesi. Religion has ceased to be determining. Ethnicity remains. They were in fact Albanian. The gardens of the Villa Comunale feature an impressively martial bust of the fifteenth-century Albanian hero Skanderbeg. It was donated by the People's Republic of Albania in 1968. The red flag of Albania flies in various prominent places. There are no statues of any garibaldino or Risorgimento figure. But later that afternoon, some way from the centre, broken and derelict, we came across the monument to Pietro Piediscalzi, a native of this village who fought in Piana beside Rosolino Pilo when the Bourbons were repulsed here on 16th May 1860, only to die, as Pilo did, a few days later on 21st May in the battle above Monreale. With the garibaldini scuttling into Piana on the afternoon of the 24th, then hurrying out again a few hours later in the direction of Corleone, the Bourbon strategy of concentrating all their forces around Palermo was beginning to look like a smart move.

Apparently the tide had turned.

Piana degli Albanesi

Drums and trumpets, flags and fires. These, Giuseppe La Masa explained, were his best weapons when he set up camp at Gibilrossa, a high plateau seven miles south-east of Palermo. Bereft of guns, he would make so much noise, put on such a show, that the Bourbons would think there were 50,000 men there, not the four or five thousand who eventually gathered.

Looking for somewhere to eat in the evening in Piana, we saw plenty of flags and heard much honking of horns. Italy were playing Austria in the Euro Football Championships. If the two-headed Albanian eagle was to be seen on many buildings around the little town, it was the tricolour now streaming from the windows of passing cars and draped over balcony railings. The locals might prize their ethnicity, the Sicilians may believe they were better off before Italy became one nation, but when it comes to football they are all joyfully Italian. And Austria, of course, far from representing the immensely powerful oppressor of the past, is just another sporting minnow for the Italian giants to gobble up. People like winners, Garibaldi observed. Opposite the Villa Comunale, the tables of the Antica Trattoria San Giovanni were empty. When we wandered onto the terrace, the proprietor, dining alone in a corner, seemed almost shocked to have a customer. "Perhaps after the game," he said ruefully.

Certainly La Masa was shocked by what happened on 24th May 1860. Marching towards Parco on Garibaldi's orders, which meant precipitous paths across high mountains, he ran into the remnants of the six hundred men who had been sent ahead the previous day. They had been fighting in the frontline, they said, when they realized the garibaldini on the hill behind them had fled. It was a terrible betrayal, they thought. La Masa immediately threatened instant death for anyone talking of flight or betrayal. Garibaldi, he claimed, had thought up a clever ruse to deceive the Bourbons. Very likely he was afraid his own troops would fall apart without the magic of the general's name. In reality, he had no idea what had happened. There had been no counter-order for him.

Forty years old, hailing from the coastal village of Trabia twenty miles south-east of Palermo, La Masa was a polemicist, a rhetorician and a theorist. Exiled from Sicily in the mid-1820s, he had returned to be one of the main players in the revolution of '48, when he was made commander in chief of rebel forces. After the revolution was overturned, he had fought for the Republic of Rome in 1849. Later, in exile in Genoa, he had written the influential pamphlet 'On Insurrectional War in Italy Aimed at Achieving Nationhood', which laid out a blueprint for combining revolution in the south with political manoeuvring from Piedmont in the north. Reduced to poverty, he had married an heiress, Felicita Bevilacqua, herself a patriot, who had nursed the wounded in the Republic of Rome.

"La Masa was an extraordinary man," remembered Abba, "blonde, with a youthful rosy complexion and very fine features, more Scandinavian than Sicilian." By all accounts he was a charismatic speaker, blessed or cursed with a very high opinion of himself, a man determined to be at the centre of attention and play a leading role. When, in April, Garibaldi had hesitated to set out for Sicily, La Masa had offered to lead the expedition himself. The other prominent Sicilians – Crispi, Carini – were not impressed. Throughout Garibaldi's camp there was a prickly resistance to La Masa's ambitions. Sirtori insisted on addressing him as "colonel", while La Masa always protested he was a general. In Salemi La Masa tried to persuade Giuseppe Bandi to leave Garibaldi and accompany him on a recruiting tour of the island. Bandi refused. "A man full of energy," he remembered, "capable too... but he would have seemed so much more capable without that fatal flaw of vanity that earned him so much envy and hostility and had him imagining he should be commanding half the world and behaving like Caesar in Gaul."

Shortly before the battle of Pianto Romano, La Masa had fallen from his horse. Abba remembered seeing the accident. Dazed and concussed, he hadn't been able to lead his company into battle. So he said. His enemies seized on this to accuse him of cowardice. After the Thousand then entered Calatafimi, La Masa had insisted they march east towards Corleone and approach Palermo from that direction. Sirtori was in favour of the faster route via Alcamo and Partinico. Having lost the argument, La Masa asked Garibaldi if he could proceed alone, taking the Corleone route himself and recruiting as many men as he could along the way. Garibaldi said yes. Or perhaps, as other versions suggest, it was Garibaldi who ordered La Masa to go. Either way, one of Garibaldi's strengths was his ability to get people who loathed each other to give their best and serve the cause.

La Masa set out from Calatafimi on the night of 16th May, deliberately "dressing the same way I did in 1848", so that people would recognize him. Many suspected he was an impostor, perhaps an agent provocateur, since it was well known that the real Giuseppe La Masa faced the death penalty in Sicily. A meeting of provincial leaders was called in the town of Mezzojuso, fifteen miles east of Corleone, to verify his identity. Having passed the test and inspired the locals to join him, he approached Palermo from the south-east; by 21st May, as Garibaldi was attacking the Bourbons from the west near Pioppo, he had brought together 4,000 men on the mountains east of the city. It was an astonishing achievement in just five days, requiring enormous efforts to mobilize local goodwill and resources. La Masa wrote to Garibaldi in Pioppo to tell him just how brilliant he had been, how great the general enthusiasm was. And the attack on Palermo should be launched from here, from Gibilrossa, he insisted, from the east, not the west.

"This position is excellent: a very high, extensive plateau between Misilmeri and Palermo." He warned the general not to attack Monreale. Only with great reluctance did he agree to move his men towards Parco for the battle of the 24th. When he discovered that Garibaldi had retreated, he was alarmed. "I implore you," he wrote that night, on returning to Gibilrossa, "please come and join my forces here. Any retreat into the interior of the island will be a disaster." Throughout the early hours of 25th May he was receiving demands for clarification from patriots in Palermo: what had happened in Parco? Was the dream over? "There is no time to lose," he wrote to Garibaldi in another note, "I'm struggling to keep these difficult troops together. Send me your orders." His position was unsustainable. The insurrection he had theorized was collapsing.

And after ninety minutes Italy still hadn't scored against Austria. The game would be going into extra time. "And we won't get any customers till nearly midnight." The proprietor's wife had come over to ask us if all was well – a stout, cheerful lady, brightly made up and elegantly dressed. We had eaten *paccheri alla crema di melanzane*. They were excellent. What did it add up to, I asked her, the people here in Piana being originally Albanian? Did they visit Albania? Did they speak Albanian? No, she said, they didn't, though there were Albanian words in the local dialect and Albanian festivals with Albanian traditional dress. The town had a strong sense of community, she said.

Eleonora observed that Piana was much cleaner than other towns we had walked through. And this was true. It's a charming hillside maze of well-swept, narrow stone streets with flowers and water fountains where swallows swoop back and forth from nests under balconies. "There's no dumping here," our hostess said, but she knew nothing of the monument to Pietro Piediscalzi, and nothing about Garibaldi's extraordinary manoeuvre that night between 24th and 25th May that was to make Piana degli Albanesi famous to all students of the Risorgimento. A sudden roar and explosion of horns told us Italy had scored. "That's a relief," she smiled. People were more likely to eat out if the team won.

"So was it a desperate retreat or was it a clever ruse?" Eleonora asked as we walked back to our bedsit. "That was what they taught us at school."

Certainly it was what the garibaldini wanted to believe. "Garibaldi," thought Capuzzi, "whose life was a string of brilliant successes, would not negate his glorious past with an act of weakness. So our retreat could only be a strategic move, never a flight."

"The general only pretended," says Zasio, "to throw up those earth-works [in Parco] to strengthen the position, as if we were planning to defend the place: it was a trick."

In a sort of mini diary sent to his wife some days later, Nino Bixio wrote: "24th [May]. Menacing attack of more than ten thousand men. Show of resistance to draw them on."

All the same, as Abba said, it *felt* like a flight. Both his diary and Capuzzi's take on a more sombre tone writing up the events of these difficult days. Abba recalls a conversation with a young monk, Father Carmelo, who was eager to join in the revolution, but was held back, he said, by the fear that the garibaldini's goal was not after all so revolutionary. They only wanted to "unify Italy", but what was the point if people were to remain as poverty-stricken as before? "United or divided, if the people suffer, they suffer." The real revolution would be "a war not against the Bourbons, but by the oppressed against their oppressors". Church included. "Didn't Garibaldi see that Sicily was still as it must have been at the time of the wars of twenty centuries ago?"

Abba did not know how to respond. Perhaps he could have said that in a modern state with a constitution and a parliament there might at least be the beginnings of a mechanism for redressing inequality. But it did not occur to him. "That monk has left me strangely uneasy," he reports. "Vaguely I realized that the unity of our country wasn't everything."

Capuzzi also recounts a meeting, this time in Piana dei Greci, after the retreat. The men had settled in a field outside the town with orders not to move. Those in charge of supplies had the usual bread, cheese and wine brought to them. Courtesy of the local monastery. But Capuzzi, always so particular about his food, begged permission to go into town to buy something decent. Having picked up artichokes, sardines and lemons, he called into the doorway of a house to ask for water. A woman in her fifties brought him what he wanted, but was suspicious, diffident. Capuzzi tried to get her to talk, and she told him a tale of poverty. Hadn't she heard, he asked, of the garibaldini and what they were doing? Yes, she said, but the soldier sensed she wasn't impressed; she thought they had come to Sicily to fight and steal. "I tried in every way I could to open her eyes, but they were words tossed to the wind." Leaving, he gave her a silver coin, which she eagerly took, "but from her face you could see she was thinking: money comes easy to ruffians like this."

Perhaps, when seeking to achieve some crucial change in the world, it is important to stay focused, not to wonder whether there aren't other more momentous changes to be made.

Back in the camp the men were "tired, restless, lost in their thoughts". They knew the enemy could show any minute. There had been at least 5,000, the carabinieri reckoned, attacking Parco. Two of their best men were missing. Others had died. No one knew what Garibaldi was planning. Unusually, he had called a war council with all his top staff.

Back in our bedsit, we too began to plan the coming day. The problem is, I told Eleonora, that even now no one is quite sure what route Garibaldi took the night of the 24th, in many ways the decisive night of the whole adventure. We began to study the map. The good thing was that the route most textbooks give is the shortest, just fifteen miles, and since we were expecting another day of sirocco misery, this seemed important. "And the bad thing?" Eleonora wanted to know. "The route I think they really took is about twenty-two miles." Outside there was an explosion of car horns. Italy had won. The party could begin.

Giuseppe Buttà was disgusted with the partying in Parco on the night of 24th May 1860. His account too undergoes a change of tone at this point in his story. Entering the village after the Bourbon infantry, he tells us how the garibaldini had forced open the shops and sacked the place. "Small-town thieves," he says. "They'd taken everything." This flies in the face of all the reports of the garibaldini being taken into people's houses and fed and clothed, and, more in general, the total non-cooperation of the local people with the Neapolitan army, which the Bourbon generals themselves complained of.

But was it the garibaldini who had forced the shops? "Here I must report" – Buttà goes on, and we remember that he arrived after the soldiers – "that Colonna's brigade, who occupied the town, committed crimes unworthy not only of their uniform, but of anyone born in a civilized country. Inspired by the thieves who went before them and desperately hungry, thanks to the carelessness of their commanders who often left their troops without food for many hours, they ended up sacking shops already sacked and others that hadn't been sacked. Some even looted houses whose owners had fled."

The local women and children, Buttà tells us, had taken refuge in the church at the top of the town, where he personally made it his job to reassure them. One has the impression from his book that Buttà was entirely sincere in his Christian mission. Initially he assumes the women had run from the garibaldini. Only later does it occur to him that they were afraid of the Bourbon troops. "That evening," he remembers, "Parco was an indescribable havoc. The soldiers were almost all drunk, and neither cajoling nor threats could make any impression on them." This, he adds, when they should have been chasing the garibaldini and finishing off the job. The only explanation, he decides, is that certain treacherous officers were deliberately fomenting this disorder so as to dishonour the Bourbon cause. "Saddened and ashamed... I climbed a little way up the hill to the cemetery, where the 9th Infantry were camped, and spent the night sleeping on the graves." Exactly as Capuzzi and Abba had the night before.

In Piana we were favourably impressed by how quickly the partying dampened down. Perhaps Austria wasn't a big enough scalp to crow about. To have defeated Garibaldi, on the other hand, was huge. The morning after the events at Parco, the official newspaper of Sicily published the following bulletin:

On 23rd May the band of Mediterranean buccaneers led by Garibaldi took up a position at Parco, fortifying it with four cannons.

Yesterday two columns of royal troops attacked the invaders with determination, driving them from their positions, putting them to flight and chasing them into the mountains of Piana dei Greci.

The royal columns are in pursuit of the band. Some were detained and treated with great respect, despite their having no right to be considered prisoners of war.

Marineo

We don't know what was decided at Garibaldi's council of war in Piana dei Greci the afternoon of 24th May. No minutes were kept. Bandi, who would have given us a lively version, was still in his bed in Calatafimi. Very probably it was the events that day at Parco that led to the rumour he heard that Garibaldi had been beaten.

We do know that Sirtori, Türr, Bixio and Crispi were all present. And that Sirtori thought they should withdraw to Castrogiovanni (now known as Enna) in the centre of Sicily to regroup and gather new forces for a longer war. But also that Türr, Bixio and Crispi disagreed, on the grounds that revolutionary enthusiasm was strong in Palermo and that, as La Masa had insisted, if they let this moment pass, it might not come again.

There were three routes into the city. The road from Partinico through Monreale, where they had tried to attack and failed. The road from Corleone through Parco, where they had tried to defend and failed. And the road from the east, along the coast, above which La Masa and his Sicilian bands were camped at Gibilrossa. However, any move in that direction, eastwards across the wide valley below Piana, then north up another valley towards the town of Misilmeri, below the heights of Gibilrossa, would surely draw a massive attack from the Bourbon forces presently in Parco and up at the Portella above Piana.

On the other hand, they could not stay where they were. Piana, on the flat, at the bottom of a mountainside, would be much harder to defend than Parco; it was already a relief that the Bourbons had not followed through that afternoon when the garibaldini were in disarray. But the king's men would surely be on the move at dawn, if not before. Crispi later claimed that Garibaldi had asked him, as a Sicilian, if he knew of any locations beyond Corleone that would offer ideal conditions for a strenuous defence. Giuliana, Crispi told him, a hilltop village some twelve miles south of Corleone, which itself was twenty miles away. At this point Colonel Orsini, commander of the artillery, was summoned and told to get the cannons ready to roll.

"Towards evening" – Abba – "the companies got the order to march, and once again it felt like a hurried retreat." The artillery and carts went first, as you would expect in a retreat. It was the road to Corleone. "'The Bourbons are coming,' men were saying to each other. 'There'll be ten thousand of them.'"

We let ourselves out of our bedsit at 5 a.m. and walked steeply downhill through a zigzag of cobbled alleys where scores of swallows ruffled their feathers beneath the eaves. Along the main street, lamp-lit, deserted, we picked up signs for Santa Cristina Gela, or Sëndahstina; all road signs are in both Italian and Albanian. Also for Ficuzza, a village on the old road to Corleone, famous for the huge wood that lay behind it.

"So is this the mainstream route, or your better-informed-theory route?"

"Both, for the moment."

Beyond the town centre it's easy walking, still downward, through a small industrial area: concrete forecourts, red and blue railings, prowling guard dogs. At the bottom of the slope, to the right, is the big lake, in fact a reservoir. This wasn't here in 1860. The valley was flooded in 1923. There are fifteen square miles of water surrounded by extensive fields of corn stubble that take on an almost copper colour in the pink sunrise. Closing the horizon, as if in a vast arena, are the steep walls of mountains, which once again have the form of long ridges, or plateaus, where an enemy could easily gather. We walked eastward along the northern shore of the lake, past the so-called "Tent of Divine Mercy", a modern-day sanctuary where the Madonna's tears are regularly celebrated, and arrived, beyond the lake, at a staggered junction with six tracks and roads forking in all directions. This is where we have to decide.

"We know for sure that the artillery and the carts and perhaps a couple of hundred men, some wounded, some *picciotti* from the interior of the island, set off on the Corleone road – which is to say, south."

"But we're going to wind up in Marineo, which is due east."

"Right. Straight ahead from here. That's where the garibaldini, minus their artillery, arrived at 10 a.m. on 25th May, the morning after the stop at Piana."

"So if this is the short route, why would he take a longer one?"

"So as not to be seen. Or to delay his decision."

This is the moment that is always described as the clever trick that won the day. But it was a huge risk. And it depended on the Bourbons not realizing what he was up to.

"As you can see, we're still in full view of Piana and of course the Portella above, the high pass."

We looked around. It would be hard to imagine a place more visible from all directions than the crossroads in the middle of the plain where we were standing.

"But it was night time."

"'Towards evening', Abba says. And it was to be a bright night. Garibaldi was pleased, because he was able to see his lucky star, Arcturus, brightest in the northern sky. The Bourbons would have had their scouts at prominent points. Bayonets are known to gleam."

"So what's the alternative?"

"Having walked a few miles on the main road" – this is Capuzzi – "we turned off onto smaller paths and walked on and on, till ten, when we stopped to rest till dawn."

And Abba: "Our column followed Orsini, convinced that Palermo was no longer an option. The rumour was that Garibaldi would disband us and leave every man to himself. Time passed miserably, but after walking a while, and night had fallen now, we were led off the main road into a wood, where we slept."

"A wood?"

"In the *Military Review* in 1911 Colonel Casimiro Vagliasindi compared a dozen versions of events. Four different woods are mentioned. One version says they followed the Corleone road for two miles, one for ten."

"Ten would mean into the mountains, beyond the lake."

"Right, where Ficuzza is, and a huge wood – 'so thick and leafy you couldn't see the sky,' Zasio says. From Ficuzza there's a track that leaves the Corleone road to the left and triangles back north-east to Marineo across the mountains. Most of all – and nobody else seems to have noticed this – the times fit. Looking at the distances, they could have reached Ficuzza around ten or eleven in the evening, absolutely out of sight of Piana and the Bourbons. Then, setting off around dawn, they would have arrived in Marineo at ten."

"25th May" – Bixio. "At dawn we march towards Marineo."

It's 6.45 a.m. The village of Santa Cristina Gela is just up the slope to our left. Hoping for an early coffee, we cross a field, climb through a clutter of low-cost housing and reach the Bar del Centro just in time for its 7 o'clock opening.

"Why do people care" – Eleonora stirs in her sugar – "exactly which way they went that night?"

"It has to do with the debate about Garibaldi's genius. Or luck. His devotees would soon be putting around the story that he had already had this ruse in mind even before attacking Monreale. It was planned from the start: a couple of fake offensives followed by fake retreats to draw the Bourbons' most effective forces out of Palermo and then send them off to Corleone after a decoy – Orsini, the artillery commander – while the main body of the Thousand circled round to attack the city from the east. His denigrators said the retreats weren't fake at all, they were a shambles, and the famous ruse more accident than genius, to the point that Buttà, the Bourbon chaplain, claims that Garibaldi only reluctantly agreed to turn back to Marineo on the insistence of Crispi and Türr."

"Your verdict?"

"There's a brief, written by Crispi, for Orsini, dated 24th May, Piana dei Greci. That's the evening of the retreat."

COLONEL,

Lieutenant General Giuseppe Garibaldi, commander-in-chief of the national forces of the Island of Sicily, has charged me to order you to take the cannons in your care to the town of Giuliana. Once you have made your way there, you will fortify your position and organize a force that is not only able to defend it, but also to move to those locations where you may be ordered to go...

"So the decision was taken in Piana."

"It's a long document. Maybe three pages. Crispi was probably writing it in the Ministry of War, their one carriage, as they escaped along the road to Corleone. In the end, even with the brief written, Garibaldi wouldn't have to make the final decision and give Orsini his orders until the moment they actually split from him. Sometime in the night. The men weren't aware of any clever tricks or brilliant strategies and went to sleep, in the wood, 'humiliated and melancholy', Abba says. With strict orders not to talk, and not to smoke."

"You wonder Garibaldi didn't tell them what he had in mind."

"Still hedging his bets perhaps. He had scouts out to inform him of any movement from the Bourbons. They could easily have cut off the road from Marineo to Misilmeri and Gibilrossa, where La Masa was, by taking the short route themselves."

So we drank our coffee, mulling over this drama of a hundred and sixty-one years before. It had cost the garibaldini an enormous effort to bring their cannons with them thus far. And Garibaldi had brought them because cannons could be so decisive in battle. To give up all his artillery and all his luggage carts, plus around a hundred and fifty men to accompany them, was a major sacrifice. On the other hand, precisely the knowledge, from the tracks on the muddy ground, that the cannons and carts were headed to Corleone, might be decisive in convincing the Bourbons he had gone that way. And Garibaldi sorely needed to get the excellent Colonel Von Mechel off his back.

We got up and went out into the square, where the sun was already noticeably warmer than ten minutes before.

"Do we know of anybody," Eleonora asked, "who took the short route to Marineo? I mean, for sure."

"We do. A party of *picciotti* split with Garibaldi at Piana. They didn't want to retreat to Corleone, where they assumed he was going. He hadn't told them anything different. So they headed east across the plain, in the direction of Marineo, then turned into the valley that led north to join up with La Masa."

"We've followed the garibaldini often enough," Eleonora said. "And yesterday we followed the Bourbons. So I propose today we follow the *picciotti*."

Given the heat that was about to hit us, this turned out to be a wise decision.

The road is a one-lane track, winding, rising, dipping between a thousand and two thousand feet, through an utterly parched landscape of white-gold grass, stained here and there with dark clumps of pine, a patch of dry bracken, occasional olive groves. Perhaps a jeep is parked beneath the trees, in the shade. No towns or settlements are to be seen in any direction. The sea is beyond the mountains to our left, the heights above the village of Belmonte Mezzagno, where La Masa's scouts will be watching. Sometimes the slopes close in each side, forcing you to twist through a narrow gorge, then open again onto undulating emptiness and hills that seem to move with an ancient, lava-flow energy, shimmering under the glare of another impossible day.

"The path was hard work" – Capuzzi speaking of the march from Ficuzza to Marineo – "because of the endless ups and downs, but the views were so many and so beautiful the spirit was cheered and we had no time to feel tired."

We felt pretty weary when shortly before nine we had our first sight of Marineo, clustered at the top of a spectacular cliff face. The view itself was enough to exhaust you, because the cliff rose the other side of a steep gorge. The road plunges down a thousand feet, amid a great slide of rocks and soil, but with the occasional stone farmhouse here and there, bright with bougainvillea, defended by sagging fences. There are vegetable gardens on crumbling terraces, and I remember a snake kept us company for part of the way, slithering along the edge of the road where a concrete wall shored up the hillside. It was a long, black, shiny creature; he must have sensed our footsteps and was anxious to escape, but could find no hole in the cement. He writhed like dark lightning, stopped dead as a broken stick, then slithered off again as we caught up. None of the garibaldini mentions snakes. Or insects. Or even mosquitoes. People were more used to them, no doubt. Finally, our noble serpent found his hole and was gone, sucked away into the hillside.

At the bottom of the descent, a stream trickles from a boulder-strewn crevice. You cross a bridge and the climb begins, steep and unrelenting in the heat. First a thousand feet down, now a thousand feet up. Hairpin after hairpin. We were soaked in sweat. Far above, to the right, the grey walls of the town, built into the mountain, give it the look of Dino Buzzati's fortress in *The Tartar Steppe*: airy fortifications rising to fairy-tale battlements. "The crenellated Marineo," Crispi calls it. Not a bad choice if you need to hide a few hundred men for the day.

To save ourselves a couple of long winds in the road, we struck up a path that climbed straight to the base of the walls. It was as near vertical as a footpath can be, and mercilessly exposed to the sun. Every step started a little avalanche of stones. My heart was beating hard. Shoes full of earth. Sometimes you had to grasp tufts of grass with your hands. Eleonora scrambled ahead, lighter and faster. Eventually we went to ground where a clump of gorse offered a handkerchief of shade and drank the last of our water supply. It was only ten o'clock, and the thought that the day might get any hotter was frightening.

At last we emerged on the final stretch of road, cliffs rising to the right and the valley that leads north to Misilmeri falling dramatically away to the left between humped mountains. Taking refuge in the deep shadows of the town we found a collie with his tongue hanging out, head cocked in amazement that any humans should be out and about. Now there was just one more climb, up Via San Francesco d'Assisi, to the castle at the top, which was exactly the sun-drenched semi-ruined pile that castles in hot countries should be. From here you turn left into Corso dei Mille. Once again it's a long narrow street with unbroken façades each side, until you reach a piazza with a statue of San Ciro – doctor, hermit and martyr – looking across to the Chiesa Madre di Marineo. This is modest baroque, but with a sumptuous eighteenth-century ceramic on the outside wall, perhaps five metres by two, showing San Ciro in brilliant orange, green and blue. Martyred in Egypt in the year 303, Ciro became patron saint of Marineo in the seventeenth century when the Pilo family obtained the holy relic of his skull. And it seems Ciro is still the most common boy's name in this town, though neither I nor Eleonora have ever met anyone thus christened. The street names are familiar, though: Via Crispi, Via Mazzini, Via Fratelli Cairoli, Via Unità d'Italia – and, inevitably, Via Giuseppe Garibaldi.

"We entered the town" – Capuzzi – "and dived into the shops for refreshments, drinking raw eggs, lemon water, diluted wine. Lunch was warm bread, straight from the oven, and salami, or 'fellata', as the Sicilians call it."

We sipped lemon granitas under the awning of a pasticceria. Elegant ladies were buying pastries for Sunday treats, while men in white vests smoked out in the street. Resting, we discussed our next move. Since we had been unable to find a place to stay in Marineo, we were facing another few miles' walk to the smaller town of Bolognetta, further east. Which meant we needed water. I went looking for shops and came to a major crossroad, a drab place of randomly parked cars and uninviting window displays. But, raising my eyes, I was startled to see what Capuzzi saw immediately after his meal: "an exceedingly high rock, that looks like a wall, a work of art, not of nature. Completely isolated, it towers massively over the houses and palaces, with grasses and wild flowers clinging to its rugged crags and an ancient tree, right at the top, raisings its arms to the sky. It would be hard," continues

Capuzzi, "to describe its beauty in words, and harder still to say the effect this enchanting vision had on my spirits."

What cheered me was the thought that I was seeing what he had seen, and that it was indeed exactly as he described it. Though I didn't respond as he did. To me the great rock seemed more threatening than beautiful, or perhaps just sad – a monstrous, badly decayed incisor rising spikily into the sky.

Back at the bar, we took turns in the bathroom to freshen up. That last steep path had reduced us to a seriously dishevelled state. Our faces and hands in particular were all grime and sunburn. Years after the event, Colonel Orsini would begin his account of the expedition to Corleone and Giuliana with a description of the men Garibaldi assigned to him that night. "They looked ridiculous, what with the dust and mud encrusted in their clothes after marching and sleeping in the rain, their shirts and trousers shredded by brambles and thorns, some wearing top hats, dinner jackets with lapels and pockets hanging by a thread – and the footwear of these men, who were soldiers only for their political ideals, was simply laughable, though they did wear their filthy stuff with dignity, often substituting the shoes they'd lost in the mud with handkerchiefs."

None of our diarists report having to go without shoes, but, on arriving in Marineo, Capuzzi was worried that he hadn't be able to shave. "Full of the thought," he wrote, "that we might soon be in Palermo, I realized that my clothes and toilette were in a horribly plebeian state… I went to the barber – or rather, to report the word that appeared in huge letters over his shop, the BLOODLETTER – to get my hair cut and beard shaved." However, just as a man "with two feverish eyes" had begun to "shear me like a sheep with clippers that hadn't been sharpened in years", a peasant came into the shop complaining of toothache. After some haggling over the price, the barber sat the man on the floor, "produced a pair of small rusty pincers and thrust them into his mouth. There were three solemn minutes during which the poor patient squirmed wildly, shrieking his pain, then the tooth was out. Grabbing the thing between bloody fingertips, the bloodletter came to me and held it up as proof of his prowess. But my patience was at an end. In a rage, I jumped to my feet, beard still uncut, tossed a couple of coins onto the table and escaped, cursing my tormentor over my shoulder."

Garibaldi spent nine hours in Marineo. "The town is busy," writes Bixio, "we rest." The men were ordered to stay as much as possible inside the churches, where they could lie down. Perhaps this is why Abba has not a word to say about the place. Nor Nievo. Nor Crispi. We wandered around with our packs, peeking into the churches, which seem to be the only places of interest, but they were busy with mass, and we didn't want to disturb.

"Why did he spend so long here," Eleonora asked, "if it was so important to meet up with La Masa and get to Palermo?"

"He was waiting to see what Von Mechel and his troops would do. Would they fall for his trick? Because once he moved into the valley, towards Misilmeri and Gibilrossa, he was a sitting duck. Particularly in daylight."

On receiving La Masa's anxious letters the morning of 25th May, Garibaldi replied from Marineo with his usual brevity, "I hope to be in Misilmeri tomorrow."

We hoped to be in Bolognetta in time for lunch. We walked downhill through the outer sprawl of Marineo, then along the mountainside. Unfortunately, there was no alternative to the main road, which is fairly new and fast with crash barriers both sides, no pavements and no shade. But it was only three miles. Arriving in another ramshackle little town, our host, seeing the state we were in, graciously insisted on carrying both our backpacks up the stairs to the second floor. As to where we would eat, he said, setting the packs down in our room, there was nothing open in Bolognetta at Sunday lunch. Just one pasticceria-cum-*alimentari*, in the street right below us, but that would be closing at midday. It was five to. I too would have to wait before my shave.

Misilmeri

Why is something more an achievement if all planned from the start? Be it a novel, a product launch or a military campaign? Isn't this dream of total foresight and mastery rather absurd? How much more canny and realistic to be constantly weighing up options, gathering new information, prodding, experimenting, waiting for the fleeting opportunity to strike.

Marineo is just twelve miles east of Piana degli Albanesi. With its customary slow-but-sure approach, the Bourbon military machine occupied Piana at midday on 25th May. Expecting a fight, they found Garibaldi had gone. All eyes had seen his column leave on the Corleone road. Colonel Von Mechel spent the day consolidating his position, considering the next step. There was never any question, with the Bourbons, of responding immediately. Many thousands of men were involved. They did not want to arrive at a conflict unless with overwhelming superiority in numbers.

Meantime, Giuseppe Buttà rushed around Piana trying to find the locals, who had fled, eager to convince them that the Bourbon soldiers (mostly Bavarian) were their friends. This was not easy after the drunken mayhem in Parco. Coming across a pretty eighteen-year-old "tousled, depressed and afraid, pressing an image of the blessed virgin to her breast" ("Kill me now!" she exclaims), the chaplain becomes besotted with "her long, crinkly raven hair, her great black eyes, swimming in tears" and spends long pages describing his visits to her and his decision to give her a small silver reliquary in the shape of the cross containing tiny relics of the twelve apostles. "I would not have given this," he says, "to a queen. But with the utmost pleasure I gave it to Annetta." So for a short while the good chaplain forgets to berate his superiors for their treachery and incompetence.

In Marineo, Garibaldi watched and waited. Refusing invitations from local notables, he ate his bread and cheese on a hill – Calvary – to the south side of the town, gazing from his telescope. What would

Colonel Von Mechel do? From Gibilrossa La Masa sent another anxious message claiming that more Neapolitan soldiers would soon be arriving in Palermo by sea from Messina. Haste was of the essence. But haste would be of no use if the garibaldini were caught down in the valley on the way to join him.

The Bourbons had a problem, Garibaldi knew, when it came to gathering reliable information; the local people would not betray the cause, and, if sent out alone, or in twos and threes, Von Mechel's couriers and scouts very often did not return. Hence the colonel's chariness. Garibaldi, on the other hand, was constantly receiving reports from *picciotti* and advice from the local peasants. Someone told him that if he climbed the great Rocca that had so impressed Capuzzi, he would be able to watch both the road to Corleone to the south and the road to Misilmeri to the north. Garibaldi climbed up there mid-afternoon, returning towards evening in a positive mood. At 7 p.m. he had his men ready to move. Since, in 1860, the clocks were not moved back in summer, this was equivalent to 8 p.m. in our time today. Sunset for 25th May, in Sicily, is 20.17.

"We leave at dusk" – Bixio – "for Misilmeri."

"In good order" – Capuzzi – "two by two, with instructions not to smoke and to observe strict silence."

"Out on the mountainside" – Abba – "you could hear the goatherds calling, gathering their flocks."

We slipped out of Bolognetta at 5 a.m. The sky was indigo. After a mile or so, striding downwards into ever-lusher vegetation, we reached the bottom of the valley and joined the road they would have been taking from Marineo.

"Suddenly, after it had been dark for a while, the column stopped" – Abba. "We were at the lowest point of the valley. Word passed down the line that the advance guard had run into the enemy. It wasn't true, luckily, because we would have been trapped."

We had no such worries. Yet there was something odd and menacing about that early morning. The sun rose as if through thick dust, its murky orange light catching an old stone viaduct crossing the valley to our right. We were on a bigger road now, climbing steadily along the flank of the hillside. You could feel the pull of the traffic towards a larger settlement. People driving to work. And now a strange wind stirred, gritty and warm. We noticed it at once. Hot air drifting across the hillside. At 6.30 a.m. Laden with dust, or sand.

Was there going to be a storm? We drank some water and waited. It was as if someone new had stepped into the room. Someone we had never met before. The birds had stopped singing.

We began to march, leaning into the hill, pushing hard on our poles. Everything felt hushed. Even the passing cars seemed slow and silent. Then, in a gust, this light breeze became a gale. It swept across the landscape whirling leaves and litter into the air. At once we had dust in our eyes. We were walking straight into it. I was luckier, with my glasses. But it was the heat that was so surprising. The wind carried a burning midday heat, at dawn.

We had grit on our lips, in our noses. Imagining that torrents of rain must surely follow, we marched faster still. I stuffed my hat in my pocket. Dark pines bent above us. Bamboo rattled. Leaves and litter came rushing towards us down the slope. A hedge of oleander shook itself into a small panic of pink and white. A ribbon of red plastic clutched at my ankle. For twenty minutes, with every step forward, we experienced a constant hot pressure pushing us back. Then, as suddenly as it had manifested itself, this strange visitation was over. The wind didn't so much drop as disappear. Everything was ordinary again. And rounding a bend to the left we had our first sight of Misilmeri.

"Finally we emerged" – Abba – "from the frightening twists of the valley – and there in front and above us were a myriad of lights. Misilmeri, lit up to greet us."

The town is tucked under the hillside, below the castle built in the early eleventh century by the Emir Jafar II. "MISILMERI, or MENZEL EL EMIR, Castello dell'Emiro." I took a photograph of the sign at five to seven. Towering above it was a huge supermarket billboard. PAGHI POCO. Low cost. Parmesan 59 cents a hundred grams. Bavaria Beer only 69 cents for 66 cl.

Von Mechel's Bavarian soldiers had let the garibaldini slip by. Palermo was just eleven miles away, beyond the heights of Gibilrossa, which form the eastern rim of the Conca d'Oro.

Almost at once there was a disagreement with the locals. The authorities, very much on the rebels' side and working in close collaboration with La Masa, had ordered the townspeople to put lights in their windows, but hadn't arranged anywhere for the men to sleep. "Eventually we were assigned to a big cattle shed" – Capuzzi – "except it was so filthy we went back to the piazza." Bixio, who wanted his men rested as soon as possible, demanded that the churches be opened. When the priests refused, he threatened to break down the doors if the keys weren't brought at once. "We entered the temple," Capuzzi remembered, "lay down on the floor and slept wonderfully."

Not so Garibaldi. Having ordered the people of Misilmeri to extinguish their lights, he scribbled another of his marvellously terse messages.

11 p.m. Misilmeri

To Signor General La Masa, wherever he may be

DEAR LA MASA,
I hope to see you here at 3 a.m. to settle some important matters.

We needed to settle in a bar for a few minutes, but found nothing open, We walked up the inevitable long, straight, cluttered street with its low flat-roofed houses and apartment blocks, its palm trees in pots, the bright colours of fruit-and-veg stands, a petrol station. After half a mile or so, we were getting desperate and hence stopped at the first place that looked vaguely possible, the rather melancholy Roxy Bar, strategically placed at a widening of the street that declared itself "Piazza Cosmo Guastella", but was known in 1860 as Piano delle Forche, "Gallows Field", in memory of the many hangings that once took place here. As recently as 1837 seventeen local men had been executed in the piazza for plotting against the Bourbons. By firing squad. Perhaps with their backs to the large baroque fountain that we contemplated through the window from our table in the Roxy Bar.

Seventeen men here. Thirteen in Palermo on 14th April, a little over a month before the garibaldini arrived in Misilmeri. Hundreds of others in any number of Italian towns and villages throughout the long process of the Risorgimento. It was this willingness to sacrifice their lives in apparently hopeless insurrections that seems so impressive now. Colonel Orsini, for example, heading south on the road to

Corleone and no doubt aware that, if Garibaldi's plan worked out, he would have the whole Bourbon army on his heels, could hardly have fancied his chances of survival. Years later, in a conference in Bologna, Crispi would claim that after the two forces split at Ficuzza, Garibaldi had whispered in his ear: "Poor Orsini! We're sending him to the sacrifice."

Was it a cynical thing to do? Orsini was forty-three, Palermo-born. He had studied at the elite Bourbon military college, the Nunziatella, become an artillery officer in the Neapolitan army. Then he converted to Mazzini's national republicanism. He sided with the rebels in 1848, helped kick the Bourbons out of Palermo and led the defence of Messina months later, when it was pounded by cannon fire for days. In exile he had risen to the rank of colonel in the Turkish army, fighting with distinction in the Crimean War.

"In short," I told Eleonora as we drank our coffee, "he knew the territory, he knew his enemy. If anyone was up for it, it was him."

"Did he survive?"

"Seems he had forty carts full of munitions and baggage, about a hundred garibaldini, many wounded, with twelve rifles between them and a hundred and fifty *picciotti* – only a few of whom had shotguns."

"And?"

"He reaches Corleone on the morning of 25th May, around the same time Garibaldi arrives in Marineo. At the point we're at in the story now, on 26th May, as Bixio's men are waking up in church here in Misilmeri, Colonel Von Mechel is only just setting out from Piana dei Greci, on the Corleone road. He still hasn't reached the crucial point where the two forces divided. And Orsini was already south of Corleone heading for Giuliana. There was still everything to play for."

We should have waited a little to take our coffee break, because some ten minutes further down the main street – Corso Vittorio Emanuele – which narrows as it climbs, one arrives at Piazza Comitato 1860, a gracious open space with two tall palm trees and a scatter of café tables under a bright-white awning. From here we could have contemplated the sandy baroque façade of San Giovanni Battista at the top of the square, where Capuzzi and his company slept, or, looking across the piazza to the right, we might have read this plaque, placed between the balconies, air-conditioning units and sagging cables of a triumphantly shabby palazzo:

ACROSS SICILY WITH GARIBALDI'S THOUSAND

> IN THIS HOUSE
> UNDER THE CHAIRMANSHIP OF VINCENZO RUMBOLO
> IN MAY MDCCCLX
> THE CENTRAL COMMITTEE
> OF THE PROVISIONAL GOVERNMENT OF SICILY
> CREATED BY GIUSEPPE LA MASA
> HAVING SET UP CAMP IN GIBILROSSA
> DECIDED THE DESTINY
> OF THE SICILIAN REVOLUTION

So we have a square named after a meeting. Held in the middle of the night. A year later, in 1861, fighting for his reputation, La Masa would publish *Some Facts and Documents about the Revolution in Southern Italy in 1860*. It includes a quantity of letters and declarations he had written himself while setting up the camp on the heights of Gibilrossa: requests for money, for food, for armaments, for clothing; invitations to the authorities of all the surrounding towns and villages to cooperate; orders to scout the mountains far and wide, to light bonfires on every hilltop to keep the Bourbons guessing; directives on discipline, on noise, on soldiers' pay (three denari a day, conditional on presence at roll call). You get a sense of what an immense organizational effort it all was and how little La Masa must have slept in those six frantic days when more than 5,000 men were recruited. Less attractively, he brings together dozens of signed avowals from "eyewitnesses" testifying to his activities and courage throughout the campaign; all these endorsements share the same legalese style and all are relentlessly focused on their admiration for La Masa, who had studied law.

Never mind. The description La Masa gives of the meeting in the early hours of 26th May suggests that Garibaldi was hesitant. All the usual suspects were present, plus a delegation of Sicilians from Castrogiovanni who were trying to coordinate uprisings around the island. Outlining the two strategies open to them, a withdrawal to Castrogiovanni or an immediate attack on Palermo, Garibaldi appeared, La Masa claimed, to favour the first. Not because he lacked courage, but because Sirtori (La Masa's arch-rival) thought the *picciotti* hopelessly unreliable. In this version only La Masa's insistence convinces the general to go up to Gibilrossa in the morning to review his forces and consider an attack.

We sat on a bench beside one of the palm trees, listening to water tinkling into a trough from the mouths of a dozen stone lions and preparing ourselves mentally for the climb ahead. The emir's ruined castle looms above the town.

"Seems strange," Eleonora reflects, "that Garibaldi would bring his men here only to propose a withdrawal."

"He was talking to the local men, the Sicilians. He puts the options before them. It's their revolution. He wants to see what they're thinking. The truth is, the moment they climb the mountain to Gibilrossa, their one line of retreat will be vulnerable. At the time of the meeting, in the middle of the night, Von Mechel still hadn't left Piana. He could have been in Misilmeri in about five hours, exposing the garibaldini to an attack on two fronts. It was all pretty precarious."

"At dawn" – Abba – "I went into a hole of a bar for a coffee and ran into Bixio in such a bad mood that I went straight out again. On the piazza there was a water seller rocking his big bottle back and forth like a bell and pouring drinks for our men crowding round his counter. He looked at them with such a smile in his eyes, like he wanted to poison their glasses."

The place where we are sitting seems the only place you could possibly refer to as "the piazza". We got to our feet and went to read the plaques on the town hall.

"To the people of Misilmeri, who kept the conspirator's secret… Francesco Crispi, 1890." At that point Crispi was prime minister of a united Italy.

"To the glorious people of Misilmeri, who faced trepidation and danger with Sicilian determination… Menotti Garibaldi, 1901." Two years later, Menotti would die of malaria.

"I was wondering," Eleonora says, "why Bixio would have been in such a bad mood."

"The colonel [Bixio]" – Capuzzi – "assigned a mule to every company, to transport our food. Which suddenly made us think that we might be up in the mountains for some days… This, together with the discomfort of a burning sun, put us in a bad mood, which just got worse and worse as we got hungrier and thirstier."

"So the attack wasn't quite decided."

"Maybe not."

We consulted our trekking app, checked that our water bottles were full and struck up the road that opens between the town hall and the church, Via Generale La Masa.

It's a steep one.

Gibilrossa

The emir's castle is a ruin on a solitary hilltop. The road snakes round and above it, so that we find ourselves looking back and down on the one remaining tower through a tangle of prickly pears and olive trees, over roofs of corrugated iron held down by blocks of cement. Beyond is the valley we've just come along, and beyond that, to the east, the mountains of the interior are silhouetted in a grey haze.

The climb is only about a thousand feet, but it feels like hard work after our break. Finally, the road straightens and flattens a little, heading due west, Palermo-bound, across a rolling upland with the low cone of Montagna Grande to the right. The garibaldini spent the day of the 26th here, amid the pines and canebrakes and endless prickly pears. As ever, Capuzzi was concerned about lunch: "When the provisions finally reached us, the meat couldn't be cooked, because we had no pots or pans to boil it in. So it was handed out raw. Men were lighting fires, but it wasn't easy, because there wasn't much to burn. We toasted the meat on the embers and tried eating it half cooked, still dripping blood."

"I hope we're not going to stay here too long" – Abba – "or we'll shrivel in the sun and go mad. It's like having a cap of fire on your head."

On the plus side, there really were four thousand and more *picciotti* waiting to greet them. "They wore sleeveless goatskin jackets over cloth blouses," wrote another garibaldino, Giuda Sylva, "leather sandals with straps wrapped round their legs up to their knees; black berets, cartridge belts across the chest, guns or knives in their trousers and a shotgun on the shoulder." But many had no more than sickles, hatchets or pikes.

The camp "seethed with men," says Abba, "sending up a sound like wind sweeping across a forest." When Garibaldi went to review them – "under the pleasant shade of the olive trees," says Nievo – a great cry went up, with much waving of shotguns and tricolours, though Garibaldi makes no mention of this moment in his memoirs. Nor do the *picciotti* find much space in the official report that Crispi would write some days later. Like almost every other aspect of this adventure, the Sicilian combatants are a subject of controversy. The northern Italian narrative that dominated in the years immediately after the Risorgimento presented them as undisciplined primitives, perhaps more a hindrance than a help – at best, a necessary evil. The revisionist spin that began in the 1920s, then again with new vigour in the 1990s, supposes these men to have been utterly ignorant and ingenuous, tools in the hands of international freemasonry and local Mafia. But if one goes to the archives, it turns out that many of Pilo's and La Masa's men were recruited from the middle and professional classes, and in fact Buttà mentions a local lawyer being among the prisoners taken by Von Mechel's Bavarians outside Monreale. For many educated Sicilians, a united liberal Italy presented itself as the obvious solution to their unhappy relationship with Naples. In any event, on 26th May 1860 the *picciotti* made it abundantly clear that they wanted action, and pride of place in the attack. Which posed a problem for Garibaldi. Were they up to it?

We were attacking a narrow road, climbing gently between low walls and flourishing vegetable gardens. Like the Conca d'Oro, the heights of Gibilrossa have been invaded by second homes and light industry. It's hard to imagine a military camp here now. But at a crossroads, between a tall hedge and an iron railing, we found a stone with the following inscription:

> IN THIS PLACE ON 26TH MAY 1860
> THE LEADER OF THE THOUSAND
> CAMPED HIS BRAVE MEN AND
> WAS WELCOMED WITH EXULTATION
> BY LA MASA AND THE PICCIOTTI

We turned up the hill to the right, then left along its flank, beginning the slow ascent towards the pass that leads back into the Golden Bowl. The air was pleasantly scented on the higher slopes, earthy and honeyed, and as the road climbed, you could look left across the land where the garibaldini gathered that day and get a sense of why La Masa was so positive about the place. It is spacious and fertile, close to Palermo, but well hidden – and, if attacked, the men could easily disperse into the higher mountains all around.

It would have been right around this time of day, as the garibaldini were trying to cook something to eat or mingling with the *picciotti*, that Colonel Von Mechel and four thousand of the best Bourbon troops, having set out from Piana dei Greci, at last reached that fork in the road – Ficuzza – twenty miles to the south of Gibilrossa, where Orsini had split from Garibaldi some thirty-six hours before. They realized at once that there had been a parting of the ways here – that one group had left the Corleone road and turned back towards Marineo. We remember there had been hours of torrential rain just a few days before. The ground was soft. But this simply made it all the clearer that everything on wheels, above all the heavy cannons that made deep ruts, had gone towards Corleone. It was a sign, Von Mechel assumed, that the rebel army was breaking up. In the coming weeks and months, Major Bosco, Von Mechel's second in command, would claim that he had proposed they follow the group that had turned off to Marineo and hence was staying closer to Palermo. The Reverend Buttà, in his account of events, would lament Von Mechel's obsession with a few antiquated cannons, his Teutonic pig-headedness, as if everyone but their dumb Swiss commander had understood. But Von Mechel was a career soldier and far from dumb. All his military training and experience would have told him that where the artillery was, there was the strength of an army and its ambition. He would have been aware of the lengths Garibaldi had gone to get his cannons over the Renda Pass and down to Parco. It was unimaginable that he had simply relinquished them, sent them off on a road to nowhere. Why would he do that?

The colonel dispatched an encouraging message to General Lanza, the king's lieutenant in Palermo, who immediately passed it on to the king in Naples: "Garibaldi's band breaking up and retreating in disorder towards Corleone." Whence, Von Mechel promised, he would pursue the scoundrel and finish him off. At once Lanza had posters printed and displayed all over Palermo: "The rebels supporting Garibaldi have dispersed, disheartened that they allowed themselves to be deceived by foreign invaders bent on bringing civil strife to Sicily."

So after the near disaster of 24th May in Parco, around midday of 26th May, Garibaldi saw a narrow window of opportunity opening up. A turn of the road and a gap in the trees presents a breathtaking view. We are now above the Gibilrossa Pass, which is visible a couple of hundred feet below, to the left. It's a flattish hollow of scrub, stone and pine, dominated by a white pyramidal obelisk so elegant and out of place in this rugged landscape as to seem a spaceship on its launch pad. Immediately beyond, where the mountain drops precipitously into the Conca, under a ribbon of low hazy cloud, one can just make out Palermo. Ten miles away. There were no Bourbon troops between Garibaldi and the river Oreto skirting the eastern side of the city. It was a clear run.

Exactly at this vantage point, on the other side of the road, stands the Santuario di Santa Maria di Gibilrossa, an abandoned monastery. "In this sacred place," reads the plaque, "Giuseppe La Masa gathered four thousand Sicilians... ready to win or die at the bidding of Giuseppe Garibaldi." And here, or very nearby, towards four in the afternoon, a last council of war was held. All the main men were present. It was agreed the attack must be made at once. "Nino," Garibaldi famously turned to Bixio, "tomorrow in Palermo." "Palermo or hell," Bixio replied. By now his mantra.

"Every face smiled" – Capuzzi. "Every heart beat harder when we got the order."

"Solemnity of the moment" – Nievo. "General joy."

"Such a shiver ran through those men" – Abba – "as seemed to animate the very rocks."

But Garibaldi had other meetings that day which were to feed conspiracy theories for years to come. The road climbs beyond the convent to the bluff above the pass. A big white dog, languishing outside a locked gate, shook the dust from its fur and decided to follow us. The road turned sharply downward, and in a few minutes we were at the obelisk. From here, where the army gathered in the early evening, you can look down through a steep valley to Palermo spread out in the plain with the graceful curve of the blue bay to the right and the mountains to the west beyond. In the bay, on 26th May 1860, among scores of ships at anchor, the huge 91-gun HMS *Hannibal*, flagship of the British Mediterranean Fleet, was the closest to the waterfront. On 15th May, Rear-Admiral Mundy had been cruising the eastern coast of Sicily when he heard of Garibaldi's landing on the other side of the island and immediately proceeded by steam and sail to Palermo. His orders, which he quotes in full in his diary account of events, were: to protect British property, to offer refuge to British and other foreign nationals in Palermo and to avoid all involvement in the struggle. At noon on 24th May, Mundy recounts, in honour of Her Majesty Queen Victoria's birthday, "a royal salute was fired by the ships of the combined squadrons [fifteen Austrian, American, Piedmontese and Neapolitan naval craft], the report of which must have astonished the combatants, who at this time were engaged in skirmishes on the distant ranges of the mountains." Which is to say, Parco and the pass above Piana degli Albanesi. At the "full-dress dinner" held that evening, the bigwigs of the other fleets were "astonished" that, despite the conflict in progress, the Admiral was still allowing complete liberty "towards British naval officers, who, in the uniform of their rank, went ashore for the sake of exercise and amusement, and without a wish to intermeddle with the affairs of the islanders". He felt, Mundy wrote, that this freedom was "advantageous to public order". So it was that, in the early afternoon of 26th May, Lieutenants Wilmot and Cooper and the paymaster Mr Morgan were taking a drive eastwards along the coast and turned inland to the "village of Misilmeri". Rapidly informed of this development, for his scouts were everywhere, Garibaldi invited the British officers to the camp at Gibilrossa."

"As soon as we reached the place" – Capuzzi – "someone told us that some English naval officers had come to the camp to greet Garibaldi; that visit was proof of sympathy for the general, for us and for the Italian cause, coming from a powerful nation. It cheered us up."

Abba was delighted, because "these seamen in white trousers" brought news. "They talked to the general, then started wandering round the camp. What firm brotherly handshakes!" Their news fired the garibaldini up: "The government in Naples is calling us 'pirates', their newspapers say we were beaten at Calatafimi... that we've been routed, and they're hunting us down to stop us taking to the streets and murdering people."

For sure, there is no one to murder on this quiet road today. No cars pass by, no one is in sight, only the big white dog, who won't let us be, sniffing at our sunburnt legs as we move round the obelisk reading the plaques. The monument looked so handsome and graceful from a distance but, alas, is miserably neglected and defaced close up. The stone plaque on one of the three sides has been torn out. On another the words DUCE GARIBALDI have been cancelled with a thick line of orange paint. One text reads:

ACROSS SICILY WITH GARIBALDI'S THOUSAND

HERE THE HEROIC RANKS OF THE THOUSAND, READY TO DIE, AWAITED THE MEMORABLE DAWN WHEN GARIBALDI, THEIR LEADER, UNLEASHED THEM ON THE ANXIOUS IMPATIENT CITY

Admiral Mundy quotes in full the report that his three officers immediately delivered to him. The heroic ranks of the rebels were for the most part "mere boys". Garibaldi's tent "was composed of a worn-out blanket, supported on pikes". The *picciotti* were armed with "old muskets, spears, scythes and rusty cutlasses", but waved "innumerable tricoloured flags" and "were furnished with a host of musicians to incite them to martial deeds".

So picturesque were the revolutionaries that one officer pulled out a sketchbook and began to draw them, including Colonel Carini, who in all the photos we have sports wonderfully waxed moustaches. "The Englishmen seemed pleased to find we were polite, well-educated people," Abba enthuses. "And we loaded them with letters, scraps of paper torn from whatever we had, scribbled in pencil. Greetings, cries of affection, that they will deliver to our families on the first ship leaving Palermo."

On returning to the city, the naval officers had to push away a man who claimed to be a friend of their driver's and tried to hitch a ride hanging on to the side of the carriage. "We conceived that he might be a spy, who, under the protection of the British uniform, might desire to pass through the royal outposts and then return with intelligence for the insurgents." Despite this scrupulous exhibition of neutrality, on hearing about his men's experience, Mundy was alarmed and put a stop to all leave on land: otherwise, he worried, "reports would arise of encouragement given to rebels".

The ban came too late. Once the story was known, rumours were inevitable.

Abba: "The naval officers said the city is a garrison, but they made us hope we might win out. Everyone knows they brought the general a map of Palermo with indications of Bourbon barricades and guard posts."

Needless to say this remark would be seized on by the enemies of the Risorgimento as proof that the evil imperial power that was Great Britain was meddling in Italian politics. But if the British officers didn't bring maps and other sensitive intelligence, who did? Because, as events show, the garibaldini were certainly well informed.

On that same day, 26th May 1860, a man called Nando Eber was determined to join the garibaldini. Thirty-five years old, Hungarian, a liberal who had fled Hungary after the collapse of the 1848 revolution, Eber was now war correspondent for *The Times*, much admired for his adventurous reports from the Crimea. And he had an agenda of his own: to shift British public opinion in favour of liberal national causes, in Italy and consequently in Hungary. Landing in Messina on 23rd May, Eber was in Palermo on the 25th, and soon in contact with the local rebels, who took advantage of his journalist's freedom of movement to send him to Gibilrossa with details of Palermo's defences. The most poorly defended of the city's gates, Eber told Garibaldi, was Porta Termini, being closest to the sea at the extreme eastern side of the town, when the Bourbons had expected an attack from the west. István Türr, another Hungarian, would later confirm that it was the information Eber brought that was decisive. But Abba's rumour about the English stuck.

The meeting that decided the attack must have come after the arrival of the naval officers, but before they left the camp. Because Bixio, who had quickly scribbled a letter to his wife "which I'm placing in friendly hands, so it will surely reach you", had already signed off. But managed to add a PS: "Great day... attack on Palermo decided."

Meantime, we were ready to move on. I wanted to linger a little, because this really is a magical place, with its obelisk, its fragrant highland stillness, its views of the city and the sea. You can imagine how the distant roofs and streets must have called to the men. "We were approaching the trial that would decide the fate of Sicily," says Capuzzi. But Eleonora was eager to get going. So we left the garibaldini behind, organizing themselves for their march.

"An hour before dark" – Bixio – "all forces were concentrated around the monastery." Five hundred Sicilians were to march up front, but led by thirty or so of the toughest garibaldini. After them came the Thousand themselves, or the seven hundred or so who were left. Then the rest of the Sicilians. They would walk through the night so as to launch the attack at dawn. "Great fires of the peasants on the mountains to give the impression we're not moving camp," wrote Nievo. "A solemn wait" – Abba – "It seemed a spirit from eternity breathed over us. I was lying between two rocks, still warm from the intense heat of the day, and I felt such a sweet glow in my limbs, stretched out in that sort of coffin, face turned to where the sun had set, that I was overcome by a melancholy desire to be good and dead."

As we began our descent, the sun was approaching the zenith. The air swooned over slopes of thistle and dry grass. The distant city shimmered. We were longing for a cool shower.

PART THREE
TAKEN AT THE FLOOD

Descent on Palermo

To anyone who has come through a Covid lockdown, Admiral Mundy's description of Palermo as he saw it from his open barouche on 21st May 1860 will sound all too familiar. "It was as if passing through a city of the dead, or one decimated by the plague. Containing two hundred thousand persons, not an inhabitant was to be seen, nor was there a vehicle abroad, save that which I occupied."

"All public offices are closed," wrote the island's governor, General Lanza, the same day. "The workers have deserted their desks. Threats of dismissal have no effect on them."

How had this come about?

After the revolution of 1848 was quashed, General Filangieri had encouraged Ferdinand II to make a tour of Sicily to reset his relationship with his subjects. In the autumn of 1852, after visiting towns in Calabria, the king crossed the sea to Messina, which had been so heavily shelled four years before. There, and further south in Catania, he received rapturous welcomes. Dignitaries fell over themselves to deny any involvement in the city's rebellious past. The king smiled and made a few random concessions. Anyone with a beard, and hence possibly a liberal, was told to shave. "A sublime spectacle," commented one French journalist. "The most extraordinary reconciliation of a legitimate sovereign with his people."

But Ferdinand did not visit Palermo. He wanted to teach the people of the capital a lesson, since that was where the revolution had started. It was a mistake. "Palermo would have been delighted to welcome him," observed Raffaele de Cesare, "and instead they resented this spiteful snub." To keep their resentment at bay, rather than a visit from the king, they got a police chief whom history books present as a pantomime villain. In his late forties, Salvatore Maniscalco was obsessed with repressing every manifestation of political liberalism. He employed a network of informers and agents provocateurs all over the island reporting directly to him. Torture was the norm.

On 27th October 1859, Maniscalco was stabbed in the back outside the cathedral in Palermo, where he attended mass, but the policeman didn't die, and from that point on became even more ruthless, though nevertheless aware that he was fighting a losing battle. "Discontent is on the rise," he wrote on 11th February 1860. "No one believes authority can hold. God save the king and his kingdom."

When Garibaldi landed at Calatafimi, Maniscalco sent his wife and children to Naples, to be away from the danger. One way or another the city was emptied, and placed in a state of frenetic expectation. At the same time, the garibaldini knew that their fate lay in the willingness of the city's men and women to support the cause. To break through the Bourbon defences and find that the people were not interested in a fight would mean certain defeat and very likely slaughter.

We left the obelisk for the descent to Palermo around 9 a.m., after four hours on the road. They left at dusk, around eight in the evening, after a long day in the hot sun with little to eat or drink. The road leads steeply down, and at the first hairpin a track leads off to the left, straight down the side of the mountain. Discesa dei Mille, says a sign. "Descent of the Thousand."

"A precipitous path, where it was hard to stay on your feet," says Capuzzi.

The order as always was: no talking, no smoking, keep close to one another.

"Having to follow a narrow, arduous path" – Garibaldi – "our column of three thousand men stretched out in an endless line, and for the same reason it was impossible to ride back and forth to tighten the men up."

Unfortunately today, after a couple of hundred yards, the Discesa peters out into rugged scrub. There are private properties. It seems there is no way down.

"It was barely a path at all" – Abba – "dropping down from crag to crag. If you missed your footing, you fell forward on your comrade below, and then he fell on someone else, and so on until eight or ten of you were rolling about together on a ledge."

They were scrambling down the slope on a clear moonlit night. We were toiling in forty humid degrees along the straight of a long hairpin, a sharp drop to our left, where Palermo was a hazy mirage, the usual pines and prickly pears on the slope above us to our right.

Garibaldi picked his way down the path on a black horse. Bixio, Türr and other officers were also mounted. After a mile and more of hairpins, we reached a point where the road crosses the gorge they descended. You can look up through reddish outcrops and thick brush to a radio antenna far above. On the other side of the road, the ground drops sheer to the coastal plain. Out at sea, a big oil tanker is leaving port. And now we are entering a tunnel, with the narrowest of pavements. A van swerves and hits its horn.

The garibaldini also faced a minor panic. "Having lost a lot of time getting everyone in order at the foot of the mountain" – Abba – "the column set off again marching slowly, silently... Suddenly, right where I was, commotion. Shouts of "Cavalry!" The gravelly earth thudded with galloping hooves... we jumped aside, broke lines, men diving into the fields beyond the low walls each side of the road, or sitting up on the walls. And, in the confusion, shots were fired at a white horse racing towards us like a phantom. Poor creature! It was carrying Captain Bovi yelling, 'It's only me!'"

"To describe the disorder, the jumpiness, the drowsiness of this slow march would be impossible." Thus Bixio. And he knew whose fault it was. "La Masa... brings confusion everywhere." The Sicilian simply couldn't control his *picciotti*. "At the merest neighing of a horse they trampled all over us, pushing me and my horse bodily twenty paces into a canebrake."

"The hubbub died down" – Abba – "and we walked on, ashamed, in a severe silence imposed by Colonel Carini. All around, near and far, dogs barked endlessly."

At last, we were able to turn off the main road into a narrow lane that led down towards the plain and the sea.

It was the early hours of the morning for the garibaldini, "almost cold," says Abba, "because of the heavy dew." "The moment of truth was approaching" – Capuzzi – "and we marched towards it silently, confident in the sanctity of our cause and the valour of our leaders."

"An emotion we had never felt before" – Zasio – "and the thought of the approaching battle made each of us more confident, prouder."

"In the darkness" – Abba – "you could hear the heavy tread of the men walking ahead of you. 'But who will be in the advance guard?' we kept asking each other."

It was a good question. This was no ordinary battle. Garibaldi needed the thousands of *picciotti*, militarily and politically. But he had no idea how they would behave when the fighting began. And they were adamant they must be the first to enter their city. He knew that the initial clashes would be crucial. Any outlying guard posts must be prevented from raising the alarm. Then they must get through the city's outer defences before reinforcements could be called in. La Masa was commanding the *picciotti* as a whole, but Garibaldi asked a priest, Agostino Rotolo, to head an advance group of fifteen Sicilians. Already a squad commander, Rotolo wore a priest's broad brimmed hat and held a rifle slung across the crucifix on his chest. He begged Garibaldi to be spared this role. He had no military experience, he said. At best he could walk ten paces ahead of the others and get himself killed. "Walk ten paces ahead without getting killed," Garibaldi told him.

From among the garibaldini, the Hungarian Lajos Tüköry had asked to lead the way. He was thirty-two, had fought in the 1848 revolution in Hungary, then, like Orsini, in the Turkish army, in Lebanon and the Crimea. Garibaldi gave him twenty-four of the best men and put him beside Rotolo and his *picciotti*.

So the attack on Palermo was led by a local priest and a foreigner, except in Giuseppe La Masa's account of events, where it was led by Giuseppe La Masa.

"When you fire on the enemy" – Crispi, reporting Garibaldi's words – "you have to kill him: to fire without wounding will only puff up his confidence and give him a low opinion of us."

"After the advance guard" – Abba – "came five hundred *picciotti*, then the Genoese Carabinieri and all the companies of the Thousand. Finally, at the back, the great swarm."

"Now came the order not to fire unless told to" – Capuzzi – "and to keep the ranks tight. The column was reorganized in rows of four, rifles on our shoulders."

Our lane dipped down through orange groves straight towards the sea. After half a mile we were among low ramshackle houses. The village of Ciaculli. Palms in pots. Carpets hanging from balconies. An alley named after Francesco Nullo, who was in the advance guard with Tüköry. A chapel the size of a garden shed with a pair of moccasins on the doorstep. Bright-blue columbines climbing a wall. Only some time after passing through a black gate did we realize we were crossing an extensive gated community. A quarter of a mile on, the gate at the other end of the community was closed. It seemed so disheartening, in the intense heat, to have to turn back and find another route. We stopped, staring at the rusty gate, fifty yards away, and to our great delight as if by power of suggestion it began to swing open. A Piaggio Ape appeared, a tiny three-wheeled van piled high with scrap metal, driven by a dark wiry man in a white vest; he raised an eyebrow when he saw us hurrying to get through the gate before it closed, but didn't stop to ask who we were.

"Then the head of the column took a wrong road" – Garibaldi – "and we had to stop to get everyone on the right one."

"Down in the Palermo plain" – Bixio – "La Masa managed to get lost and made us all take the wrong road."

The road Garibaldi wanted to avoid was the one we had now foolishly turned into, running arrow straight towards Palermo, but narrow. There was barely room for a car to pass, and high stone walls either side. If they were attacked here, they would be trapped. Garibaldi took them to Favara, closer to the coast. Then turned.

"Things only go well," notes Bixio, "when Garibaldi is in command."

"The road ran between dry stone walls and olive groves" – Abba – "with occasional houses, dark and silent. From one of these came the tinkling of a piano – and that sound, coming and going, instilled the kind of melancholy that is made of grief, of love, hope, yearnings, a touch of all that is sensitive in us."

If anyone was playing a piano when we passed, we didn't hear it. The traffic was a constant thundering stream along a road that seemed to have been conceived at best as a farm track or private drive. Trucks, vans, tractors, SUVs. The whole coastal plain here is choked with crumbling buildings and car exhaust, made just about bearable by the pressure of vegetation – bamboo, palms, oleanders – all determined to fight back against everything human. And the walk was taking much longer than we expected. We were spending far too long pressing ourselves against walls to let dusty trucks get by. When the road finally widened and rural dereliction morphed into low apartment blocks, with awnings and laundry and piles of rubbish, it was already eleven.

"We passed an immense building" – Abba – "asleep and empty, then turned into a big road leading to Palermo."

"At the first houses" – Zasio – "the *picciotti* marching with us started, as always, to yell at the top of their voices: long live this, death to that. It was imprudent, the alarm that woke the Bourbons."

"Around 2 a.m." – Bixio – "we come to the first houses, which to our surprise are occupied but not guarded, and the *picciotti*, who are supposed to be marching in silence, start yelling at the top of their voices."

"Our hearts were already beating hard" – Abba – "when suddenly there came a tempest of shouting and gunfire from up front… Many of the *picciotti*, overcome by panic, stopped, turned and pushed back against the carabinieri, causing the whole column to move back in disorder. Bixio arrived, furious with La Masa. Then Garibaldi, to calm them down."

"Generale La Merda!" Bixio told the Sicilian to his face.

"The air began to freshen with the coming dawn" – Abba. "We were told to walk four by four and stay close to the orchard walls, then we quickened our pace."

Not far behind them, we at last came across a café, the first since Misilmeri. Domenico's Bakery, a modern, air-conditioned place, at the bottom of a block of flats. Inside, at the till, a fat surly man in shorts and T-shirt demanded a surprising price for a coke and a fruit juice. At the bar, a girl who struggled to take her eyes off her phone placed two plastic cups on the counter.

"In glasses, please," I asked. "And ice in the coke."

The girl eyed me, my pack, my trekking poles, as if trying to decide whether to refuse. The whole bar, full of bright-red chairs and tables with no one sitting at them, contrived to feel hostile in its very emptiness. She sighed and reached for a glass. We felt we'd won a little battle.

Ponte dell'Ammiraglio and the Oreto River, the map told us, were now just a mile away. Resuming our march, we crossed the railway lines, turned into a busy road, Corso dei Mille, and almost at once came across a shop called Ortopedia dei Mille. "The Thousand's Orthopedics." Fifty yards on, there was a sign for a hospital emergency room. The road is wide here, lined with lush ficus trees and taller apartment blocks. The whole suburb was throbbing with trucks, trams, scooters, vans, drawing you towards the battle: Palermo. You could feel you were nearly there.

"Approaching the city, our marching is more orderly" – Bixio – "and dawn is already breaking to bring a little reality to those fearful minds that darkness reduces to worse than sheep."

Garibaldi had wanted to arrive while it was still night and surprise the Bourbons at Ponte dell'Ammiraglio. Instead, with all the delays, the shouting and the firing, daylight was coming up and the soldiers were alert and ready.

"In the early light" – Abba – "the humpback profile of the bridge and its ten or dozen supports appeared through the smoke, seething with men and rifles."

"A hard core of brave men," – Garibaldi – "led by Tükory and Missori, marched in the advance guard. Among them were Nullo, Enrico Cairoli, Vigo Pelizzari, Taddei, Poggi, Scopini, Uziel, Perla, Gnecco and other most courageous men whose names, it pains me to say, I no longer recall."

Those he doesn't recall, in particular, are the Sicilians.

"At the first light of dawn" – this is the Sicilian Vincenzo Fuxa in an affidavit written for La Masa the following year – "we found ourselves near Ponte dell'Ammiraglio, where the Bourbons attacked us and the battle began – a fierce battle, because the Bourbons, who had taken positions in the trees and houses surrounding the bridge, were firing at us from all sides. General La Masa, racing in front, settled the momentary hesitation of our column, something natural when you're attacked by an enemy lying in wait, and with just a few men carried the bridge."

Other eyewitness accounts described the hesitation of the Sicilians as more than momentary. They ran for cover, leaving Tükory's advance party dangerously exposed. Bixio galloped forward and threw his company into the fray.

"From the head of the column" – Abba – "we heard gunfire and a cry of 'To arms!', yelled in desperation. Then a terrible howl, a sudden barrage, everyone moving at a run – '*Avanti! Avanti*" – and we were in the battle."

You do not actually cross Ponte dell'Ammiraglio to enter Palermo these days. Even in 1860, there was no water flowing under it. The tiny river Oreto was split in two channels, and the channel under Ponte dell'Ammiraglio had long since dried up. The main channel, a hundred yards nearer the town, flowed under Ponte delle Teste Mozze, so named because of the decapitated heads of brigands that would be fixed on posts to reassure travellers that they were entering an area of law and order.

"We ran into a crowd of *picciotti*" – Abba. "We pushed some of them into the gardens either side of the road, and took others forward with us. One, maybe a company commander, was yelling furious accusations at his men and came with us waving his sword. But in his anger, he shouted 'God!', turned around, tottered sideways like a drunk and fell in the ditch beneath two tall poplars."

Ponte dell'Ammiraglio now stands in a small public park to the left of the modern thoroughfare. It's an antique Norman structure, about a hundred yards long by ten wide, not exactly humpbacked, more a low pyramid shape sitting on three arches, its cobbled surface infested by shrivelled weeds.

"We pushed quickly forward for a good stretch" – Abba – "but at Ponte dell'Ammiraglio the resistance was ferocious. Along the road, on the arches, under the bridge and in the surrounding gardens, a massacre of bayonets. Dawn was coming up, and everyone had something savage in their faces."

> CELEBRATING
> ON THE FIRST CENTENARY
> 27TH MAY 1860
> THE REGION OF SICILY
> RECONSECRATES THE MEMORY
> OF
> ROCCO LA RUSSA
> PIETRO LO SQUIGLIO
> TOMMASO LO CICERO
> PIETRO INSERILLO
> WHO FELL HERE
> THE GLORIOUS FIRST

All Sicilian names. There were between two and three hundred Bourbon soldiers at the bridge. The battle lasted half an hour.

"Seeing the Bourbons" – Zasio – "we began to fire, and were met by an immediate barrage that had many men falling at once. Reinforced, we attacked again."

Any cover is below the bridge, between its arches. Above, there is only a low wall, not even three feet high.

"A wounded soldier" – Abba – "was banging his head on the little wall of the bridge trying to smash his own skull, but Gerolamo Airenta gently pulled him away from it, then with his usual calm went on firing."

"Needless to say" – Bixio – "from being the first the *picciotti* were now the last."

Long after any of them, we walked round the bridge on the dry grass under the hot sun, reading the endless plaques.

> SPIRIT AND EYE OF THE STRATEGIST
> GARIBALDI
> MADE THIS BRIDGE GLORIOUS
> AT DAWN ON 27TH MAY 1860
> PASSING WITH THE SICILIANS AND THE THOUSAND
> VICTORIOUSLY ONWARD
> TO LOOK FOR ITALY
> IN THE HEART OF PALERMO
> 1860–1910

"By dint of sheer stubbornness" – Zasio – "we took the bridge from the Bourbons, and were ready to carry on the attack to the principle barricade."

"Advancing with bayonet and volleys of rifle fire" – Bixio – "almost at a run, putting to flight all the resistance we met... each man fighting in his own style."

"The Neapolitan army," historian De Cesare later commented, "felt impotent to fight an enemy that was not afraid of death."

We rejoined the main road, packs on our backs and poles in hand, and crossed what is now a very modern bridge carrying four lanes of traffic. The river is a muddy trickle choked with reeds. The surrounding city is a nondescript expanse of apartment blocks, rather posher than those on the east side of the river. After about half a mile, the main flow of traffic turns left and Corso dei Mille narrows into older buildings, colourfully cluttered, cars double- and even triple-parked, hoots, cries, heaps of rubbish, abandoned supermarket trolleys. On a wall to our left, swathed in cables, by a noble door, a plaque reads: "Benedetto Cairoli, soldier of liberty, here consecrated with his blood the glorious day of redemption." In fact Cairoli wasn't wounded here, but given shelter afterwards. Below, a notice offers rooms to let for female students or workers only. No men.

Another hundred yards and you reach a crossroad, Via Lincoln, which, to the right, runs straight to the sea a half-mile away and, to the left, takes you to the railway station and Piazza Sant'Antonino. Across Via Lincoln, where Corso dei Mille becomes Via Garibaldi, is where Porta Termini once stood, one of the city's ancient gates. This is where the Limited Traffic Zone now starts.

"We resumed our march" – Capuzzi – "in the midst of gunfire, till we came to the crossroads where the first barrier had been built."

You can find one or two illustrations of the old Porta Termini on the Internet, but no photographs. Dating back to Norman times, it had been redeveloped in the seventeenth century: a narrow arch supporting an extravagant baroque oratory two storeys high, complete with saints and Madonna. But this was torn down, in 1852, by Carlo Filangieri, the Bourbon general who reconquered Sicily after the 1848 revolution. The narrowness of the gate made it too hard, the general felt, for an army to get into the city, should it rebel. Also, Porta Termini was close to Piazza Fieravecchia, which had always been a rallying point for subversives. Ironically, the removal of the gate created precisely the weak point Garibaldi needed to penetrate the town. The Bourbon soldiers, however, had erected a high barricade across the street, "solid and well built", says Zasio, "with sacks of earth".

"The big road that the invaders now have to cross to get to Porta Termini" – Crispi – "is swept by cannon fire from a ship placed at the opening of the street and also by the rifle fire of the troops."

"The Bourbons" – Capuzzi – "were sending a hail of bullets from the Piazza Sant'Antonino to stop us making progress."

So the advance was now faced with a heavy crossfire, from right and left, along what is now Via Lincoln, and from straight ahead, behind the barrier. Lajos Tüköry went down, his knee blown away. We waited for the traffic light to turn green and walked across. It's a totally anonymous crossroad now. A wide-open space of asphalt, without even any lane markings to break it up. Shops, scooters, satellite dishes. Sweltering heat. And now, from the left, came the sound of cavalry.

It's curious that neither Abba nor Capuzzi, Zasio or Crispi ever describe their own personal exploits. Never mention killing. Or being hurt. Yet they are always ready to tell us of the courage of others.

"Faustino Tanara from Parma," Abba tells us, "with his company, and the Sicilian priest, Antonio Rotolo, with a big squad of *picciotti*, kept the cavalry at bay." Vincenzo Fuxa, Crispi tells us, with another group of *picciotti*, headed seawards along Via Lincoln to meet gunfire from that direction. The Sicilians were taking courage.

"Chased ourselves and chasing others" – Abba – 'we gathered at the crossroads of Porta Termini, blasted by cannon fire from a ship and rifle fire from the barrier."

It was here that Benedetto Cairoli went down, together with his brother Enrico.

"Before entering the city" – Bixio – "I was lightly wounded in the right collar bone and could not keep my men together with the same energy."

"Bixio, raging up and down on his horse" – Abba – "himself wounded, berating, insulting… unleashing his fury on someone who dared to warn him his chest was covered in blood."

"It was wonderful to see Garibaldi at moments like this" – Crispi. "On the battlefield his face shone with joy: it didn't seem he was involved in a struggle where men were falling all around, dead or wounded, more like a wedding ball. He stopped his horse opposite the street that now bears his name, at the point where it crosses Via Lincoln. From the right the Neapolitan fleet was firing grapeshot, from the left the Bourbon infantry shot their bullets. Firm, imperturbable, he did not move until the last of his volunteers had entered the town."

Having crossed the street, we stop for a moment and turn. If ever there was a place for an equestrian statue, this must be it. Garibaldi stock still, on his horse, under fire. "A marvellous confidence and calm stamped on his face," remembered Abba. "Türr was beside him." The traffic frets, waiting for the light to change.

"Nullo from Bergamo, reckless as ever" – Zasio – "grabbed a flag from a desperate *picciotto* and under heavy fire planted it in the sacks of the dreaded barrier."

"Garibaldi gave the signal" – Abba – "and the terrible step was taken: at a run we poured into the street that led to Fieravecchia."

Barricades

"Whit Sunday, 27th May" – Admiral Mundy's diary. "I was awoke at 4 o'clock this morning by continuous discharges of musketry."

The admiral was not surprised. The previous evening, "at a late hour", he had received a letter inviting him to send an observer to the Prince of Lampedusa's tower for a bird's eye view of the imminent assault on the town. "Almost everyone knew for certain," the brothers Filippo and Gaetano Borghese would later claim in their memoir, "that the attack would come the next morning." But if this were the case, Mundy wondered, why didn't the Bourbons take appropriate measures? And why didn't the population rise up the moment they heard gunfire?

"Is this really Piazza della Fieravecchia?" asked Abba after dashing the four hundred yards from Porta Termini to their first objective. To the dismay of the garibaldini, there was no one about.

Now called Piazza della Rivoluzione, Fieravecchia is an irregular space where five streets meet, with a fountain and statue in the middle: the Genio di Palermo, a crowned and bearded old man clutching a sea serpent. In 1852 General Filangieri had had the statue removed and placed in storage, so that it could offer no incitement to revolt. The piazza was expected to be the heart of any uprising. Instead, as the revolutionaries arrived at a run, nothing happened. Not even a bell ringing.

"Garibaldi almost turned pale" – Abba. "From the gap between two shutters someone shouted '*Evviva!*' A few windows opened, a few heads leant out, but no one came down to the street, armed or unarmed. A tragic moment."

"Meantime, we ran through the alleys and piazzas" – Nievo – "two here, one there, like sheep, looking for Neapolitans to kick out, or Palermitani to have them get on with their revolution, or at least build a barricade or two."

"Since the population of the capital was completely unarmed" – Garibaldi – "people couldn't at first expose themselves to the tremendous fire going on in the streets."

Nor could church bells easily be rung, since the police had removed the clappers. "The lawyer Giovanni Muratori," recounted a certain Antonio Beninati in his diary on 26th May, "wants me to find someone to shut himself up in the convent of the Ospedaletto and get the bell ringing before tomorrow. I contacted one of our trusted men, the master blacksmith, Antonino Pirconti, but he wouldn't do it: he told me he wasn't ready to die like those in the April revolution."

We approached the piazza walking against a one-way stream of traffic in Via Garibaldi, stopping to read the many plaques, hopefully from under the shade of a balcony. These are solid city buildings, five or six storeys high, centuries old. Palermo was in full swing. A man with a cat on his shoulder stopped us to ask for money. Our holiday rental was still a mile off.

"We barricaded the streets leading from the piazza" – Zasio – "with empty barrels and tables dragged from the surrounding shops."

Today the surrounding shops are mainly milliners and jewellers. The Berrettificio Mascari Francesco, for example, which we pass on our left, has a fine display of tartan berets. "Camarrone has raised the prices of his English-style velvet berets again," wrote the same Antonio Beninati, "the ones the revolutionaries are wearing, such is the demand."

In general, the change of mood passing from suburban sprawl to city centre, the sudden leap in quality of the cafés and the goods on display, could not be more emphatic. For all the crusty antiquity and elegant disrepair of these monuments and buildings, you feel at once you're in a modern cosmopolitan space where tourists are welcome and rubbish will be collected. Arriving in the piazza, we find the Genio is back on his pedestal in the middle of the fountain, hugging a plump serpent to his breast. "27 MAGGIO 1860," says the plaque. Not another word is needed.

"Where are the people?" Abba asked a man who appeared at a door armed with a dagger. "Why aren't they here?"

"Three or four times, *signorino*, at dawn," the man replied, "the police fired off shots yelling 'Viva l'Italia, viva Garibaldi.' Anyone who came down to the street was arrested and shown no mercy."

Described as "notes scribbled in pencil by a modest elderly patriot", Beninati's diary confirms this claim: "Tonight, as on others," he begins his entry for 25th May, "lots of rifle fire from the police... they think they can fool people and get them to come out of their houses."

What mainly emerges from Beninati's diary, though, is the total uncertainty in which the people of Palermo had been living since the April revolution. They did not believe official news bulletins, hence were convinced, for example, that Rosolino Pilo was still alive and well. Day by day all kinds of imaginary scenarios, triumphant and catastrophic, were conjured up by word of mouth and the many clandestine printing presses. Whatever the claims of the Borghese brothers, a teacher and medical student who compiled their memoir with feverish hindsight in the days after the fighting was over, the committed patriot Beninati did not hear of the coming attack until almost midnight of the 26th, and only then because, on returning home, he ran into someone who had spoken to the head of the city's secret Revolutionary Committee. They had got word from Gibilrossa and were trying to warn people to be ready. "The police look glum and beaten," Beninati enthused.

We noticed a surprising number of police on the streets of Palermo, having seen very few on our trip so far. Blue trousers with red stripes. Guns and truncheons. A certain swagger.

It was police behaviour "tending to exasperate" that Admiral Mundy found "beyond comprehension". On the evening of Saturday 26th May, he reports, citizens of Palermo who had taken advantage of an open invitation to visit British and Piedmontese warships anchored in the bay were arrested on returning to shore. Two hundred were marched to jail. "Lucky that our boatman realized what was happening," jotted Beninati, "and changed direction."

"From Porta Termini I rode to Fieravecchia" – Garibaldi – "and from there to Piazza Bologni."

Hard on his heels, or his horse's hooves, around six in the morning, Abba was briefly able to forget his panic about the lack of citizen support: "Clutching an iron grating just above us with hands that looked like lilies, three young maidens dressed in white, all very beautiful, were looking out."

"The girls asked:
"'Who are you?'
"'Italians. And you?'
"'Nuns.'
"'You poor things!'
"'Viva Santa Rosalia!
"'Viva l'Italia.'"

From his window, barely a hundred yards away, Antonio Beninati had seen the Bourbon soldiers fleeing from Porta Termini towards the Royal Palace, and, after waiting a little while, for safety, went down to the street where the Sicilian bands were arriving in fits and starts, "each bearing a flag with the patron saint of their towns. Misilmeri: San Giusto; Bagheria: San Giuseppe; Marineo: San Ciro." Pushing through the crowd to get close to Garibaldi, the first words Beninati heard the general say were, "Go and get the wounded."

"More than a hundred men were lost just getting into the town" – Zasio. "Many dead, many wounded."

We were trying to get close too, following the rebels' lead through a disorienting mix of twisting alley and noble square, deep shade and dazzling sunshine. No pretty nuns, but an awful lot of flesh on display. Shops spill their wares onto the streets, horses tug open carriages packed with tourists, scooters are weaving far too fast between cars and pedestrians, bumping on the uneven stone flagging. There is much bloated baroque and obscene graffiti, many tangles of cable beside battered shutters, balconies cluttered with satellite dishes, dog kennels and bicycles, laundry lines sagging with sheets and tablecloths, tropical trees in giant pots, weeds sprouting from the paving, rubbish overflowing from collective bins. And people, people, people. A tall toothless Arab man with a white fez dances to a wail of music from the sound system throbbing beside his begging bowl. A cyclist with a cigar in his mouth stops to greet him. All in all it's a huge injection of life after the rather gloomy towns we've been walking through so far. Palermo seethes. But it is time to give the reader some idea of the geography of the place. Otherwise we will soon be lost.

The bay of Palermo curves from south-east to north-west, and the city clings to the shoreline like a wasps' nest to a roof beam. Developed when the island was under Arab control, the settlement was planned around a single dead-straight thoroughfare running from the centre of the bay at one end inland to the main city gate at the other. Now called Via Vittorio Emanuele, in 1860 it was Via Toledo, named after a sixteenth-century Spanish viceroy, or simply the "Cassaro", its old Arab name; on the low uneven hills either side of this magnificent street were a maze of meandering alleys. Another viceroy cleared up some of the confusion by adding a second, arrow-straight street, Via Maqueda, which crosses Via Toledo at right angles creating a central hub, the Quattro Canti, named after the four elaborate early seventeenth-century façades that look down onto it. Via Maqueda links Porta Vicari on the south of the town to Porta Maqueda (now demolished) to the north. The distance is little less than a mile, about the same as the distance along Via Toledo from the Cala, the old port, to the Duomo and the Royal Palace.

Given this admirable geometric simplicity, whenever you set foot on Maqueda or the then Via Toledo, you know exactly where you are in relation to the city's key features. But within the four quarters carved out by these great, rigorously straight streets, everything is a labyrinthine tangle and nothing is easier than to find yourself back in Maqueda when you thought you would come out at Toledo, or at the seafront, or the Royal Palace. Disorientation is the norm. It is true that another large road, Via Roma, now cuts across the town, more or less parallel to Via Maqueda, but this was not built until the late nineteenth century, to link the new railway station to the port.

The garibaldini had penetrated the city in the south-east quarter. Their urgent strategic goal was to control the Quattro Canti, the central crossroads. The main body of the royal troops, some 12,000, were stationed in and around the Royal Palace, at the western (that is inland) end of Via Toledo. Other substantial groups of men were billeted along Via Toledo, at the Mint, which was at the sea end of the same street, and in the fort of Castellammare a few hundred yards to the north of the Mint, on the shore. For most of their supplies, and particularly their munitions, the soldiers around the Royal Palace relied on access to the port and their numerous fleet; they needed to keep Via Toledo open at all costs.

Following the rebels from Piazza della Rivoluzione to Piazza Bologni, one crosses Maqueda in the direction of the Royal Palace, and advances down a long narrow alley that emerges in the square which is about eighty yards by twenty, perfectly rectangular, and opens at the far end on Via Toledo. Here, wrote Garibaldi, "seeing it was hard to keep together a strong core of men when spreading out through a big metropolis, I got off my horse and set myself up in a doorway".

It is always a pleasure when your various sources agree: "Here he dismounted," echoes Abba, "and sat down. Yes, he sat down! His calm was almost frightening."

The pleasure is even greater when today's physical reality fits perfectly. Arriving in Piazza Bologni, following the same streets, we know immediately in which doorway the general must have sat. Three storeys high, the seventeenth-century Palazzo Ugo delle Favare occupies the whole western side of the square. Magnificently shabby and apparently unoccupied now, its grandiose central doorway seems the perfect place to take a rest after eight hours on horseback. Framed between two black pillars, it must have lent an architectural authority to Garibaldi's orders. Above the door, between the elaborate wrought iron of a balcony railing and the scrolls of a great coat of arms, a fading plaque reads:

> In this illustrious house
> on 27th May 1860
> for only two hours
> GIUSEPPE GARIBALDI
> Laid down his weary limbs.

But that would be later in the day. The general could hardly sleep at 6.30 a.m., barely inside the city, with the people of Palermo still mainly in their houses and a garrison of many thousands of well-armed men just a few hundred yards away.

"Four or five bold Bourbon officers" – Abba – "each leading half a battalion to the centre, sowing death and destruction, would have been enough to overwhelm us."

To increase everyone's jitteriness, there was an accident. "Lowering my horse's saddle and gun belt on the ground" – Garibaldi – "a pistol struck the cobbles and went off, the bullet grazing my right foot and taking away a scrap of my trousers."

Garibaldi has nothing to say in his memoir about his leadership under fire at Porta Termini, nothing about the exhausting business of trying to command a makeshift army in chaotic circumstances. The only personal anecdote he gives us is this moment of clumsiness that had all those round him in a panic. "'They've killed him!' we cried," recalls Abba. But the near miss cheered the general up: "'Such strokes of luck,' I said to myself, 'never come alone.'"

"Desperately hungry" – Zasio. "Someone brought us food and a branch of Japanese persimmons."

"The bells began to ring out" – Abba – "the city was waking up."

"The inhabitants" – Capuzzi – "came down into the street with cockades, armed with shotguns, daggers, swords, pistols."

"A young Piedmontese" – Beninati – "asked me for food. I took him to my house."

"The persimmons were delicious" – Zasio – "an intense golden yellow."

Looking around Piazza Bologni from the shade of the famous doorway, the space certainly looks big enough to gather a thousand men or so. Today, a couple of cafés have spread their tables at the Toledo end; otherwise, the sun-baked flagstones are surprisingly empty. It's thirty-six degrees. There is no sign of a persimmon tree, though weeds are sprouting between paving stones and from the gutters of the roof above.

"Meantime" – Abba – "men were arriving from every direction with confused, contrasting, even absurd news."

Very likely one of these was Giuseppe La Masa. Here our sources are in ferocious disagreement – but that can be a pleasure too. Witness statements in La Masa's book describe him as among the first to pass the barricade at Porta Termini, then striking off alone through half of Palermo "to reconnoitre the points where the Bourbons were concentrated", before rushing back to report to Garibaldi.

"The last battle for the barricade" – Bixio – "was carried by Captain Bassini wielding his sabre, while La Masa fled." Later, he reports, "we saw La Masa coming out of a house, where I have no doubt he had been hiding."

It was hard to compete with Bixio in moments like this.

"Bixio appeared on foot" – Abba – "clenching a broken sword, furious, terrible. He wanted twenty determined men to go and get himself killed with them at the Palazzo Reale. 'Since in a couple of hours we'll all be dead anyway!' he yelled, and was already at the corner of Via Toledo when Garibaldi called him back."

Barricades, the general ordered. They must make it impossible for the soldiers to penetrate the city's narrow streets. This was something ordinary, unarmed citizens could do.

"Furniture was thrown down from the windows" – Capuzzi – "the paving stones torn from the streets."

"From the windows" – Garibaldi – "rained down seats, mattresses, furnishings of every kind to build the barriers."

But these were not the only things to rain down.

"Towards seven o'clock" – Abba – "came a great boom from Castellammare, a roar in the air. The first bomb crashed down."

"Enormous shells were fired from the seafront" – Zasio – "and two noble lives extinguished. A member of the commissariat, struck in the stomach, and Richiedei, whose head was split in two."

"The fire from the fortress then opened" – Admiral Mundy – "and, shortly after six o'clock, the whole of the Neapolitan squadron opened an indiscriminate fire of shot and shell upon the town, which was very soon in flames in several places."

"A bomb falls on San Giuseppe [dei Padri Teatini]" – Beninati – "shattering the vault and going through the floor to explode in the Church of the Madonna della Provvidenza beneath, killing one of Professor Scandurra's nieces."

Civilian deaths had begun. The exploding shells came at five-minute intervals, the time required for the fortress's big cannon to cool. Hour after hour. One essential quality of anyone wishing to change the world is a readiness to accept that huge suffering may result from your decisions. "Perhaps nobody," Abba reflects of the citizens who now flocked to welcome Garibaldi, "realized that this man... had come to bring down upon their city, and himself, and his men, utter carnage."

"A convent on one side of the street was burning" – Zasio. "Clouds of dense smoke rising from its roof along with gigantic flames."

The bells rang out. The barricades went up. Gunfire was brisk all over the town as the rebels pushed outwards and the Bourbon troops made their first incursions from the Royal Palace and other barracks. "Fighting at Sant'Antonino," Beninati jotted, "at Porta Carini, at the cathedral, in Via Castro."

We walked between café tables and turned left onto Via Toledo, or rather Via Vittorio Emanuele II, now a busy pedestrian street. Fridge magnets, tee shirts, tourist information, street food. Tricolours are on sale for Italy's next big game, the quarter final against Belgium. Standing at the door of a restaurant, seeing us approach with our backpacks and poles, a young waiter quipped, "For Everest, signori, take the next left."

"If he only knew," Eleonora shook her head. We had been walking eight hours.

"Both our lot and the Piedmontese are looking tired" – Beninati. "Famished, exhausted from their march, sleepless. How will they manage?"

We passed the huge complex of the cathedral with barely a glance. A right turn, another three hundred yards and we had found our holiday let. The landlady led us up eight dark flights of stairs. They seemed endless. Once inside the flat, another steep staircase led to a sitting room and bedroom and yet another to a big terrace on the roof. You could lean out and imagine heaving chairs and wardrobes down into the street far below, for the barricades. Or tossing plant pots at Bourbon soldiers. "Perhaps none of them dared push towards the centre" – Abba – "for fear of being buried under a bit of everything, from all the houses: furniture, stones, burning oil."

Tired and hungry, we showered, changed and hurried back down the stairs to look for somewhere to eat.

"Feeling hungry" – Beninati – "I go home and grab a piece of bread and some olives. Two bombs fall, one in the Canella courtyard, one in the piazza. The first sends Neli Fuso and his wife to the other world, their daughter Giuseppa, horribly wounded, is taken to the hospital at Sant'Anna… If this bombardment goes on all night, it's goodbye to Palermo."

Bombardment

"At three o'clock in the afternoon" – Admiral Mundy's diary – "the general bombardment of the ill-fated city, by sea and land, recommenced."

Three o'clock was around the time we finally managed to eat, and also, according to Abba, the moment when the people of Palermo committed themselves wholeheartedly and poured out onto the streets. "Armed with knives, axes, nails, hammers, spades, sticks and stones" – reported the Borghese brothers – "boys, old men, young men, women, priests, monks."

"My dear Adelaide," Bixio wrote to his wife that afternoon, "we entered Palermo this morning and accomplished the revolution."

"I notice," jotted Beninati, "a tearful Count Lucchesi Palli hugging common workmen and calling them 'his brothers'."

Bixio was writing rather than fighting, because his wound was more serious than he had wanted to believe. A bullet had entered beneath the collar bone. He gouged it out himself, but lost a lot of blood. Garibaldi ordered him to find a bed. "More of this another time," he promises his wife. "I'm sleepy and tired after the incredible work of these last two days and three sleepless nights."

Our landlady had advised us to go to the nearby Mercato del Capo. It was mayhem. Stalls either side of a narrow cobbled street climbing through flaking stone façades, fruit boxes on red and yellow crates displaying every edible product of this Mediterranean earth, huge red awnings stretched overhead against the pitiless sun, so that the light amid the mill of shoppers was warm and rich, voices calling "peppers... pomegranates... peaches... melons... apricots", cavernous openings stinking of fish, slabs of bloody tuna, slimy piles of silvery squid, boys squeezing oranges, men scraping ice from huge blocks to serve with fresh lemon juice, and, at one street corner, a column of blue smoke rising from a sizzling barbecue, piles of meat filling the air with heavy smells – to cap it all, somewhere in a side street, the wailing and thumping of Arab music.

We sat ourselves at red plastic tables outside Dainotti's, a popular eating place. Everything is red and yellow. Motorbikes sway by, brushing against bulging bags. The riders have no helmets. Smells of oil and sweat. Some stalls are closing now, and sharp-eyed housewives are looking for bargains. Behind the counter, which is open onto the street, a woman serves a long queue at speed, ladling a prawn soup, slicing a hunk of ham, squashing a mozzarella into a bread roll, tipping pasta from a pan. She has strong hands, thick wrists. Waiting our turn, the heat and bustle have reduced me to a kind of stupor. "Bring this... get that," a voice is calling. Four beers. Two *panelle*. Bussing the tables, a girl is wearing a black T-shirt that says "I picciotti del Capo". Perhaps it's her mother that's serving, her grandmother calling the orders, three generations with one intent.

"The women too," remembered Garibaldi, "were sublime in their patriotic fervour: throughout that inferno of bombs and bullets, they urged our men on, waving their hands and praising and cheering."

We ate a steamy *caponata*, and under the red awning everything was achingly vivid: the green of fresh basil leaves, the red and dark stew of cherry tomatoes and aubergine chunks. By the time we had finished, the market was half empty, the stalls mostly dismantled. We wiped our mouths and set out to see where the revolution was up to.

"The most violent attacks" – Beninati, writing on the afternoon of the 27th – "are at the Benedictine monastery, Via di Castro, the cathedral, Porta Carini, Via Gioiamia and Via dei Biscottari."

Porta Carini is at the top of the market, just a hundred yards from Dainotti's. This is the north-west edge of the old town. Two tall fortifications of pinkish stone stand either side of the street, ornamented up top with what look like floral vases. Passing between them you move from the bustle of the market to a wide-open expanse of heavily trafficked asphalt, where more modern streets lead off in all directions beyond the old city walls. In the heat of the afternoon, people have mostly disappeared, and we're the only customers asking for an espresso in Bar Porta Carini. Again the tables are red plastic, though the awning is white this time. And I try to explain to Eleonora what exactly happened here, so far as I have understood it.

Garibaldi had sent an order to Giovanni Corrao, who was commanding Rosolino Pilo's men, to come down from the mountains above Pioppo, bypass Monreale, enter the city from the west, wherever they could, and make sure, when they arrived, that the prisoners in the big jails on that side of the town did not escape from their cells. But the Sicilians' advance was blocked by the Bourbons at the church that we can just make out at the end of the street opposite our table. Via Carini.

"Retreating quickly inside the monastery of San Francesco di Paola," remembered Nicola Rammacca, one of Corrao's company commanders, "we returned fire from the windows of the church."

Zasio was shocked: "Christs and Madonnas and pictures of saints and everything precious was, terrible to say, destroyed. People expected a miracle – that didn't happen."

"The Church of San Tommaso dei Greci was set on fire" – Beninati. "The chaplain Millonze, the priest's nephew, perished in the flames."

We set off to one of the scenes of destruction. Santa Caterina. This took us down the deep shade of Via Volturno to Piazza Giuseppe Verdi, where Porta Maqueda once stood. The old town was really fairly small, and we have already got ourselves halfway round it. Demolished in 1877 to make way for the pillars, plinth and dome of the huge and pompous pile that is Teatro Massimo, Porta Maqueda stood at the opposite end of the city from Porta Termini, where the Garibaldini had entered. By mid-afternoon, then, the rebels were pushing out in bands from the centre, trying to get control of the city's gates, while from outside more and more armed Sicilians were looking for ways to get in. At the same time, General Lanza recalled his garrisons in Monreale and Parco – thousands of men – back to the city and the Royal Palace. Corrao's *picciotti* had retreated a few hundred yards from San Francesco di Paola when they realized that a column of troops was bearing down on them from behind, from Monreale. Corrao, writes Rammacca, "immediately ordered people to put mattresses on their balconies so we could fire on the soldiers as soon as they were in range. But rather than returning fire, they brought up two cannons and began to shell us."

Cannons were also being used in what is now the big square outside the Teatro Massimo.

"From Porta Maqueda" – Abba – "the cannons of General Cataldo began to fire along that great street [Maqueda]."

"One band of fighters leaves from the town hall" – Beninati – "to reinforce and help the band already fighting at Porta Maqueda. The barrage of fire is intense, and our men are struggling to hold on."

The Bourbons clearly preferred firing their artillery along the streets to actually venturing down them.

"However combat-hardened a professional army may be" – Zasio – "it will always prefer a regular battle to the prospect of reducing to obedience a people entrenched in their streets."

Turning into Via Maqueda towards the centre, we wonder how the rebels found any cover. What we're looking down is a pedestrian paradise, a dead-straight quarter of a mile of cafés and fashion stores, souvenirs and ice-cream parlours.

"The doors and the windows of all houses" – Garibaldi, by decree – "must be left open day and night to give refuge to the fighters…"

"This is a different kind of struggle," Zasio explains, "deadly, extreme; when their lives and property are threatened and a principle is at stake, ordinary people are transformed into warriors and perform miracles."

"Under Sant'Isidoro's arch" – Beninati – "I see more than three hundred urchins armed with big cobbles and a kind of catapult on a cart for hurling rocks."

We sauntered among ice-cream eaters and desultory shoppers, relieved not to have to do any more serious marching, not to mention fighting. The buildings lining the street are old and elegant, their original façades mostly respected, so that the shop fronts are small and quaint, including the official store of Palermo Football Club, selling the team's pink and black kits. Tourists are trundling their luggage to expensive hotels. A handsome boy with smart shades sails by perfectly erect on his electric scooter. Everyone is focused on purchases and pleasure, except a gypsy woman, cross-legged, begging, a child in her arms. Finally we arrive at the Quattro Canti, where we find the kind of barriers the people of Palermo would have loved to get their hands on a hundred and sixty years ago: big concrete girders laid across the street to prevent terrorists driving vans into the crowd. One bears a cartoon image of Santa Rosalia, Palermo's patron saint, daubed on its side for further protection.

The Quattro Canti, the town's central crossroad, is full-on Spanish baroque, the four great façades, or *canti* – brownish stone with white ornamentation – cutting the corners to turn square into octagon. Each *canto* is three storeys high and slightly concave, with a central fountain at street level and slim columns either side. Each has its statues and plaques, its saints and coats of arms, its balconies and shutters, all stylishly shabby; one is apparently derelict, top-floor windows gaping and shutters broken. The effect is oddly mesmerizing: symmetrical and alike, yet all slightly different, the *canti* cast a charming spell on a space that is at once quite contained, just a few square yards, yet offers views as far as the eye can see along its four straight approach roads. As we turn around to admire each façade, two carabinieri appear, strutting back and forth in their red striped pants, heavy blue shirts and military caps. One quails to think how hot they must be; sure enough there are dark stains under their armpits, above their gun belts. Still, one quails even more to imagine the scene here that fatal day. Because if General Cataldo's cannons were firing down Maqueda from the northern city gate, "General Lanza's", Abba tells us, "were raking the length of the Toledo from the Royal Palace", one turret of which we can just glimpse a half-mile to the west.

Nor was this all. Admiral Mundy is eloquent on the subject. In a conversation he reports with Admiral Persano, commander of the Piedmontese fleet, he advises him, when visiting a port, to "bring his ships as close into the land as the depth of water would allow". This to "show your flag to advantage". And he boasts that wherever he anchors HMS *Hannibal* "it would not be an easy matter to pick a berth between it and the shore". So on 27th May 1860 this imposing British warship was anchored just off Palermo's waterfront, exactly opposite the opening of Via Toledo at Porta Felice, a position of maximum visibility and prestige.

Yet, to the admiral's surprise and dismay, two Neapolitan "steamers of war" ("built in England," he recalls, "and armed with 95 cwt. 68-pounders") "manoeuvred with considerable skill" to get between the *Hannibal* and the shore. "Sweeping round within a few yards of the spanker boom of the *Hannibal*, he brought both broadsides alternately to bear on the Toledo, and raked with his heavy metal the whole of that magnificent street."

In short, Palermo's main thoroughfare was being sprayed with shot and shell from both ends simultaneously.

"Getting across the Toledo," reported Lieutenant Wilmot, who had been sent ashore to check on the circumstances of the fabulously wealthy wine merchant, Mr Ingram, was "unpleasant".

"So soon as the steamer drifted out of range," the Admiral goes on, "[the captain] turned again at half a cable's distance from the shore, and thus kept repeating his circuit under the *Hannibal*'s stern, and delivering his fire upon his countrymen."

We looked up towards the Royal Palace and down towards the sea, took a deep breath and crossed the lovely space unscathed. Not fifty yards further on, to the left as you head south on Maqueda, is the even lovelier, indeed magnificent Piazza Pretoria, and, behind it, the pink façade and dome of Santa Caterina.

"In discussion with Palermo's Revolutionary Committee" – Garibaldi – "we decided to establish my headquarters in Palazzo Pretorio, the central point of the city."

The Palazzo, which was the town hall, is on the south side of the piazza.

"Garibaldi had them put a mattress on the steps of the fountain" – Abba – "opposite the big door of the Palazzo, and there, at the foot of one of the tall statues that grace the piazza, he was brought news, gave orders, rested."

The fountain is a great white-and-pink circle, perhaps fifty yards in diameter, with concentric rings of bright-white nude statues (forty-eight in all), climbing up four levels of pools and waterspouts to the centre, where three putti hold up a basin on which two other putti hold up another basin, from above which a young male figure, who seems to have outgrown the putti stage, pours down water over his mates. Around the outer circle, where Garibaldi sat, Neptune and Apollo, Bacchus and Diana strike splendid postures in the spray, while around the inside of the first basin scores of noble animal heads send constant streams splashing into the various pools. The visitor seeing all this for the first time simply cannot help drawing a sharp breath: it's an extraordinary act of municipal self-celebration, wonderfully rich, exhibitionist, playful and dazzlingly out of sync with the town's other, more sombre treasures, as if a piece of Florence at its most flighty, a sort of nudist camp for gods and heroes, had been teletransported to the centre of Palermo. And, indeed, the whole stunning stone circus was originally commissioned for a Florentine villa in the mid sixteenth-century and sold off second-hand when the family went bankrupt.

Now all of this was exposed to the bombs.

"The citadel [Castellammare] opened the cannonade" – Admiral Mundy – "by throwing shells in the direction of the Piazza Pretoria, now known to be the headquarters of the terrible Dictator."

Sadly, you can no longer sit side by side with the Greek deities, as Garibaldi did, holding a map of Palermo in his hands and trying to keep track of the fighting at all points of the compass. A black iron railing fences off the monument. We climbed the half-dozen shallow steps that lead up to the piazza from Via Maqueda and sat down at the top.

"Here the fighters" – Zasio – "came to report on the progress of the various battles and were given fresh orders for the action."

As we sit soaking up the scene, trying to imagine how it must have been, the doors, directly opposite, of San Giuseppe dei Padri Teatini, open up, and a bride and groom saunter out. Apparently, they are to be photographed beside a black open-top Maserati with the white statues of the fountain behind. A crowd begins to gather.

"Here the citizens came" – Zasio again – "to bring news of places under threat as the Bourbons tried to fight their way to the centre, or of buildings that had collapsed, or they came asking for weapons, or, when daunted, for encouragement."

"The general isn't in as cheerful a mood as he was this morning" – Beninati – "perhaps because the Bourbons are attacking in many parts of the city and there aren't enough men to stop them."

"Confusion reigns" – Beninati. "And every time a bomb falls, the people shout, 'Viva Santa Rosalia!'" – in gratitude for their survival.

The couple are embracing in the front seat now, drawing cheers from the crowd. We turn back to the piazza. To our right is Palazzo Pretorio, which now boasts a grand neoclassical façade, but in 1860 was still wearing its sixteenth-century makeover. Crispi was already in there on the afternoon of the 27th preparing the six decrees that would be issued the following day. "Crimes of theft, murder and pillage" – one of them read – "of whatever kind, will be punished by death."

Behind the fountain is Santa Caterina: outside, a pleasantly shabby pink baroque façade; inside, a veritable cascade of marble ornamentation of the most extravagant kind. Every inch of the lofty space is smothered in putti and saints and shields and bas-reliefs and inlays of lapis lazuli and amethyst, altars dripping with gold.

"Part of the church of Santa Caterina has come down," wrote Beninati, mid-afternoon of the 27th.

Attached to the main church was a convent, cloistered home to the daughters of the rich – the unlucky ones, that is, who weren't going to be given a dowry.

"The fire began in the roof" – Abba – "thanks to a bomb that exploded up there."

We wondered at the fact that none of this damage could now be seen. Only the following day, Abba recounts, with the fire burning on, did it occur to anyone that the nuns were still in there.

"Finally some men went into the oratory and found them like white ghosts weeping in the dark."

The women were terrified.

"They knelt, arms writhing, offering their throats for the slaughter."

In the end, they had to be brought out by force.

"Girls of heavenly beauty, young as the dawn... old mummified hags..."

"The holy virgins" – the Borghese brothers – "run through the streets half dressed, barefoot."

The nuns weren't the only women horrified at the thought of what might happen to them in war. Leaving Garibaldi and his staff behind, we decided to end a long day with a look at the sea and the fort that was pitching the bombs into town. This meant half a mile down Via Toledo – I can't call it Via Vittorio Emanuele – to Porta San Felice. It's a gate very like Porta Carini: two grandiose bastions either side of the big street. And in 1860 the waterfront was right here, immediately beyond the gate; hence the Bourbon warships could swing close by and fire between the bastions. Now the shore has been pushed back about a hundred yards, and the space filled in using rubble from the bombing of the city's docks in the Second World War. So, instead of HMS *Hannibal*, what we're looking at as we come through the gate is a flat stretch of grass and wide gravel paths, people with their dogs, children flying kites, kiosks offering snacks and soft drinks, joggers, skateboarders and, beyond them, a sparkling blue, utterly empty sea. Not one of the two hundred ships that were anchored offshore here in 1860. This morning's oil tanker is long gone.

The port where cruise ships and containers actually dock is a short walk to the north – our left, that is – beyond the Cala, an inlet packed with countless private yachts, its waterfront lined with palm trees and luxury cafés. Just the other side of the inlet is the castle – or, rather, *was* the castle. The once-imposing fort that pounded the city with "thirteen-inch exploding shells" (Mundy loves to show his expertise) is now a ruin. The "Archaeological Area" that surrounds and includes it is "temporarily closed". All we can see are stumps of old towers in an expanse of wasteland – and, beyond that, warehouses, cranes, the upper deck of a liner.

It's perhaps a bit mad, since we've been on our feet since four this morning, but to wind up our day we go on walking north along the broad Via Crispi, keeping the docks to our right. It was in this area, famed for its prisons, that the young Giulia de Beaumont came for an extended visit in February 1860. Giulia was born in Naples in 1842. Her father was an officer in the Bourbon army; her mother had died giving birth to her, and she was sent to Palermo to live with an aunt who had married a local nobleman, Antonio De Gregorio. In 1857, when Giulia was just fifteen, a young writer and naturalist, Paolo Lioy, fell in love with her, married her and took her to his home in Vicenza almost nine hundred miles to the north. Now in 1860, together with her husband Paolo and his mother, she was making a first visit back to her old home, her aunt and uncle, her cousin Camillo and his pregnant wife Lilla. So she was in the city throughout the April revolution, the consequent police repression, the executions, the long nights lit up by the fires on the mountaintops around the town: "Not a Golden Bowl," she wrote, "but a bowl of flame." Events had prompted her to keep a diary. Living close to the port, Giulia watched streams of nervous citizens fleeing the town throughout the month of May: "Families crowding onto ships… endless carts full of furniture and packing cases." Woken by gunfire on 27th May, she looked out of the windows, and "you could see the castle vomiting shells and cannon fire". In the evening, when darkness fell, "the cannons rumbled on, and the bombs fell like balls of fire in their thousands on the poor city". Eventually "we closed the shutters – it was too painful to watch".

But closing their windows on the world didn't make them safe: at three in the morning, "the wet nurse came in and said: the convicts are hacking off their chains; they'll get out any moment". Just across a narrow alley from their villa was the port's naval arsenal, which also served as a prison. Giulia and her husband went to listen. "It was true: you could hear the creaking of the chains and the sound of hammering. We were terrified."

And we were beginning to feel extremely weary. It was early evening. The De Gregorio villa is a mile and more beyond the fort or castle. To our right, behind high railings, are the docks: storage yards, gantry cranes. To our left, an interminable march of anonymous apartment blocks.

"Eight hundred assassins," wrote the eighteen-year-old Giulia de Beaumont, "escaping at night at a time when there was no police protection."

Finally the blocks give way to the Ucciardone Prison, the city's largest, a long grey wall topped with glass lookout posts. Then at last you turn right onto the leafy Via dell'Arsenale, which leads, in about half a mile, to the Molo Nuovo, the new wharf, completed in 1590. Near the end, on the left, stands the sumptuous De Gregorio villa. Three storeys of golden-pink stone, tall windows, long balconies – a girl is sitting on one with her back to the street – a handsome colonnade porch, a pompous tympanum, a coat of arms. Just beyond the villa, before the street ends in the dock gates where a container truck is waiting to enter, is the old Arsenal. It's a long, low, grim building, its ground-floor windows heavily barred. You can even walk up the alley between villa and Arsenal and see the crumbling walls of what was the prison part of the structure.

We had expected magnificent sunset views. Giulia's diary speaks of looking back from the house along the waterfront, past the castle, towards Palermo. But now a string of modern warehouses have been built between the villa and the sea. There's a low hum of machinery. We're all boxed in.

"A terrible crash, the great iron gate came down, and a flood of convicts dressed in red rushed out of the prison, each urging the others to keep quiet, and us behind the shutters holding our breath in case they heard and came for us."

General Lanza, despairing of keeping isolated groups of soldiers at various points of the city, had ordered all troops except those in the castle to return any way they could to the Royal Palace. Fearing for their lives, the prison guards and police at the Arsenal had followed the soldiers.

"The hunt for the 'rats' has begun," wrote Beninati. "Hatred of the police knows no limits."

The Arsenal is now a maritime museum. We sniffed around for a few minutes, listening to the monotonous bleep of a truck reversing, examining an old iron anchor outside the main door, enjoying the deep shade of the trees behind the villa, then set off back towards our apartment, following the route that the Bourbon soldiers took to return to the Royal Palace. Unable to go up Via Toledo, raked by fire from their own ships, they marched around the town to the north, joined up with General Cataldo's forces at Porta Maqueda and, proceeding together, found themselves clashing both with the rebels inside the town and with Corrao's band of *picciotti* trying to reach the prisons to make sure no one got out.

"Arriving in Piazza Croci [behind the Ucciardone jail]" – Captain Rammacca – "we ran into the convicts – whom, as in 1848, the Bourbons had freed."

All in all, around two thousand men escaped their cells to add to the general confusion.

"One thing is certain" – Beninati – "there'll be no sleeping tonight."

Having failed in their mission, Corrao's men turned back to Porta Maqueda, which General Cataldo had now abandoned.

"All of a sudden" – Giulia de Beaumont – "just when it seemed those villains were slipping quietly away, scores of them started pounding on our front door."

In the middle of a broad avenue, we passed a bronze statue of Francesco Crispi, arms folded in a handsome tailcoat, bearded face gazing up at the sky. "27th May 1860," runs the inscription. "The Monarchy Unites Us."

Eventually, we reached the greyish pink walls of San Francesco di Paola, where there are indeed low windows that a soldier might shoot from. It was a night of dangerous encounters.

"A cavalry party had come riding by" – Beaumont – "and the convicts, terrified, were begging, 'For pity's sake, don't kill us.'" In the event, Giulia's men helped them get their chains off, and the convicts embraced them, "calling them brothers and promising never to steal or kill again."

We picked up some food at a convenience store, climbed the endless stairs to our flat and ate dinner on the rooftop terrace, whence we could see the spire of the cathedral at the top of Via Toledo to our left and the Church of the Guardian Angel much closer to our right.

It was a warm evening and our landlady had begged us to water her plants for her: flowering shrubs and cactuses, geraniums and pittosporum, the kind of things that can survive hours of intense sunshine. I stood splashing them with a hosepipe. The darkness had a sweet dusty fragrance.

On the other side of the city, the last incident Beninati recalls of 27th May is that of a number of families taken hostage by Bourbon troops as they retreated to the Royal Palace, "victims of outrages and iniquities that cannot be written but can easily be imagined". Two hours later nine hostages were released. "They had not walked eighty paces when they were cut down from behind by rifle fire… They are still lying in the Piazza now. We don't even know who they are."

"What I still don't get," reflected Eleonora as we were climbing into bed, "is how these twelve thousand soldiers, or however many there were, at the Royal Palace, with all their cannons and gear and everything, could fail to make headway in the town."

It's a good question.

Stalemate

Giuseppe Buttà is scathing: "General Lanza knew everything and did nothing." "To bomb a populous and monumental city" – the Bourbon chaplain goes on – "with no military objective, when he had all the means to prevent a revolution and prevent Garibaldi getting into Palermo, was the worst of crimes – infamy, madness."

"Lanza didn't want to win," wrote Giacinto de' Sivo, great apologist of the Bourbon dynasty, "or even to fight."

Still, "he wasn't mad," explains Buttà. "He knew exactly what he was doing. Bombing Palermo he succeeded in stirring up hatred against the innocent king, who was thus betrayed."

Butta's book was published in 1875, and essentially repeats and elaborates De' Sivo's claims, made in 1867 and now reproduced as if proven truths on dozens of revisionist websites and chatlines, as if what happened in May 1860 were of the utmost topical interest in Italy today. Garibaldi's men "were always beaten," says Buttà, "by the Bourbon soldiers, but the soldiers withdrew every time, because Lanza ordered them to do so."

So Lanza was a traitor. He "arranged for Garibaldi's easy entry into Palermo", his goal being to come away with "sixty thousand ducats" from the Bank of Sicily, the rest of the five million's worth going to the garibaldini."

Does this make sense?

Hitherto commander of the king's forces in Naples, General Ferdinando Lanza had been offered the position of king's lieutenant in Sicily on 15th May, just twelve days before Garibaldi's entry in Palermo. His name had been put forward by the elderly General Filangieri, a man beyond suspicion. Lanza had been beside Filangieri in 1848 when they reconquered the rebellious Sicily by bombing its towns into submission. Bombing was, and still is, a successful strategy. ("What is so discouraging for us" – Beninati on the evening of 27th May – "is the constant, unrelenting bombing.") Before 15th May, Lanza couldn't have had any inkling he would be in line for the lieutenant's job, since up to that moment the king was still trying to give it to three other men, who all turned it down. Invited to go to Palermo, Lanza accepted and set off immediately, arriving on the evening of 16th May to find the city rejoicing at the news of Garibaldi's victory at Calatafimi. His predecessor, Prince Castelcicala, disgusted by his summary firing, did not hang around to brief the new lieutenant, but left the following morning. That same day, 16th May, the king received a letter from the head of the police in Palermo, Salvatore Maniscalco, which read: "Everyone is terrified; the government workers have deserted their offices; there is no sense of duty; society is disintegrating."

Lanza himself was originally from Palermo: it was his home city, but he did not belong to one of its noble or powerful families; this circumstance did not make his position easier; people knew him, but didn't respect him. Nor initially had he had any idea of what awaited him. On the evening of 15th May, having barely got through the door of the Royal Palace, he summoned the lieutenant's permanent secretary to enquire whether the horses and carriages in the stables of the palace were his to use so long as he was lieutenant; having been assured that they were, he sent instructions to his son in Naples to sell his own horses and carriages, which were no longer necessary. This was hardly the move of a man who was planning to hand over his power and prestige to the enemy. Yet only the following afternoon, in his first report back to the king, he would write: "Palermo is just waiting for the right moment to rebel... the position is desperate." A few hours had sufficed to open his eyes. Days later, writing to the Ministry of War in Naples, he confessed that he wished "to die now at the age of seventy-three, after sixty years of service."

The first words of the young king in his immediate reply to Lanza's report were: "No one knows better than you that if we briefly lose all of Sicily yet hold on to Messina, we can successfully reconquer the island."

What a thing to write! Of course, it was an allusion to 1848, but it was also setting his lieutenant up for the idea that the loss of Palermo would not be judged a disaster, so long as he could hold on to a bridgehead close to the mainland. Filangieri, too, wrote to Lanza the same day suggesting it might be wiser to abandon the defence of Palermo in order to fight the rebels in open country. How disorienting. From this point on, day by day, the twenty-four-year-old king wrote compulsively to the seventy-three-year-old, obese and disconsolate Lanza, assuring the general he had carte blanche to act as he thought best – after all, he was the one with the experience and the man on the spot – but also plying him with the most varied and detailed proposals as to what he should be doing and sending him new, heavyweight advisers with every ship that arrived from Naples. It is clear from these letters that the king still believed his army had won at Calatafimi – no one had dared to tell him the truth – and he writes long paragraphs encouraging Lanza to distribute medals to the bravest soldiers, even reminding him which medals should be awarded for this or that achievement, as if a senior officer with sixty years' service might have forgotten. One can only imagine the lieutenant's relief when on 26th May Colonel Von Mechel, who fortunately was one of the king's favourites, sent the news that Garibaldi had been beaten at Parco and had now fled to Corleone. It was a complete vindication of his strategy of launching attacks on the rebels from a strong base in Palermo. "I firmly trust that now Garibaldi's band has been eliminated the insurrection will collapse," the lieutenant concludes his triumphant letter to the king, sending with it, as proof and trophy, three red shirts taken from dead or captured garibaldini at Parco. How could General Landi, in these circumstances, have supposed the rebels were about to attack? Von Mechel's report was surely worth more than the frenzied rumours of the citizenry.

Having completed our long march from Marsala, we have an easy day before us and set off after breakfast up the gentle slope of via Matteo Bonello towards the cathedral. To our left, cascades of ivy are spilling over what's left of the Cappella dell'Incoronata, where the Norman kings of the island were once crowned. The building was blown away by Lanza's artillery on 28th and 29th May 1860, all its archives destroyed. But the portico that still stands is charming, in its way.

"The bombardment is very violent this morning" – Beninati. "It seems the troops are more determined. The bands and the Piedmontese are attacking them with great violence in the vicinity of the cathedral."

Which is immediately beyond the Cappella.

The garibaldini had not been allotted anywhere to sleep on the night of the 27th, nor had there been any organized distribution of food for them since the fighting began.

"Lots of men are sleeping in open shops" – Beninati. "I've even seen some stretched out on the fishmongers' counters… hungry, exhausted."

"One fought everywhere" – Abba – "forgetting everything else."

"It's very strange seeing everyone armed" – Giulia de Beaumont, 28th May – "some like soldiers, some with just a dagger. Boys of seven among groups of soldiers. Convicts in prison uniform, others in the latest fashion."

The cathedral stands towards the western (that is inland) end of Via Toledo. Assuming you approach it from the Quattro Canti with the sea at your back, it lies to the right of the road, while, opening up to the left just a hundred yards beyond, are the extensive grounds of the Royal Palace, where the Bourbon troops were camped. So this was a key position. The sheer size of the church is astonishing. Set well back from the street, the nave runs parallel to it for a hundred yards and more, flaunting a generous hotchpotch of styles – battlements, bell towers, turrets, a high dome, an elaborate tympanum, Gothic arches, Roman arches, even a sixteenth-century clock tower, all built in a sandy pink stone that is darker or lighter depending on how the surface has been worked. It lacks the clarity of a great work of architecture, but is immediately eye-catching and endearing, affirming a vast process of accumulation and assimilation over many centuries. Even before you get into the building, a wealth of statues and plaques invites the mind to meander among saints and martyrs, popes and virgins, posturing for the most part in dreamy baroque. The combination of the richly ornamented façade and the quieter, almost austere gardens, where melancholy palm trees raise tufts of green high into the sky, casts a powerful spell.

"It was a fine and great achievement on the part of the 8th Company" – Abba – "which, staying more compact than the others in their determination to take the cathedral, finally managed to do so around 14.00 on the third day [29th May]. At the same time, with an unspeakably loud crash, the palace of Prince Carini, just across the street, collapsed."

The 8th Company was made up entirely of men from Bergamo.

A period photograph taken from behind the statues in the cathedral grounds shows the once-handsome Palazzo Carini completely gutted.

"It was set on fire by a bomb" – Abba – "like Palazzo Cutò, Palazzo D'Azzale and others. All ruined."

But this is getting ahead of ourselves. For the whole of 28th May the cathedral was easily held by the Bourbon troops, who used it as a base for launching attacks down Via Toledo into the city. Standing at the corner, looking down the thoroughfare from the cathedral square towards the distant sea, you can see the problem the Bourbons faced. Since the street is just twenty-five feet across, only so many men could advance down it together. "Every house," wrote the anonymous author of the pro-Bourbon *Chronicle of Events in Sicily*, "becomes a stronghold for the rebels, whence they can fire from close range on the king's troops, while the soldiers can only fire at the walls."

The surrounding streets and alleys are even narrower, sometimes barely six feet wide.

"From the windows and balconies," proceeds the chronicler, "the troops are battered with falling furniture and slabs of marble."

"In the house of the lawyer Matteo Muratori" – Beninati – "we climbed the stairs to the terrace and then the roof to throw the tiles down on the troops."

"The balconies" – Buttà – "were turned into little fortresses with woollen mattresses and sandbags, and loopholes to shoot through without being seen."

"The only choice left to the enemy" – Abba – "was to burn down the city, or leave it to us."

On the other hand, it's also easy to see how difficult it would be for the rebels to take the cathedral with the big open space outside it, where the Bourbons could deploy their cannons.

Inside, the church is disappointing. The long nave is a late-eighteenth-century makeover which, for all its regimented rows of polished pillars and stock statues, its elaborate candelabra and symmetrical, well-lit side chapels, is simply too polite, too rational to excite much interest, let alone religious awe. It seems out of sympathy with the raw energy of the city and the twisted baroque of the other churches. Arguably, that "renovation" in the previous century did more damage to the church than the fighting of 1860: a lavish sixteenth-century apse had been broken up, and its fine statues shared out among the countless side chapels; many frescoes were simply destroyed. So we find ourselves having to be satisfied with a precious detail here or there, rather than the overall effect: two elaborate baroque fonts, a white-marble Assumption, somewhere between bas-relief and statue, showing the Madonna with her hands joined in prayerful wonder while seven fluttering angels clutch at her robes to fly her up to heaven. It was hard to get excited.

But the roof is extraordinary. Or perhaps I was just too focused on the battle now to pay much attention to anything else. First you climb some regular flights of stone steps, then a suffocatingly narrow spiral staircase. Emerging at the top, stopping a moment to take in the astonishing views all around, we realize that the sirocco is finally over. After a week of heavy humidity, the air this morning is fresh and clear – still burning hot, but not hazy. Walking back and forth between low railings along the top of the nave, you can see the whole arc of the mountains around the Conca d'Oro with spectacular clarity. Likewise, the panorama of the city, its towers and domes, battlements and roof gardens, then the curve of the bay beyond. Everything is sharp and sparkling. And though you cannot climb the bell tower at the southwestern extremity of the pile, you can see that it looks down, not just on the gardens below the cathedral, but over the top of the surrounding houses to the grounds of the Royal Palace.

"At two in the afternoon" – *Chronicle of Events* – "the insurgents occupy the bell tower of the mother church, whence they can fire down with advantage, causing many deaths among the soldiers and artillerymen of the Royal Palace."

From where we are, on the roof, looking past the bell tower, we can just see the treetops in the grounds and the upper walls of the Royal Palace behind. The top of the tower is lavishly ornamented with delicate pinnacles at each corner. You can even see between slender pillars into the bell chamber, where the men were shooting from.

"Captain Bassini" – Abba – "gave the order to fire with a hunting whistle while smoking his pipe, entirely exposed to the enemy, who sent a storm of bullets his way without ever hitting him. He firmly believed he was invulnerable."

Back at street level, between the cathedral and the Royal Palace, hence right beneath the trajectory of bullets fired over 160 years ago, we sit at a café and order almond granitas. At the table beside us two middle-aged Bavarian women, one stout, one lean, seem extremely uncomfortable in the hot weather. On the morning of 29th May, as the battle for the cathedral was in full swing, Admiral Mundy noted "two large steamers... approaching at full speed from the direction of Naples, the decks and paddle boxes of which were crowded with armed men... riflemen of the Bavarian Contingent." Meantime, Colonel Von Mechel and his two thousand Bavarians, who had chased Orsini's ragtag column beyond Corleone to within twenty miles of Sicily's southern coast, had finally received news of Garibaldi's entry into Palermo and begun the long march back.

The nationality of the various troops on the Bourbon side was important. For while the Germans were mercenary and had no ideological position on the future of Italy, the Neapolitans were susceptible to Risorgimento propaganda.

"Desertions began" – Abba – "among the Bourbon officers. Lieutenant Achille De Martini, commander of the cannons at Calatafimi, came to Palazzo Pretorio and gave himself body and soul to Garibaldi."

"Perhaps in their eyes," General Rodolfo Corselli wrote of these deserters fifty years after the event, "the *ideal* of one great Italian fatherland had begun to take shape."

"The more the confidence of the volunteers grows,' wrote the *Times* correspondent Nando Eber, "the more the discipline of the regular troops breaks down."

It was almost always the officers, the educated men, who deserted, not the common soldiers. And almost always the common soldiers who got killed, not the officers. "Of the king's troops," summed up historian De Cesare, "only four officers were killed, while 204 soldiers died and 600 were wounded."

Despite all the wealth of archive material on the battle for Palermo, I have found no account of what life in the Royal Palace was really like during these days of fighting. Looking into the huge open space outside it, "we saw," says Abba, "I don't know how many thousand men camping there. They were eating lettuce like sheep."

Having gathered all his formidable army in the same place, General Lanza was facing logistical problems.

"Our bands had occupied the roads connecting city and country" – Garibaldi – "so that the troops in the Royal Palace... found themselves absolutely isolated and began to suffer shortages."

Of food and ammunition, of course. But this was not the only problem. In the early morning of 28th May, the second day of battle, Admiral Mundy received a visit from Captain Kosscvich, commander of the Bourbon naval force, who confessed that "all land communication between the royal headquarters and the fleet was cut off by the insurgent population, and therefore messages could only be received through the medium of the semaphores on the turret of the Royal Palace."

Today the space where the soldiers camped is a lovely park, perhaps two hundred yards by two hundred, where broad pink gravel paths meander through a lush forest of palms and shrubs. Like the cathedral, the palace is huge, built in the same sandy pink stone. Again the structure has absorbed a mix of styles over more than a thousand years. It was here the Norman kings resided in the eleventh and twelfth centuries. Then it was redesigned as a fortress. Then the Spanish viceroys of the fourteenth, fifteen and sixteenth centuries transformed it into a residence again, aiming at the most extravagant pomp. Unlike the cathedral, there is nothing remarkable about the exterior – no decoration, no pretty inlays or spiral columns, just a long, high, bare façade whose wings and centre, built at different times, are of different heights and set at slightly skewed angles to each other. Row upon row of windows – some square, some with the pointed Norman arch – offer the only variation. Inside, however, the building is sumptuous and labyrinthine beyond belief. Great stone staircases climb around airy wells, giving on elegant courtyards sporting three levels of loggia, whose shady galleries are richly decorated with frescoes and mosaics. The grand reception rooms seem endless and offer every variety of decoration, from the most intricate Arabic patterning to the most vainglorious eighteenth-century mannerism. At the heart of it all are the twelfth-century mosaics of the Cappella Palatina, bringing together Byzantine, Latin and Arabic motifs in teeming biblical narratives of green, blue and gold, all framed with wide borders of intricately patterned stone inlays. To enter the chapel and move slowly forward up its central nave – white, grey and pink to the sides, then overwhelmingly gold above, everywhere alive and glittering with men and women and animals, wonderful clothes, wonderful gestures – is to enter a state of awe, to feel oneself wrapped in beauty. Although every inch of wall and window-surround, arch and ceiling is fabulously decorated, one never experiences the sense of overkill that churches of the high baroque provoke. There is no cloying sentiment, no focus on individual pathos, no contortion, no posturing. The whole project feels seamless, lavish in materials, but austere in gesture. The stern, bearded face of Christ Pantocrator gazes down the nave from the apex of the dome above the altar, utterly unimpressed by historical events.

How curious it is to think of General Lanza spending his days in this magnificent building, his new home, while trying to come to grips with a revolution seething in the city outside, his home city, where he must have realized he would be hated for all time. Did the splendour all around give him an illusion of power and invulnerability? Or did he feel dwarfed by something so much greater than himself and his immediate troubles? Did he come to these mosaics from time to time for a few moments' relief, craning his neck to lose himself in the wonderful story-telling high up on walls and arches Noah climbing into his ship to escape the flood; Mary and Joseph fleeing Herod on camelback? Did he fall on his knees and pray? Or did he simply ignore it, having no time to lose? Beside him was Salvatore Maniscalco, the chief of police, who had taken refuge in the palace along with many other policemen and officials in Palermo.

"From time to time" – Abba – "you would hear a commotion of furious shouting, women who had been lying in wait for a policeman and caught him, yelling 'Rat, rat!' – and they mauled him and tore him to shreds."

This was why one of the six decrees Garibaldi issued on 28th May forbade murder and pillage on pain of death. To no avail.

"The police are hunted to death" – the Borghese brothers. "As soon as they are found, they are massacred by the crowd, and their bodies lie naked and mutilated in the streets."

High up on the walls of the Cappella Palatina, a grim Cain swings his axe over a sprawling Abel; Abraham has his knife poised above his blindfold son.

"But if by chance" – Abba – "a garibaldino arrived in time to get his hands on the hapless policeman, then the women were almost happy to give the man up alive. Many were saved that way, and held in the cellars of Palazzo Pretorio, where at least no one could torture them."

Of the other decrees issued in the palazzo on the 28th May, three were administrative: Crispi would be in charge of the provisional government's finances; chiefs of police were nominated for the city itself and the surrounding districts; the city council was dissolved, and a new council nominated. Throughout this trip, it has astonished me

how determinedly the garibaldini planned ahead, even when it looked like their adventure might be over within hours.
The sixth decree was more urgently practical. It set up a Barricades Committee for the rebuilding and systematic organization of barricades throughout the town.
"Solid barricades will be set up every hundred paces... built with paving stones, boxes filled with rocks, timbers roped together, bags of earth... to be erected under the supervision of intelligent people with building experience... there will be an earth depot where bags are to be filled in their thousands... barricades are to be guarded at all times by courageous people living in the same street where the barricade is located... every half-hour a messenger will be sent to the Barricades Committee to inform them of developments."
"Perhaps there were too many barricades," Garibaldi later reflected. "But it certainly got people fired up making them."
The Barricades Committee had a budget and kept accounts.

To Rosario Alfano: for 300 baskets and 200 large baskets in good condition: 20 onze.[1]

To Franc. De Luca: for 60 large barrels and 22 mast timbers: 40 onze.

The list is long.

Total expenditures: 1,641 onze.

Leaving the Royal Palace, we continued our progress southwards around the walls of the old city, now reduced to a stone stump here and there. It's hard, reading the diaries of the various protagonists, and even Garibaldi's account, to discern anything as elaborate as a plan for victory on the part of the rebels. The barricades offered some defence, but would hardly win the war. There doesn't seem to have been any intention to attack the palace and its grounds head on, but rather to force the soldiers back to their camp and isolate them there, perhaps shooting from a distance, harrying them constantly, until logistical issues forced them to make a move and expose themselves. So there

---

[1] *onze*: The onza was worth 30 tarì (a tarì was worth 2 carlins or 20 grana; a ducat was worth 10 carlins).

was fighting at the former Benedictine monastery of San Giovanni degli Eremiti, just a couple of blocks from the Royal Palace. It is no more than a shell of thirteenth-century masonry now, surrounded by a lush garden of palms, cactuses, banana plants and orange trees, but with five delicious little red domes still exotically intact, one topping the bell tower.

"Antonio Mosto fought here with his carabinieri" – Abba – "shooting from the tower at the artillerymen at the Porta Montalto bastion, forcing them to abandon two cannons."

We take the opportunity to sit for a while in the shade of the church's charmingly melancholy cloister. Again the Arab and the Norman seem perfectly at ease together, in the elaborately decorated rectangle of columns and the ancient well placed in the centre. Amazingly, we are the only visitors aside from some stray cats lurking in the grass. There are twisted pines, knotty prickly pears, lemon trees, a tall, dusty cypress and a pleasant earthy fragrance. It's hard to think of the place as anything other than a haven of peace and meditation.

"Calmly supporting Mosto" – Abba – "his shots hitting their mark, was Giambattista Capurro, a youngster with a bandage over a wound in his forehead, and Ernesto Cicala, seriously wounded by bomb shrapnel."

We walked a couple of hundred yards along the Via dei Benedettini to the place the men were shooting at. What's left of it. The Porta Montalto bastion is now just a few yards of weather-stained seventeenth-century fortification, perhaps twenty feet high by five thick, marooned among parked cars and apartment blocks. The engraving on a large stone plaque has now faded to the point that the only thing I can make out is MDCCCLX. Grass and dandelions sprout from every crevice. Abba himself fought here.

"After a stout defence" – *Chronicle of Events* – "overwhelmed by the numbers of the enemy, at eleven in the morning [29th May] the Royal troops abandoned the positions of the Benedettini, the Annunziata and the Montalto bastion."

In fact the positions were soon retaken.

"Colonel Carini" – Abba – "sent me to Palazzo Pretorio to ask for ammunition. I found Sirtori there. Apparently there was no ammunition, because he told me to tell Carini that we would have to defend the bastion with our bayonets."

"Munitions are scarce" – Beninati – "and if it wasn't for Doctor Giuseppe Briuccia who opened his warehouse and gave the Revolutionary Committee enough lead to make bullets, things would be worse. Rammacca is sending powder, and they are assembling cartridges in Via Stazzone."

"Night and day" – Garibaldi – "people were putting together cartridges, but never enough for the constant fighting."

Beninati was not impressed: "Where are the rifles and cannons Garibaldi was supposed to be bringing? We were duped, and like fools we believed what we were told."

"The *picciotti* fired too much," Garibaldi thought.

Evidently, the alliance between Sicilians and garibaldini was something that could all too easily turn sour. There are no mentions of Giuseppe La Masa in the garibaldini diaries for these days. In his own version of events he was in the front line of all the fighting.

The Montalto bastion was mostly demolished in 1885 to allow for a flow of traffic into the broad street that runs due west from here to the sea, passing Porta Termini on the way. This is the same street where Lajos Tüköry had his knee shot to bits at dawn of 27th May, attacking the Bourbons at Porta Termini. And in fact it is now called Corso Tukory, which then becomes Via Lincoln after Porta Termini.

"Together with Francesco Nullo and Vincenzo Agri" – Beninati – "I go and visit the wounded Hungarian Luigi Tuchery in the house of the Prince of San Lorenzo… Outside, in the courtyard, Doctor Castellana tells us: "Either we amputate now, or the patient is at risk."

We didn't take Corso Tukory, but dived into the labyrinth of narrow streets known as the Albergheria district, between the Royal Palace and Maqueda. A flea market is doing brisk business, bringing together men and women of every colour and costume. In places it is hard to distinguish the wares they have spread on the pavements from the rubbish strewn more or less everywhere. Collapsed buildings look like they might have been shelled yesterday. On a wall dominating an open lot, a huge modern mural shows a haloed black man in a white cassock – San Benedetto, the moor – raising his hand in elegant blessing over the feverish transactions going on beneath: old radios, toys, framed photographs, chainsaws, second-hand underwear, soiled pillows, screwdrivers, a fridge, a bicycle wheel. Everything is on sale.

Some of the vendors have brought chairs to sit on. Two Arab men are arguing over a pitch. Whiffs of dope and aftershave.

Then we're in the market proper, called Ballarò, another busy street-food paradise: plastic tables under makeshift awnings in crowded alleys, hawkers crying their wares, abundant food and intense vitality. I grab a table while Eleonora goes off to order *cazzilli*, cigar-shaped potato croquettes. I wait until she's popping one in her mouth before offering a detail from Beninati.

"In an alley in the Albergheria, Salvatore Morello hunted down the soldier who had killed his brother. The man was still wearing the ring he'd taken from his victim. And with a bite Salvatore Morello tore off the finger and the ring of his brother Andrea."

Eleonora demands a truce for lunch.

Being so near the Royal Palace, the Albergheria was one of the most hotly contested areas.

"Every house that the troops were forced to abandon," Capuzzi wrote, "was sacked and burnt."

"The whole district," Admiral Mundy would later write, "about a thousand yards in length by a hundred yards in width, is a crushed mass of ruins, still smouldering in its ashes."

"Most of the houses are so badly built" – Eber – "that a single bomb is enough to reduce them to a heap of rubble."

"Unburied corpses in the streets" – Zasio – "an unspeakable stench."

"There were so many dead soldiers lying there" – Abba – "it was hard to understand how they could all have been killed."

"Wounded everywhere" – Beninati – "and generous people pulling them from the rubble of the bombing."

Still too weak to leave his bed, Bixio wrote to Garibaldi advising him how to proceed: divide the city into sections, he suggested, allot specific bands to defend each of them, keep the garibaldini in the centre as a reserve to reinforce the Sicilians wherever required. "My thoughts were well received," he says. To his wife Adelaide, on the 29th May, he writes. "Once again, all we have here is an inferno of gunfire. The city is crawling with armed men all fighting mostly on their own initiative."

"The second day then was like the first and worse" – Abba – "but the third [29th May] surpassed all imagining. The streets were packed with people, since, under the bombs, staying inside was more dangerous than being out."

On the afternoon of 29th May, "with vigorous attacks" – *Chronicle of Events* – "the king's troops, now reinforced, retake Montalto and San Giovanni degli Eremiti, and... the bell tower of the cathedral." "From the grounds of the Royal Palace" – the Borghese brothers – "the cannons were trained on the fatal bell towers; the range was so close that the grapeshot smashed the columns and capitals and sent splinters of arabesques flying into the air."

After lunch we walked east, across Maqueda, towards the sea. This part of the town was safely in rebel hands. Narrow streets, two-star hotels, sagging walls shored up with old timbers. There were the usual youngsters on their scooters, old men smoking on chairs beside their doorsteps, laundry hanging limp between balconies. A woman on a roof terrace beating a carpet. Flaking stucco, a smell of cats. But also a wonderful green-and-gold dome held up by four patient statues, a small motorized three-wheeler selling ice creams. In one workshop open on the street I glimpsed a man sanding the corners of a sumptuous coffin.

After twenty minutes or so, we reached Santa Maria dello Spasimo, an extensive complex of ruined church and ancient bastion, alas closed now – for renovation, one hopes. On the afternoon of 28th May, Beninati gave his arm to a wounded man and helped him reach the hospital here. He found seventy patients, under the care of a twenty-three-year-old monk; most were being treated for wounds caused by the bombing. "I was amazed," he says, "to see that the nurses were whores from the hospital." In fact this was ordinarily a hospital for prostitutes. With syphilis. "Those lost women look after the wounded with such compassion, such love, such fervour, I was moved."

Of all the diaries that present these dramatic days, Beninati's is the most engaging, perhaps because, though knowing almost nothing about the man, you sense that war is opening his eyes and changing him. "Dear God," he tells himself, "those women deserve our respect and admiration!" He blunders about the town in a hallucinatory stupor, carrying messages, helping where he can, seeing things he never expected to see. "To fulfil my duties as priest and citizen here," the monk at Santa Maria dello Spasimo tells him, "I abandoned my father and mother." "His answer left me speechless," says Beninati. In a corner he sees "a beautiful girl, about eighteen", whose leg is to be amputated, yet the girl's only request is for a comb and a mirror. "Such courage is amazing." The monk goes on to tell the diarist how he defended a wounded policeman whom the crowd had tracked down to the hospital. "Taking his crucifix from his breast... he had shouted: 'Get out of here, in the name of Christ.'"

Most of all, Beninati is amazed by the general atmosphere of defiance: "The people don't seem worried about the dead or the wounded, or the destruction of the city, much of which is in flames: they just shout 'Viva l'Italia, Garibaldi, Vittorio Emanuele, Santa Rosalia!'"

"People went wild" – Abba – "carried away by a kind of grim enthusiasm for the slaughter."

The wounded were not just an issue for the rebels. From Santa Maria dello Spasimo we walked northward, in parallel with the waterfront, along the very straight, very narrow Via della Vetriera, towards what was the Bourbon military hospital, in the complex known as Palazzo Finanze, now home to the Guardia delle Finanze, the customs and border police, in Via Cavour. It's a stone's throw from the sea and the Castellammare fortress that was shelling the town.

"Thanks to the treason of the chaplain" – *Chronicle of Events*, 28th May morning – "and the cowardice of the commander, the hospital is occupied by the insurgents and the soldiers forced to retreat with a number of wounded."

Built in 1840, the hospital was modern and well equipped – a solid, extensive pink rectangle organized around a grassy courtyard. All the same, having walked through all these streets to get here, you sense what a problem it must have been for the Bourbons having their hospital at the opposite side of town from the troops and the main scene of the fighting. Reporting the recapture of the cathedral, *Chronicle of Events* notes: "The wounded increase to 356, and due to the loss of communications with the port they are not getting the food and the medications they need." The day before, the chronicler, whose work gathers together the daily communications of the various Bourbon generals, commented: "Colonel Buonopane arrives from Naples with doctors, surgeons, hospital staff, mattresses, medicines and medications." But the men had not been able to land their precious supplies because of the fighting.

So aside from having little to eat, the soldiers in the palace grounds had to listen to the groans of 356 men. A number that would rise to over five hundred in the coming hours.

The Risorgimento Museum is in Piazza San Domenico, heading back to Via Toledo and Piazza Pretoria.

"At nine in the evening" – *Chronicle*, 29th May – "the fortress recommenced its shelling, and a huge fire developed around Piazza San Domenico."

I had high hopes for the museum, which we recognized at once in a corner of the piazza thanks to the tricolour flying over a wooden door with flaking brown paint and ancient iron knockers. But up close we found a washed-out piece of A4 fixed to the wood with four drawing pins, announcing that it was "temporarily" closed.

So we went into San Domenico, which, after the cathedral, is Palermo's second most prestigious church. It houses a "Pantheon of the Illustrious Men of Sicily", meaning fifty and more funeral monuments and plaques in the quiet side chapels. Rosolino Pilo is there. Sculpted in white stone, a handsome, bearded face with deep-set eyes looks out from the top of the monument, while beneath him a young woman mourns over his cremation urn. At each chapel there are long rows of electric candles, with the invitation to pay a little for the privilege of turning one on.

So it was, amid a wealth of painting and sculpture, that we stumbled on Tüköry's tomb:

CRIMEA, COMO, CALATAFIMI...
PALERMO WANTED HIM FOR HER SON.

The stone memorial is set vertically against the wall in a quiet corner. A round bronze bas-relief shows another fine-looking young man with thick hair swept across his forehead, hooded eyes, a strong moustache.

We walked back towards our apartment along Via Toledo. Of the chronicles and diaries I have been reading, some are more credible than others. I'm not convinced, for example, by the tale that the Hungarian, Eber, tells about the moments after the Bourbons retook the cathedral, when they began to advance down this very street threatening to strike at the heart of the rebellion in Piazza Pretoria. "Garibaldi was dining when this news reached him," Eber elaborates. "Getting to his feet, the general said, 'I suppose I'll have to go there myself.'" His entourage begged him not to expose himself to danger, but "Garibaldi stood in the middle of the street, rousing and encouraging his men." This is believable enough, but then "One of the *picciotti* standing right beside Garibaldi was hit by a bullet in the head, and the general, seeing him fall, caught him for a few moments with his arm."

It's too much. If it happened, why do none of the other writers mention it? Why don't we know the victim's name?

"But the effect was already achieved," Eber goes on. "The trumpeter who was always at Garibaldi's side sounded the charge, and the Neapolitans fled."

It all seems too easy. On the other hand, we can be sure, I think, reaching the grand Quattro Canti crossroad, of something that initially seemed to Beninati like another hallucination.

"We've gone back to Lent!" the diarist announces out of the blue. "They have hung the banner of the Church of San Giuseppe ai Quattro Canti across Via Toledo to interrupt the semaphore communication along the street between the Royal Palace and the Neapolitan fleet."

Other sources confirm he wasn't dreaming. The banner was usually displayed at Lent.

"It was an immense tapestry" – Abba – "with beautifully embroidered figures, and it was sad to see it punctured by shot from Bourbon cannons."

"It seems a bit of a joke to me" – Beninati – "because even with the banner across the street you can still see the ships' signals from the observatory on top of the palace."

But whatever their obscure points and exaggerations, all the diaries and memoirs agree that by the evening of 29th May, after three days of fighting, a substantial stalemate had been reached. The rebels didn't have the numbers or the weaponry to take the Royal Palace. The Bourbons were becoming casualty-averse and had no appetite for advancing into town. "Via Toledo was shattered," says Zasio, "with buildings collapsed and burning just a few paces from each other." Both sides were overwhelmed by the numbers of wounded. "I don't think I exaggerate when I say that the dead and wounded are truly infinite," Beninati writes.

Something would have to give.

"That evening" – Abba – "even Garibaldi almost despaired. News came that two battalions of Bavarians had landed at Castellammare, fresh from Naples."

These were the same men Mundy had seen arriving on paddle steamers in the early morning. Now they had safely disembarked together with the men sent the day before with medical supplies.

There was worse.

"During the afternoon" – *Chronicle of Events* – "from the Castellammare fortress, lookouts saw Von Mechel's men arriving in the distance across the bay near Villabate [five miles to the east of Palermo]; four strong infantry battalions, partly under the command of the valiant Major Del Bosco." They had made it back from Corleone.

"When he realized we had given them the slip and entered Palermo" – Abba, reporting later conversations with Bavarian soldiers – "Del Bosco nearly lost his mind and had them march as fast as possible, promising fire and plunder, hardly caring who collapsed with exhaustion along the way."

The curious thing about the story of the Thousand is that while one knows that in the end they won, or at least came out on top – after all, so many of the city's street names are spoilers – nevertheless at every point it seems impossible to understand exactly how this could have happened, so great were the odds against them. And it is this of course that feeds the many conspiracy theories and accusations of betrayal.

"Evening," writes Giulia de Beaumont from her uncle's villa by the sea, "shots fired close by. Soldiers coming off the boats into the streets yelling, 'Long live the king!' They're bringing supplies to the palace."

Buttà, De Sivo and the revisionist camp in general are convinced that Lanza ordered the men to go round the north of the town, rather than attacking the rebels in the centre, so that he could neutralize their impact under his command at the palace – this in line with his treacherous plan to have Garibaldi win and earn himself a traitor's reward. But with 500 wounded men on his hands, it's perhaps not surprising that the king's lieutenant wanted these medical supplies at the Royal Palace as soon as possible. And if they were going to be brought around the town, they needed a considerable escort.

"The larger division" – Admiral Mundy – "sallied out from the citadel at a late hour, amidst great cheering and continued salvos of musketry."

"The rebels answered, firing from the balconies" – Beaumont. "The bands around the port are calling everyone to arms. Banging on the doors: 'Any men, come with us – if you have any arms, come out now,' they shout. And they come knocking on our door. They want to shoot from our balconies. It was the most frightening moment of my whole life. Any minute they might open the door and take away

Paolo and Camillo [her husband and cousin], or the soldiers could come in and burn down the house."

"The whole body of men" – Mundy describing the Bourbon reinforcements – "about seven-hundred strong, were clad in light-grey uniform, and admirably equipped... flanked by several squadrons of cavalry."

"Finally" – Beaumont again – "thanks be to God, my aunt... had the courage to go to the window and say, 'Friends, do you really want the soldiers to burn down our house? Don't you realize that if they see you shooting from here the castle will send some bombs our way? You can go to the fifth house along the street, which is empty. Do us a favour.'"

And they did.

"In the night" – *Chronicle of Events* winds up the story – "bayonets at the ready, following a devious route through secluded streets and not without some losses, the soldiers arrived at the Royal Palace and delivered the supplies that Colonel Buonopane had brought, though he personally had stayed behind at the castle."

We were already in bed when fireworks awoke us. A crackle of explosions. Back on the terrace in my boxers, I watched rockets flaring up from a point on the northern edge of town. Typical summer stuff. Celebrating a local fête, or some such.

"Families are preparing big illuminations," wrote Beninati on the evening of 27th May.

Every night of the battle, the people of Palermo kept the city as bright as they could.

"Bizarre and mysterious contrast" – *Chronicle of Events* – "seeing houses lit up as though to celebrate the imminent triumph of the revolution, and at the same time the lights of cannon and rifle fire flaring in the dark."

I stood beside one of the oleander bushes on the terrace watching green and yellow stars shower from the sky against a distant profile of dark mountains.

"The windows of the houses began to light up" – Abba – "so that the streets were bright as day almost."

Down in the street below me, a young man and woman were walking by in the fresh evening air. I thought of Giulia de Beaumont's aunt going out onto the balcony to confront the armed rebels. And for a moment I shared Beninati's wonder at how unpredictable people can be, how courageous in the face of great danger, and how fearful sometimes when there is no risk at all.

Truce

On 26th May, the day before Garibaldi's entry in Palermo, the *Giornale officiale di Sicilia*, the island's main newspaper, published a decree nominating Angelo Maniscalco as collector of customs duties in Messina, the main port for goods entering Sicily from the mainland. A lucrative appointment. Angelo was the eldest son of Salvatore Maniscalco, Palermo's chief of police. He was five years old. Published on the paper's front page, the decree carried the signatures of Prince Cassaro, prime minister of the Kingdom of the Two Sicilies, and General Lanza, the king's lieutenant in Sicily. Apparently the nomination had been promised to the boy at his baptism by the previous king, Ferdinand II. Only days before that decree was published, we remember, Maniscalco had sent his family to Naples for their safety, while Lanza had spoken of Palermo being on the brink of revolution. Yet these men went ahead with this provocative arrangement and allowed its prominent publication. Perhaps it was impossible for them to imagine a world without this sort of privilege, even if common sense told them that the writing was on the wall. It's worth keeping this strange blend of presumption and defeatism in mind as we watch the bizarre events of 30th May unfold.

One reason we know that the church banner strung across Via Toledo wasn't blocking the semaphore between the Royal Palace and the Bourbon fleet is that Admiral Mundy reports receiving messages from the palace via the fleet. On 28th May, the second day of the fighting, Captain Kossovich, commander of the Bourbon ship *Parthenon*, had asked Mundy, on behalf of General Lanza, to provide an escort with the British flag to bring two Bourbon generals from the palace to HMS *Hannibal* for discussions. About what exactly wasn't clear.

Mundy, like the commanders of other foreign warships in the bay, was anxious to do something to stop the bombardment of the city – "one of the most awful scenes of destruction from civil discord that modern history has recorded," he writes. HMS *Hannibal* was harbouring quite a number of the city's residents, who were spending their days on deck watching their homes being bombarded, so the admiral would have been aware of their grief. But the neutrality imposed on him by the British government meant he could hardly parade the Union Jack on the town's main street at the request of one of the warring parties to the possible detriment of the other. It was up to Garibaldi, Mundy told Captain Kossovich, to concede safe passage, and he sent Flag Lieutenant Wilmot to Garibaldi to ask for this concession, which was immediately granted. But Lanza refused to be involved in any negotiation that involved even indirect recognition of his enemy, so Wilmot had to go back and tell Garibaldi the arrangement was off. "As darkness had set in and the cannon fire from Castellammare continued unabated, the performance of this duty entailed considerable danger."

This frustrating exchange was repeated, almost blow by blow, on 29th May, the third day of fighting. Lanza made the same request; Mundy offered the same response: all he could do, he said, was offer the neutral territory of his ship to both parties as a safe place for negotiation, nothing more. But Lanza continued to demand the protection of the British flag to pass through the rebel-held part of the town. "These proceedings," says Mundy, "were a mystery I was unable to solve, and I ceased to puzzle my brain with further attempts to unravel them."

A cornerstone of the neo-Bourbon version of events is the assumption that Admiral Mundy was in cahoots with Garibaldi to destroy the Bourbon kingdom. Yet it's clear from the admiral's diary that for all his disgust at the bombing of the city, he remained very much a royalist. On a number of occasions he fervently wishes that "the youngest sovereign in Europe" – Francis II – "would put himself at the head of his faithful soldiery" and "make himself a name". Certainly on 30th May he was appalled to discover that instead of using his, the admiral's, good offices to ask Garibaldi to concede safe passage along Via Toledo for negotiations on HMS *Hannibal*, Lanza had written to the rebel leader directly, making exactly the same request he had refused to allow the admiral to make on his behalf: "General Lanza to His Excellency General Garibaldi," the letter begins.

"What must have been the distress of the royal army," Mundy wonders, when shown the communication, "before the alter ego of the sovereign could have condescended to pen so humble a letter as this!"

"Worth noting" – Garibaldi makes the same point in his autobiography – "that the commander of the Thousand, hitherto referred to as a pirate, has suddenly become 'His Excellency', a title he would now be afflicted with for all subsequent transactions, and which he personally has always despised."

Despite the dire situation on the streets of Palermo, news that negotiations were to begin was not met with universal joy.

"If Garibaldi settles for some meagre concessions" – Beninati – "for example, the proposal of a constitution by the king of Naples, I'm sure the people will tear both Garibaldi and the garibaldini to shreds."

"[Lanza] is hoping" – Bixio to his wife – "in a constitution... I fear a generous constitution would undermine the unity of the country."

Nevertheless, when Lanza's letter was brought to Garibaldi around 9 a.m. of what promised to be the fourth day of fighting, together with the proposal of a twenty-four-hour armistice, the general accepted at once and ordered an immediate ceasefire. "God knows we needed it," he observed, "obliged as we were to assemble cartridges that were fired as soon as made."

This hardly fits with the idea of a man benefiting from an international conspiracy.

"We had no arms or ammunition" – Garibaldi – "from any of the warships in the port and the bay, which included an Italian [Piedmontese] frigate."

Mundy, meantime, was experiencing feelings of "infinite satisfaction", thinking of the prestige involved in his hosting the peace talks; the Royal Navy would be credited with stopping the bombing of a historic city. But the hour of the conference had barely been fixed (two in the afternoon) "when, to my utter dismay" – Mundy – "I heard a loud report of musketry in the direction of the Consular House, followed by continued discharges at intervals, as if from file-and-volley firing." What could this be but "a contemptuous defiance of every understood law of honour, and a marked affront to the majesty of the British flag?"

The British consul's house was close to the Fieravecchia, and that is where we went for our morning coffee. Rather than a proper piazza, it's more an odd triangle formed by the accidental encounter of five crooked streets, the resulting space barely ennobled by the famous statue of the Genio di Palermo in the middle. Mid-morning, the sunlight glared on lava-black flagstones. The few potted bushes round the bar were still damp from an early-morning soaking. Our waitress brought out a fat croissant bursting with ricotta cream which we just about managed to finish between us. The Sicilians love richness and abundance. Needless to say, the garibaldini were not eating so well.

"Nothing but bread," says Capuzzi of these days of fighting, "washed down with a cup or two of strong spirits."

"When hunger got the better of you" – Abba – "the monasteries had been turned into soup kitchens."

On the wall to the left of our table, by the door of the piazza's tobacconist's, a stone plaque beneath a fading image of the Madonna promises forty days' indulgence to anyone reciting an Ave Maria. By concession of the archbishop of Palermo, 1797.

"Crowds of white-wimpled nuns watched from the doors," says Abba. "Some would stretch out their arms to hang a relic round the neck of the nearest soldier, then run off in bliss, as if they'd ravished a soul from purgatory."

Apparently it was impossible to keep religion and war effort apart.

"The people" – Zasio – "claimed Garibaldi was related to Santa Rosalia, which was why she looked kindly on his exploits."

There are two other plaques on the same building, once a nobleman's palazzo: between upper windows elegantly framed with fake columns, an inscription recalls Niccolò Garzilli, who was executed by firing squad in this piazza in 1850, "His only crime to have yearned for the freedom of his country."

Lower down, between a little stone cherub and the window of a pub, another plaque recalls the piazza's revolutionary heritage and "inextinguishable days of glorious conspiracies". But there is nothing on any of the buildings around us to record the arrival here, in the heart of the city, on 30th May 1860, of Colonel Von Mechel and Major Del Bosco supported by about four thousand Bavarian soldiers, something that very nearly extinguished this particular revolution in decidedly inglorious fashion.

Timing is crucial. On 28th May Von Mechel had heard of Garibaldi's entry in Palermo and ordered his men to turn back towards the city. A forty-five-mile march through mountainous country. The weather was hot. Oddly, he did not inform General Lanza, his commander-in-chief, as to where and when exactly he would arrive. No doubt he felt he'd been made a fool of. Or perhaps he tried to inform Lanza, but his messages didn't get through.

"Having arrived in Villabate" – Buttà – "Von Mechel sent a Sicilian sergeant to Lanza, in disguise, with a letter saying that he would attack the city the following morning... Nothing more was heard of that poor Sicilian sergeant – perhaps Lanza made him disappear, to avoid any risk of having to confess he had received the letter."

Buttà is the only one who has this story.

"I'm in Fieravecchia" – Beninati, the morning of 30th May – "when news arrives that General Del Bosco is coming from Villabate with the Bavarian column to surrender to Garibaldi... The news was welcomed with great excitement... The bells were set ringing."

Although this is hard to imagine, two other sources give the same story: that Von Mechel was bringing over his men en masse to the revolutionary cause. Perhaps that would explain why the rebels were so unprepared when, instead of surrendering, Del Bosco, as Beninati says, "greeted us with cannon shot".

This time Buttà actually saw the action: "I was assigned to Porta Termini – and I was delighted, because I knew that that was where the fighting would be fiercest. And it was."

"The rifle fire is ferocious" – Beninati. "After fifteen minutes our bands have to fall back into the gardens [the city's botanical park]."

"At the beginning, quite a few soldiers were killed and wounded" – Buttà. "It was at that point that they decided to burn down the houses to flush out the rebels."

"Commanded by La Masa" – La Masa speaking of himself in third person – "[the Sicilians] would have held their position victoriously, if they hadn't run out of ammunition."

"It was 11 a.m." – Abba in Piazza Pretoria – "when a cry of treachery was raised."

"In vain" – Eber – "did the garibaldini raise the white flag to signify that there was a truce."

All the recorded descriptions of this engagement are strikingly different – perhaps because the attack was two-pronged, with one column of men coming through Porta Termini and the other across the botanical gardens, closer to the sea. Then the outer defences were held by Sicilian bands, and only after they had retreated did a group of garibaldini arrive, led by Colonel Carini.

Rushing into a friend's palazzo to throw down roof tiles on the soldiers, Beninati saw "the lawyer's daughter in the kitchen – a lovely blonde girl, Rosina – trying to kill herself, yelling: 'They'll take me dead, but never alive…' It was quite a while before we were able to calm that young girl down."

Meantime, the tireless Flag Lieutenant Wilmot had been making his way to Garibaldi's headquarters in Palazzo Pretorio to check the details for the safe passage of the Bourbon generals to HMS *Hannibal* for negotiations, when suddenly he reports, "I found myself close in front of a body of Bavarian troops… firing as they marched forward."

"Colonel Carini was wounded" – Eber – "but still the garibaldini held to the instructions they had not to respond to enemy fire."

"Some of the Sicilians behind a barricade immediately returned the shots" – Wilmot – "and now I was caught between two fires."

"The garibaldini retreated from behind their barricades" – Buttà – "until, having reached Piazza della Fieravecchia, they took to their heels and fled."

"Garibaldi was on the point of declaring the truce broken" – Eber – "when two Neapolitan negotiators arrived [from the Royal Palace]. They begged pardon for what had happened and said it had been a misunderstanding, since Von Mechel's column didn't know about the truce."

"There were no more enemies to fight" – Buttà – "and the only sounds were voices begging for mercy."

Accompanying the Neapolitan officers to the scene of the fighting, Garibaldi, says Abba, "ran into Colonel Carini, who was being carried on a stretcher, seriously wounded in the shoulder and shouting to hurry, hurry, before all was lost."

"Now, exactly as victory was smiling on the Neapolitan troops" – Buttà – "a man appeared in the uniform of the 6th Regiment… and shouted at the soldiers: 'By order of His Excellency the king's lieutenant, General Lanza, stop here, because the revolution has been beaten and subdued.'"

Again, only Buttà has this version. It's hard to understand how the officer could claim the revolution was subdued when the soldiers had just been fighting the revolutionaries.

"Not many minutes subsequently" – Wilmot – "Garibaldi himself reached the spot, accompanied by thirty or forty of his Italian band.

He was furious, and a very angry conversation took place between him and the Neapolitan colonel."

We wandered back and forth along the narrow Via Divisi, where the Neapolitans had begun to advance from Fieravecchia in the direction of Piazza Pretoria when they were informed of the truce.

"At the sight of the Bourbon colonel holding a white handkerchief" – Abba – "the Bavarians stopped at once, as if someone had waved a wand."

There are no plaques here, but a hum of air conditioners on narrow balconies, beside laundry gleaming white in the sunlight and a few tricolours flying for the imminent football game.

"The brave and loyal Von Mechel" – Buttà – "almost died of grief."

Like all of Palermo, the street is a dense muddle of past and present: surveillance cameras screwed into ancient masonry, obscene graffiti on flaking stucco, sixteenth-century façades and bike shops. There is nothing here that might give us a clearer picture of what happened on that May morning in 1860.

"So much," Buttà concludes in disgust, "for the celebrated victories of Garibaldi!"

"If I were Garibaldi" – Eber – "I wouldn't listen to any proposals before Von Mechel's column has retreated to the positions it treacherously seized."

"The heat is suffocating" – Beninati – "the sun burns."

Now we walked out from the centre under the same burning sun, along the route Major Del Bosco had taken to come into town, which gave us an excuse for visiting the botanical gardens. Here, at about the hour the fighting was at its fiercest, we sat on a bench contemplating a massive Ficus Macrophylla, brought to Sicily from Norfolk Island, Australia, in 1845. Its multiple trunks, which cling to the ground like the tentacles of some giant octopus, its dangling lichens and endlessly intertwining branches, dry and peeling in places but supporting a vast canopy of new growth above, seemed the perfect emblem of a story that may have a fairly clear shape from a distance but is irretrievably knotted and tangled close up. No one will ever get to the bottom, I thought, of whatever was going on between the various Bourbon commanders the morning Von Mechel attacked, or exactly how desperate the rebels' position was when the Bavarians were halted. And these gardens in general, we decided, wandering down a splendid avenue of so-called "silk floss" trees with weirdly bottle-shaped trunks and dense, dark foliage, were in perfect harmony with that Sicilian mood of melancholy and magnificence, glaring light and lassitude, that inevitably imposes itself on your days here.

If one is given to conspiracy theories, it will obviously seem suspicious that General Lanza pressed ahead with the truce despite the fact that the Bourbons had finally gained the upper hand. But did he actually know that? If he'd wanted to sell out to Garibaldi, surely he would have made the truce well before Von Mechel turned up. And he wouldn't have launched the successful counter-attacks of the previous afternoon that had resulted in so many casualties. He had five hundred wounded men on his hands, many of them dying. He had proposed a truce of just twenty-four hours to get those men safe passage to the port, to bury the dead and to secure much-needed food supplies. His men had nothing to eat. He'd given his word of honour, and there was an arrangement in place with the world's greatest foreign power, which had a formidable warship anchored offshore. Anyway, the battle would be resuming the following day at noon. And, perhaps, as we shall see, he wasn't eager for all the glory to go to the Bavarians.

From the botanical gardens to the sea it's just a couple of hundred yards, then less than a mile along the shore, with the sea sparkling to your right and open grass wilting to your left, to the Cala, the inlet back in the centre of the city where Garibaldi and the two Bourbon generals stepped into a boat to be rowed out to HMS *Hannibal*. General Letizia and General Chrétien arrived "in the vice-regal barouche" – Mundy – "with its blue and scarlet liveries and attendant outriders." Garibaldi walked. But he had put on his Piedmontese general's uniform, which inevitably begged some thorny questions. "I may also mention" – Mundy – "that when Garibaldi and his son were standing at the landing place, awaiting the arrival of the Neapolitan generals, several musket shots were fired at him from the citadel…"

Mundy includes a hand-drawn sketch in his account showing Palermo and the ships in the bay and the harbour beside Castellammare, as shown in our map in the opening pages of this book.

There were nine Neapolitan warships in the harbour, five British warships lying off the seafront, and behind them, one after another, lines upon lines of French, Austrian, Spanish and Piedmontese warships. Further out still, were "110 merchant ships with refugees on board". Today there is just a single ferry plying a postcard blue. One forgets how important sea travel and sea power used to be. If the Neapolitan army had wished to leave Palermo, for example, their only assured means of withdrawal was the sea. Because when Garibaldi had entered Palermo, other Sicilian towns had seized the opportunity to rise up and rebel.

"The news arriving from other provinces" – Eber – "could hardly be better. The people are rising up everywhere, the troops retreating."

"Catania and its whole surrounding province" – *Chronicle of Events* – "are in the sights of the rebellion which is preparing arms and artillery to attack the city's loyal garrison."

No doubt these developments were very much on Lanza's mind when he decided to ask for a truce.

We tried to find the steps where Garibaldi and the generals boarded the boat – the "Landing Place" on Mundy's map – but the seafront has been rebuilt since then, and all you see now is parked cars beside the port-authority building and a grubby strip of beach. Apparently the generals hadn't understood that they would be sitting in the same boat with Garibaldi, and General Letizia, the head negotiator, "was unable to disguise his dejection". So said Wilmot, who sat beside him.

On board HMS *Hannibal*, General Letizia immediately began to complain about the company he was keeping. Mundy had invited captains from French, American and Piedmontese naval vessels into his cabin to witness the talks. And of course Garibaldi was there too, and Mundy himself. One wonders how big exactly his cabin was. Lanza's letter of invitation to Garibaldi, General Letizia protested, whose content he had shared with Mundy, had only spoken of himself and General Chrétien dealing with the Admiral, who would then mediate, referring their proposals to Garibaldi. Everyone else would have to go. He was categorical.

We sat down at a bar beside the Cala to think this over. One hears so much about the arrangements for peace negotiations, the number of people at the table, the brief and the power that each delegate has. Letizia, who was sixty-six, raised his voice "in a manner that was quite uncalled for," Mundy thought. Both Captain Lefèvre and Captain Palmer expressed their indignation and amazement at his attitude. But it made sense to me: Letizia wanted to avoid any impression of an international tribunal presiding over his government's behaviour.

"News of Garibaldi's entry into Palermo" – Raffaele de Cesare – "had astonished and moved all of Italy and liberal Europe."

If, when he finally decided to embark on this campaign, Garibaldi had hoped the tide might be flowing his way, it was partly because he had seen that liberal sentiments were on the rise throughout Europe. In 1859 the influential *Times* had abandoned its traditional opposition to Italian self-determination. The citizens of London and Paris, but New York and Washington too, were shocked when they read of the bombing of Palermo. Garibaldi might be coming to these negotiations entirely alone, but he knew he had the sympathy of the overwhelming majority of literate Europeans.

"The duel between Garibaldi and the Neapolitan viceroy," wrote *The Times*, "is being fought out under the eyes of newspaper correspondents, tourists, artists and English or American sympathizers..."

Even the people of Naples were not immune. Raffaele de Cesare was only fourteen in 1860, "but in Naples," he remembers, "the news produced an unforgettable impression, and on the evening of 29th May there was a small demonstration with cries of 'Viva la Sicilia! Viva Garibaldi!' It was dispersed by the police."

Asked if he was OK with the presence of the foreign captains, Garibaldi said yes. "I told General Letizia" – Mundy – "that I was utterly unable to comprehend the meaning of the violent conduct he had exhibited." He must take it or leave it, "consent to treat personally with Garibaldi, in the presence of the foreign captains... [or] declare the negotiations to be at an end". After conferring with General Chrétien, Letizia decided to take it, and from that moment on was operating outside the brief he had received from General Lanza.

After lunch we popped our noses into Santa Maria della Catena, a fourteenth-century church just a stone's throw away, on Via Vittorio Emanuele. Apparently it was named after a miracle when a fierce storm interrupted the execution of three innocent men. Brought into the church from the torrential rain, the condemned men's chains fell away, and they found themselves free. A fourteenth-century fresco depicts the Madonna who worked this miracle; she is feeding a baby who looks like a little old man – her face absorbed, indifferent, gazing at a spot on the floor.

Prisoners and prisons are a constant theme in Palermo. Likewise executions and vendettas. A couple of hundred yards from Santa Maria della Catena, behind Piazza Marina, we were just in time to join a guided tour of Palazzo Chiaromonte-Steri, an imposing fourteenth-century building that served as the court of the Inquisition through the sixteen and seventeen hundreds. The supposed heretics were held in chains in the dungeons. The building seems more a fortress than a palazzo, its greyish brown stone built to offer a blank face to the pitiless sun. But inside there are elaborate timber ceilings, fancy stonework zigzagging over arched windows, beautiful courtyards with tall palm trees immersed in deep silence. The guide's voice describing the sufferings of the prisoners – they lived in their excrement – seems disrespectfully loud. The only others on the tour are two Germans. Moving from one cell to another, you can't help but marvel at the sketches and graffiti that fill every inch of the walls. These poor captives had time on their hands, and some of them were talented. There is a useful map of Sicily, an elaborate depiction of a naval battle. Crucifixions. Most moving of all are the words scrawled in red capitals: CORAGGIO, ANIMA CARCERATA – "Take heart, imprisoned soul."

"Master of arms Don Giorgio Chinnici, the greatest torturer of the liberals" – Beninati – "was captured and brought before Garibaldi... Chinnici was notorious for inflicting the *cap of silence, the collar, the iron ring round the temples, pulling fingernails*... Garibaldi greeted him with courtesy and ordered that no one touch so much as a hair on his head."

"The countenance of the Dictator," says Mundy of Garibaldi while General Letizia was protesting and the foreign captains spoke their minds, "betrayed no emotion at what was passing."

Another five minutes' walk from Palazzo Chiaramonte and you're at the Cortile della Gancia, where on 4th April 1860 Chinnici and other Bourbon soldiers had won a decisive gun battle with insurgents hiding in the Chiesa della Gancia, thirteen of whom were then publicly executed, the event that had caused Garibaldi to postpone his departure from Quarto. A plaque on the monastery wall recalls Gaspare Bivona and Filippo Patti, who escaped death by hiding under the corpses of their friends.

"His father," wrote De Cesare of the young King Francis II, "had accumulated a fund of hatred in Sicily, and he would be called upon to pay the price."

The key moment in the negotiations on HMS *Hannibal* came when, sitting at "a small round table in the centre of the cabin", speaking a mixture of Italian and French, General Letizia read out the six conditions for a ceasefire that General Lanza had prepared. The first four, regarding the movement of the wounded and the displaced, as well as access to food and medicines, "were agreed to without comment"; the fifth read: "That the municipality should present a humble petition to His Majesty the King, laying before him the real wishes of the city."

Lanza was hinting at the possibility of a constitution, a new pact between king and people, to preserve the status quo.

"In a vehement and loud tone of voice" – Mundy – "[Garibaldi] replied 'No!... The time for humble petitions is passed.'" And he added, "*La municipalité, c'est moi.*"

Walking up Via Alloro to Piazza Croce dei Vespri, scene of Palermo's first great revolution in 1282, a plaque claims: "Here lived Jean de Saint-Remy, law enforcer in the name of Charles of Anjou, and here the vengeful fury of the people fell on the foreign oppressor." On the façade of a noble palazzo, now abandoned, a rusty old sign reads, "HOTEL PATRIA".

"Astonishment and indignation were depicted on the countenance of General Letizia on hearing these words" – Mundy. "'Unless this article is agreed to,' he said, 'all communication between us must cease.'"

At these words, Garibaldi "completely lost command of [his] temper", denouncing "the infamy of the royal authorities in allowing foreign mercenaries, whilst a flag of truce was flying, to attack the Italian troops."

Letizia turned on Mundy and demanded he intervene to stop this scandalous talk.

Mundy reminded the Bourbon general of the limits of his good offices.

Captain Lefèvre waded in, "burning with indignation at this renewed exhibition of violent language".

"Garibaldi had risen from his seat" – Mundy – "under the belief that the negotiations had been brought to a close."

You have to wonder whether he was bluffing. But whatever Garibaldi's intentions, his move to walk out on the talks had immediate effect. The two Bourbon generals conferred and reluctantly accepted "the expunging of the fifth article from the convention" – Mundy – "though by so material a concession he [Letizia] knew he should incur the displeasure of the royal commissioner [Lanza]."

TRUCE

After brief discussion, "an armistice was agreed to until noon on the following day".

Curiously, it was at this point that Garibaldi almost lost his nerve. The passage is one of the most surprising in his memoirs. True, he now had his one-day breathing space, but his men were desperately short of arms and ammunition; much of the city was damaged by bombs; "the enemy was now inside [the town] with its best troops... the cannons of the fleet, of Palazzo Reale and Castellammare could soon resume their work of destruction."

"I suddenly felt uncertain as to what to do," Garibaldi confesses, "whether it made sense to go on defending the town or whether we should gather all our forces together and retreat into the country."

Perhaps the sight of the rubble along Via Toledo as he walked to HMS *Hannibal* had unsettled him. He was largely responsible, after all.

"The idea" – Garibaldi – "came on my mind like a nightmare... it would mean abandoning the city to the ravages of a riotous soldiery."

Back at Palazzo Pretorio, he expressed himself frankly to the Revolutionary Committee: the Bourbons were offering a liberal constitution in return for an act of submission. Otherwise it was war.

"They told me" – Garibaldi – "to speak to the people gathered under the balconies, which I did... almost angry with myself."

"He appeared on the left-hand balcony of the Palazzo" – Abba – "the sun, already low, gleaming on the glass behind."

Returning to the piazza, we find that there are actually nine balconies across the façade of Palazzo Pretorio, all on the third floor, so you'd be hard put to say which was "the left-hand" one. They barely protrude from the building, offering little more than a kind of stone parapet to lean out from.

"'The enemy has offered conditions humiliating to the city of Palermo.'" – Beninati. "The general pronounced these words from the first balcony of the town hall."

The "first" balcony would presumably mean the one closest to the street, Via Maqueda, which is in fact on the extreme left, as you look out from inside the building. It makes sense. From here, Garibaldi would have been able to address not only the people in the piazza and Via Maqueda but also the crowd a hundred yards away in the Quattro Canti. Thousands.

"Of their demands" – the published version of Garibaldi's harangue – "one was offensive to the brave people of Palermo, and I rejected it with contempt."

"There are those alive today," Abba wrote forty years later, "who hear that voice constantly in their minds."

A hundred and sixty-two years after the event, our knowing that it was here Garibaldi spoke, from this very balcony right above our heads, only makes us more aware of the abyss of time separating us now from that voice then. Looking out across the piazza today, the general would be watching youngsters wearing headsets throbbing with music, men riding electric scooters, children licking ice creams, wearing sandals with flashing lights, girls showing tattooed calves and shoulders, a guide holding a selfie-stick in the air to gather a group of Americans. It's a peaceful, prosperous scene in breathtakingly beautiful surroundings, sunshine picking out the grain of the stuccoed façades and gleaming on the bright-white statues around the fountain. Which makes it all the more extraordinary that so many locals now believe that Palermo was a happier place under the Bourbons.

This was not the mood in 1860.

"The general" – Beninati – "concluded by asking the people if they wanted peace or war."

"We should have noticed," says Eleonora, pointing up at the wall.

It's quite a small stone, just to the other side of this balcony: "From this building, on 30th May 1860, Giuseppe Garibaldi… announced the final battle… and heard in reply, over and over, a deafening, vibrant shout of, 'War'."

"War! War!" – Beninati. "The people were delirious, wild, out of their heads."

"That roar" – Garibaldi – "decided the liberty of two peoples, and decreed the fall of a tyrant."

"Seeing the crowd's reaction" – Beninati – "the general seemed surprised, amazed, even confused."

But Beninati was confused himself: "I see many in the crowd who have lost their homes and all their goods to the bombing, yet it was they who raised the most ferocious cries for war."

"I was reinvigorated" – Garibaldi – "and from that moment on, every trace of fear, or hesitation or indecision vanished."

Portraits

It's a large claim to make, but when we were walking cross country, particularly when the going was tough – from Marsala to Salemi, from Piana degli Albanesi to Marineo – it was possible from time to time to feel close to the garibaldini. We shared the same landscape, the same fatigue and thirst, the blisters and sunburn, the same pleasures satisfying hunger or resting in the shade. Once in Palermo, we missed all this. Modern life is so present here: the shop windows, the flashing lights, an adolescent's aftershave, the young woman having a video-call rant about her grandmother. I was reminded of this loss looking at some nineteenth-century landscapes in the Galleria d'Arte Moderna – hardly things to pull in the crowds, yet they had me riveted. Antonino Leto's *Countryside with Prickly Pears* (1867) was exactly the place where we'd stopped above Pioppo to eat a peach: the same dry, feathery grass, the fierce glare of the sun on grey rock, the same twisted cactus shapes. Francesco Lojacono's *Wind in the mountains* (1872) exactly caught the mood of that morning walk to Misilmeri, when the hot wind blew up. Lojacono has the light perfectly, its layers of haze and patches of fierce chiaroscuro. His *View of Palermo* must have been painted close to where we looked down through the mist from Gibilrossa. There are the blue-green agaves, the palms and the olives. These pictures gave us the impression of something shared.

Also I notice, reading back and forth through chronicles and diaries, that it is always the small moments of physical experience and the casual encounters along the way that attract me, more than the politics and polemics. "We now had a few hours to get our strength back," says Capuzzi of the truce, "but that meant lying down on the cold hard marble of San Giuseppe, assigned to us as barracks." After "twenty-four nights in the open and three days' continuous fighting", Capuzzi decides to find himself a proper "plumped up" bed in someone's house: "There are no words for how deliciously I slept."

One is drawn into the polemics for or against the Risorgimento. You want to have your say. But this lures you away from the physical reality of events and becomes more and more an assertion of your own position, your own supposed reasonableness and powers of understanding. It's interesting that none of the fervent polemicists, even those who were involved in the campaign, offer much in the way of details. Buttà never says exactly where he was during a battle, who he was beside, whether he was hungry or thirsty. His most convincing passages are his few meetings with local people, the girl he swoons over in Piana degli Albanesi, a lawyer turned rebel whom he despises on the slopes above Monreale.

"Worse than the fighting" – Abba on the truce – "was the torment of searching for the wounded and the dead." He goes on to talk about the kind of wounds the men had: "Mostly in the head or upper torso. The barricades had saved the lower part of the body. Which was lucky, because those with leg wounds almost always died."

"This morning" – Bixio's diary – "Tüköry was amputated at the thigh."

"You lose a kingdom" – Buttà fuming about the truce – "to take care of a few wounded men." He never names a single one.

On the afternoon of 30th May the various companies of the Thousand were ordered to assemble for a body count. The men had been fighting alongside the Sicilians in small groups, a few in each band, to beef them up.

"Then friends got together who had lost sight of each other during those three days" – Abba. "Some were so stunned, so wiped out by the long sleepless hours and the effort and emotions, they couldn't even think what to say. But when someone looked well fed and rested, we were suspicious."

Officially the truce had been declared to bury the dead, care for the wounded and allow civilians to flee. And no doubt some of this went on. In the Galleria d'Arte Moderna, Filippo Liardo's *Burial of a Garibaldino* shows two young women, arm in arm, hair hanging loose, one dark, one fair, in the rubble of a bombed-out house beside a black coffin bearing a red cap. On the wall, you can just about recognize a votive image of Santa Rosalia. It's a curiously reticent, quietly intimate painting. The young artist clearly knew exactly what a bomb-struck building looks like. A native of Palermo, Liardo had fought alongside the garibaldini. When the canvas was shown in Paris in 1865, it made his name.

Certainly a lot of people took the opportunity to get out of the city. "At all hours of the day" – Giulia de Beaumont – "we can see whole families fleeing. Hatless, dishevelled women running towards the wharf and the sea. 'Palermo is finished,' everyone says."

"But only the well off" – Eber – "could afford a place on board ship."

"Many take to the countryside" – Beninati. "I saw women half naked, children in just their shirts."

"The population are heading for the fields" – *Chronicle of Events* – "or hiding in cellars and tombs."

All the same, on the rebel side, the twenty-four-hour truce was mostly dedicated to building new barricades and assembling cartridges. While the soldiers got some sleep, the people worked through the night. The Bavarians in Piazza Fieravecchia had to be sealed off. "All the women in the neighbourhood helped" – Beninati – "and the fun of it was that while we were working, anyone passing by was co-opted. The boys carried cobblestones in baskets to the upper floors. The young men on the roofs made heaps of tiles ready to throw."

"Priests, men and women" – Eber – "everyone worked at the barricades."

"The worst consequence of this truce" – *Chronicle of Events* – " is that Colonel Del Bosco and Colonel Von Mechel… find themselves almost trapped, hemmed in by a network of barricades, unable to launch a new attack."

"The city is impassable" – Borghese brothers – "because of all the rubble blocking the streets."

Abba and a friend thought they recognized a red-and-white checked shirt in the crowd.

"Where did you find it?"

"I took it from a dead man."

They ran to San Giovanni degli Eremiti to look for the corpse of their friend: "Antonio Simonetta, Milanese, nineteen years old."

"Nothing" – Abba. "Nobody knows where they buried him."

Near the church they came into contact with some Bourbon soldiers, who taunted them, "You'll see, you'll see, tomorrow you'll all be dead!"

"We're trapped in a triangle" – Beninati. "They can bombard us at will, all the more so since they've just been given a new supply of bombs from Naples."

Yet people were in good spirits: "The whole night" – Beninati – "was spent yelling 'On your guard, sentry, on your guard!' – and partying." "At night" – Admiral Mundy from the bridge of his ship – "the city was splendidly illuminated."

"There wasn't a hovel" – Abba – "however poor and tucked away in the alleys, that didn't have a light in every window."

"Regular alarms" – Borghese brothers – "warn the Bourbons that the people are awake and thirsting for revenge."

"The night passed without incident" – Beninati – "except a few Bavarian soldiers deserted."

Why would *they* change sides, you wonder, when apparently so close to victory? Surely they weren't interested in a united Italy. Describing Garibaldi's speech from the balcony of Palazzo Pretorio, I omitted one detail, out of prudence. It seemed too incredible, and I have found it in only one account. In 1926 the Sicilian historian Alfonso Sansone published the hitherto unavailable correspondence between General Lanza and Francis II in a book called *The Fortunes of the Expedition of the Thousand: New Documents*. Between one missive and the next, he offers the necessary context. "The Dictator," he writes of the afternoon of 30th May, "appeared at the balcony on the corner of Palazzo Pretorio, together with Major Del Bosco, in the role of Bourbon negotiator..."

Is it possible that Del Bosco, who was considered the Bourbons' most effective, active and indeed most handsome commander, was present at Garibaldi's speech, actually on the balcony? In which case, the people's great cry of "War! War!" would have been meant as much for him as for the general. And even if he wasn't there, the Bavarian troops whom, together with Colonel Von Mechel, Del Bosco commanded, were near enough to hear that defiant roar. What effect would it have had on them? It was clear that victory could only come after immense bloodshed.

"The Swiss-Bavarians" – Bixio – "are thirsty for blood and plunder."

But perhaps not all of them. Getting his men into Palermo and sparking off the revolution, Garibaldi had created a situation where the Bourbons and their Bavarian mercenaries were obliged to be utterly ruthless or abandon the city. How much did they really want this?

Without having entirely recovered from his wound of four days before, Bixio got out of his bed on the morning of 31st May, stumbled to Piazza Pretoria to find Garibaldi and was at once his anxious, curmudgeonly self: "There's a back-and-forth of negotiators and a confusion here such as to disgust even the best-intentioned man on earth. One can only hope things turn out well."

"A forest of monkeys and parrots" – Eber – "would seem a calm and pleasant place of retirement after having spent just half an hour in this Babylon."

Inside the palazzo that overlooked the piazza, Garibaldi was writing orders for the forthcoming battle.

"Get together as many men as you can," he wrote to Colonel Orsini, who was following Von Mechel and Del Bosco back from Corleone, bringing with him two cannons, "and march on the capital to attack the enemy from behind... Today the destiny of Sicily will be decided."

"The general sometimes seems very confident" – Bixio – "and sometimes very worried."

Beninati finally managed to get himself introduced to Garibaldi, by his son Menotti: "The general shook my hand firmly and said, 'My dear man.' But his complexion betrayed anxiety."

"Everyone" – Zasio – "had placed all the planning and power in Garibaldi's hands. Everything depended on him, and at moments of urgency and danger, when it seemed God himself would not be enough, he responded with great efficacy."

We're in the Galleria d'Arte Moderna, in front of Salvatore Lo Forte's portrait of Garibaldi painted late in 1860 from an iconic photograph by Gustave Le Gray. Le Gray, a French painter and photographer, was travelling in Sicily in July 1860 with the writer Alexander Dumas, who was busy turning Garibaldi into a myth; the general himself had asked for the photo to be taken, presumably intending to use it for distribution to newspapers.

In the photo Garibaldi leans a shoulder against a light-coloured wall, perhaps the wall of Palazzo Pretorio, slim belly slightly pushed out, head cocked, right hand gripping a sabre at his belt, left hand on his hip. A mature man of action. The lush beard is well groomed and about as full as a beard can be, almost entirely hiding his cheeks. On top, his hair has receded, revealing a great dome of a forehead, whence a thin nose rises from two deep creases. And he turns to look straight at the camera from intense, hooded eyes, one slightly more open than the other, as if staring into bright sunlight. You know at once that this is a man at the height of his powers, absolutely sure of himself. His dark shirt looks a little shabby, certainly well worn, cuffs casually turned up. The trousers are lighter and stylishly baggy. A loop of chain round his neck is presumably attached to a fob watch in his top pocket, while lower down a leather lanyard secures the sheath of his sabre to his belt. This is someone at ease with gear, at ease with his body, at ease with life. You can see the veins on the back of his hand, the scars on his strong fingers. There are no rings. The kerchief knotted under his chin adds a cavalier touch.

So much for the photo. On the wall of the gallery, Lo Forte has gentrified him, painting just the upper torso, puffing it out a little, removing the lean relaxed physicality. The arms are gone too, and the scarred hands. The painted face seems more solemn somehow, more bourgeois, the cheeks fleshier. A dignitary, not a fighter. The eyes have been opened, losing a little of their fierceness. The shirt of course is red, and more regal than the one in the photo. The watch chain is gold. Crucially, the wall that gave sense to the leaning body is gone. Now the backdrop is a sky at dusk, streaks of rosy red in a wash of indigo; just behind the top of the general's head a source of white light projects a glow over carefully combed hair. Surely the moon couldn't be so bright with the sun still pouring its light over the scene. A couple of inches above the head, dead centre and just beyond the convenient but improbable glow, a very large, very bright, traditionally star-shaped star, offers a banal symbolism. Garibaldi is the chosen one.

What remains in both photo and painting is a subtle pathos: you sense this man is looking at you from the other side of some extraordinary experience: that isolates him. I'm reminded that when Garibaldi turned his hand to novel-writing, publishing *Clelia, the Government of the Priests* in 1868, his alter ego in the book is called *il solitario*, "the loner". And thinking back on this march across Sicily, I realize that from the moment his personal assistant and assiduous chronicler, Giuseppe Bandi, was removed from the scene by multiple bullet wounds at Calatafimi, we don't have a single recorded conversation with Garibaldi. Of course he always had his main men beside him, Türr and Sirtori, Crispi and Bixio and Carini. And his son, Menotti. There were always people pressing for his attention, local dignitaries, Sicilian fighters, English officers, Hungarian journalists, and he was always careful to be welcoming and to win them over. That went with the job. But there is no account of any conversation. One remembers the moment in Partinico when he was disgusted by the charred bodies of the Neapolitan soldiers. There are the descriptions of his men watching him sleeping on the bare rocks high up at the Renda pass. Abba and Capuzzi see him galloping by at crucial moments: the aborted attack on Monreale, the sudden decision to abandon the defence of Parco. We know that he helped lift the cannons from their carriages for the night-time descent in heavy rain from Renda, and that he asked the peasants in Marineo where was the best vantage point from which to see the movement of the Bourbon troops, then climbed up there himself to keep watch for hours. He gave speeches, of course, to his men after Calatafimi, to the Sicilian bands above Gibilrossa, and we know he told Bixio: "Tomorrow, in Palermo." That's about it. He was locked up in his responsibilities. They could hardly have been greater than on the morning of 31st May, as the truce drew to a close and he and his staff made plans for the decisive battle.

"Anyone wishing to experience powerful emotions," wrote Eber that morning, "need only find a ship and come to Palermo... every hour brings a sudden change in the state of affairs... one moment all is triumph and hope, the next all is terror and despondency."

As the countdown to midday began, the mood was buoyant. "We've drunk lots of coffee and eaten a few biscuits," says Beninati. "My mother... thought to bring some rice and beans to the men at the barricades, and some bread, cheese and wine."

"It was a marvellous thing" – Abba – "that instead of encouraging people to relax in the hope that the struggle was over, the truce had got them even more fired up."

This despite the fact that "the bodies of the dead" – Borghese brothers – "assuming the many and strange shapes of death's convulsions, lie unburied in the streets, where their nauseating smell poisons the air."

"Priests and monks" – Eber – "went up and down carrying crosses and encouraging people to have faith in Providence and fight for their lives and properties."

"They gave us ammunition and food" – Capuzzi. "It was the first time a meal had been distributed since we arrived in Palermo."

The barricades were now such "formidable bastions" – Beninati – "that I don't think Bosco will be able to advance."

"I managed to do some sentry duty" – Bixio – "and to concentrate my two battalions in San Giuseppe."
"In the most crowded parts of town" – Abba – "musical bands were playing patriotic tunes."
But the Bourbons were confident too. Both Buttà and the anonymous author of *Chronicle of Events*, who must have been a Bourbon officer, give details of an elaborate plan of attack along three main streets: from the north, the west and the south-west. The men and their equipment were in place. They had their orders. Lanza was convinced of victory. It seemed the killing must resume.
"At noon the truce ends" – Borghese brothers – "the people are impatient to go on the attack."
Just five minutes' walk from the Galleria d'Arte Moderna, which is close to the Fieravecchia, you can visit Sicily's Galleria d'Arte Regionale in Palazzo Abatellis, showing paintings from earlier periods. The most arresting work is *The Triumph of Death*, a fifteenth-century fresco of about twenty feet by twenty, which you can view from close up, at floor level, or looking down from a gallery high on the wall the other side of the room. It's astonishing. A white horse, or the rotting corpse of a white horse, bursts into a lush garden, galloping left to right and occupying the entire centre of the scene. On its back a hideous skeleton rider is firing arrows into a crowd. Beneath the horse's hooves are the bodies of those already dead: popes and kings and knights and ladies, a heap of lush clothes and grim faces, "assuming the many and strange shapes of death's convulsions", as the Borghese brothers put it. Behind the horse, altogether ignored by Death, a group of poor folk, miserably clothed but still alive, are praying for a final release from their miseries, in vain. To the right, unaware that they are next for the chop, handsome men and women hang around an elaborate stone well, playing musical instruments – a lyre, a harp – and chatting together. The whole field of vision is at once extremely dense and busy, richly detailed and coloured, yet at the same time dreamlike, as if time had been suspended at a moment that was full both of ordinary life and high drama, pleasure and terror.

The fresco, painted by an unknown artist, used to be in Palazzo Sclafani, just a stone's throw from the Royal Palace. It was moved when the palazzo was bombed in 1945. One wonders if perhaps Colonel Buonopane had seen it, or if it was on his mind as the last hours of the truce ticked away. Camillo Buonopane was the kingdom's deputy chief of staff and "held to be the best-educated man in the army," remembers Raffaele de Cesare, though otherwise "he had none of the qualities required for the position he occupied". Having accompanied the medical supplies that arrived in Palermo on 28th May, the colonel returned to Naples for consultations with the king, then sailed back to Palermo, arriving on the evening of 30th May – and on the morning of 31st May "when everything was ready [for the battle]" – *Chronicle of Events* – "he arrives at the Royal Palace and persuades the commander-in-chief to relent." The new barricades, the colonel thought, were such that an immediate attack would be extremely costly. Soon enough, Buonopane and General Letizia arrived in Piazza Pretoria to ask Garibaldi to extend the truce.

"The news has not been well received" – Beninati. "The people want to fight at any cost."

"Imagine my surprise" – General Lanza's official report – "when the deputy chief of staff, Colonel Buonopane, came to see me just hours before hostilities were to recommence, charged by His Majesty (by the grace of God) to negotiate, advising me he had arranged to prolong the first truce of twenty-four hours for a further three days, when I was certain I would be master of Palermo that day."

A quite different version than the one offered by the *Chronicle*. Which brings us to the enigma at the heart of our story, the heart of all the polemics surrounding the adventure of the Thousand: Who was making the decisions on the Bourbon side? Garibaldi's solitude, his apartness if you like, in photographs and portraits, is the solitude of the Dictator. A republican and a democrat, Garibaldi insisted that in a military campaign power must be delegated, by common accord, to one man. For rapidity and clarity of decision-making. Albeit after taking advice from all quarters. When the campaign was over, he would relinquish power, as in fact he did, without delay.

The Bourbon kingdom was an absolute monarchy, one that had steadfastly refused to grant a constitution to its people. So again we have one man in charge, but in this case a man without experience, and with no time limit on his power. Before his early death in 1859, the previous king, Ferdinand II, had advised his son to maintain the kingdom's close alliance with Austria and with the papacy, the two great champions of old-fashioned absolutism. So the all-powerful

Francis, aged twenty-three, began his reign in thrall to a policy that would be obsolete only a month after his coronation, when Austria lost the war with France and Piedmont and hence could no longer guarantee the Bourbon kingdom's independence. For counsellors, Francis had three uncles (his father's brothers) as well as the eldest of his own many half-brothers, Louis, who was twenty-one. There was also his strong-willed stepmother, Maria Theresa of Austria, who would have liked Louis to be king, then his father's confessor, Padre Borelli, with whom Francis loved to explore his interest in mystical experience, and the ageing General Filangieri, who saw a need to adapt to a new liberal Europe and concede a constitution. There were also various counts and princes and generals who insisted that things remain as they were. "Not all were sincere," observes De Cesare, "and those who were sincere were not the most enlightened."

It didn't help that the king appeared to have no mind or initiative of his own. Shortly before his father's death, he had married, or been married to, sight unseen, the beautiful eighteen-year-old Maria Sophie of Bavaria, but he was unable to consummate their marriage. He suffered from a severe case of phimosis – a tight foreskin – not a difficult problem to solve, so long as one takes it to a doctor. Francis did not. Soon enough his vivacious wife became restless. Photographs and portraits of Francis show a slim, sad youth cruelly upstaged by his smart military uniform with its bright-yellow epaulettes and splendid, unearned decorations. It would be hard to think of a man more different from Garibaldi, or of a situation in which an absolute monarchy would be less likely to survive. After a long meeting with his councillors on the morning of 30th May, during which the possibility of granting a constitution and opening negotiations with France and Piedmont was heatedly debated, Francis could only conclude that "Don Peppino" – his name for Garibaldi – "has clean hands, but he is a cover: behind him are the western powers, and Piedmont that have decreed the end of our dynasty." It was hardly fighting talk.

After reading all the documents and accounts available, it seems impossible to know who was really responsible for that second truce in Palermo. It's not clear whether Lanza, as the king's lieutenant in Sicily, had the power to reject Buonopane's arguments and reopen hostilities, or whether Buonopane was acting under explicit instructions brought from the king in Naples. The impression is that no one was in control – certainly no one was eager to take responsibility.

Nor has anyone given us a proper account of the meeting between Garibaldi and the two Bourbon officers that morning. "Letizia asked me" – Garibaldi – "for three more days of truce, since twenty-four hours hadn't been enough to transport the wounded onto the ships. I accepted, and meantime not a second was lost making gunpowder and assembling cartridges."

That's it. He doesn't so much as mention the second clause of the agreement, which was to prove such a gift to conspiracy theorists.

"The Royal Bank funds will be delivered to Secretary of State Crispi, who will issue a receipt, and the detachment of soldiers guarding the bank will withdraw to Castellammare with their arms and gear."

"Have you ever read" – rages Buttà – "in the annals of war, that while negotiating a truce favourable only to the losers, these are handed the state's money?"

Still standing today, the Palazzo delle Finanze is on Via Toledo – Vittorio Emanuele, that is – about a hundred yards from the Cala, the port, and five hundred from the cannons at Castellammare. In short, the other side of town from the Royal Palace. A former sixteenth-century prison, restyled in the 1840s for use as a bank, it has a fortress look to it: four massive Doric pillars and elaborate wrought-iron gates defend the entrance. Like so many major buildings in the city, it is presently in disuse. A lose cable sags down between two pillars; the porch area inside is full of bird droppings.

"People said and wrote" – Buttà – "that Lanza syphoned off sixty thousand ducats from the five million in the bank for himself."

In fact, Crispi's receipt on taking over the bank was for 5,414,444 ducats in coin, of which only 100,000 belonged to the state, the rest to local depositors.

"The soldiers occupying the Palazzo delle Finanze" – Eber, two days earlier, on 29th May – "sent a negotiator to say they wished to leave the building. As a condition, Garibaldi insisted they lay down their arms. They refused, and now a cannon is being set up to help them see reason."

"Twenty garibaldini" – Abba – "and a host of locals have been watching the Palazzo delle Finanze day and night to make sure that Sicily's money stays in Sicily."

There were one hundred and twenty-five soldiers in the bank, isolated and deep inside enemy territory. Given that they had run out of supplies, that some were wounded and that the new truce was now to be for three days, Letizia and Buonopane had little alternative but to hand over the building. To all intents and purposes, it was already lost. Garibaldi was making a concession when he allowed the soldiers to keep their weapons and enjoy safe passage to rejoin the Bourbon forces at the Royal Palace.

So 31st May ended in anti-climax. The faithful Colonel Orsini marched into town bringing his cannons, which had now been dragged from Marsala almost to Palermo, then across the mountains beyond Corleone and now all the way back to Palermo again. They were set up to defend the barricade at Porta Maqueda. The people applauded.

Beninati went to pay another visit to Lajos Tüköry.

"He has a high fever, and I found him much weakened, but he is always cheerful... Two revolvers that had been on his bedside table were no longer there."

A last word about portraits. As we were hurrying out of the Galleria d'Arte Moderna, at the bottom of a flight of stairs in a last stretch of corridor, I happened to glimpse, through a half-open door, another painting of Garibaldi. It was in some kind of storeroom or unused exhibition space, mostly empty, forbidden to the public. But, incongruously, it was propped on the back of a little three-wheeler van, against its grey cabin; the resulting impression was of an old-fashioned figure in a red shirt looking back at the road behind as he is driven away into the distance.

Peeking through the door, we took pictures. The painting – a large portrait of the general, perhaps five feet high – looked like another version from Le Gray's photo. Almost the same pose, but with the sword on the left side, rather than the right. I've been unable to find it on the Internet. In any event, there was something disquieting about the apparition. As if the great general of the Risorgimento, together with all he stood for – his courage, his vision, his virility – were being simultaneously celebrated and taken off to a rubbish dump.

Secrets

For a further week we wander round Palermo, trying to bend our experience to the narrative of 1860. It gets harder. The city is so rich in history, the old streets and stones have soaked up centuries of pomp and violence. The monuments to Garibaldi along Via della Libertà or in Piazza Marina are only two among multitudes to other conquerors: "Triumphing in Palermo after victory in Tunis" – a plaque on the wall of Palazzo Ajutamicristo – "Emperor Charles V of Austria stayed in this building in 1535." Here's a fountain restored by Philip IV of Spain in 1663, here a memorial "To the martyrs of the criminal Fascist oppression", here a monument to a hero of the war in Abyssinia, another to the thirteenth-century rebels of the Vespri. Murals of the assassinated magistrates, Giovanni Falcone and Paolo Borsellino, look down from bare walls in the suburbs. In a narrow street not far from our apartment we overhear a tourist guide explaining how a local aristocrat of the fourteenth century tried to kill his rivals by blowing up the palazzo where they were having a party.

The penultimate day of our visit we took a bus to Monreale, and were overwhelmed by the Byzantine mosaics in the cathedral there. It's the Cappella Palatina all over again, but on a vastly larger scale. Story after glittering story unfolds on the upper walls of the great church: stern bearded faces, grand gestures, flowing robes. Simply to have conceived this space and its decoration, to have found the energy and resources required to bring the work to completion, is beyond extraordinary. You're aware of the uniqueness of Sicily, the many different influences it brings together – Greek, Norman, Byzantine, Arab – but also its intense Italianness: it is not difficult to understand the tension on this island between the desires to be distinct and, simultaneously, to be part of a larger whole. Sitting that evening in a crowded café on the Maqueda, we watched Italy beat Belgium in the Euro quarter finals, anxiously and noisily supported by those same citizens who at other moments are convinced the Risorgimento was a mistake. Another evening, in the same, now half-empty café, we had watched England play Ukraine, and noticed that the few locals bothering to follow the game were all rooting against England – the country cannot be forgiven for the power it once exercised. Certainly Admiral Mundy's diary exudes presumption. On 2nd June, the second day of the second truce, he dressed in plain clothes and had Lieutenant Wilmot escort him on an inspection of the town. "My flag lieutenant," he purrs, "seemed everywhere to be recognized – and, as it was now generally known that the moral agency of the British flag had saved the city from further destruction, the gratitude and respect of the people were made unmistakably manifest."

The only Union Jack we saw flying was a soiled towel hanging to dry from a high balcony in a dark alley.

Where Mundy always speaks of Britain and the British, the garibaldini thought only of England and the English. "These sailors of the English Navy" – Abba – "welcome us more warmly than those of Piedmont... There is no bottle they won't share with us, no knick-knack they don't offer."

"The English and American officers" – Garibaldi – "gave our men their revolvers and hunting rifles." However, the senior officers of the Piedmontese fleet "remained obedient to the cold, calculating men of the ministry in Turin... impassive witnesses of the destruction of one of Italy's most noble cities."

During his incognito tour, Mundy was shocked by the extent of the devastation, which "could scarcely be perceived" from his ship out in the bay. Near the Royal Palace "families had been burnt alive within the buildings". The once "beautiful metropolis... presented a heart-rending spectacle".

"Oh, what a wrenching sight" – Beaumont – "to see such a populous area, as big as the whole city of Vicenza, reduced to ruins – hundreds of houses that are now no more than a couple of sagging walls and broken balconies. The result of terrible fires that were set on purpose."

"Try to go into one of the ruins" – Eber – "and it won't be long before you stumble on a charred corpse; here a leg sticking out of a heap of stones, there a smoky face to frighten you. If you hear a noise, that will be a half-dozen rats... or a stray dog... Swarms of flies infest the air..."

Revisiting these streets, we came across a monument we had missed first time round, confirmation of Beninati's account of people being dragged from their homes, released, then shot as they fled. Beninati regretted that he didn't know their names; now you can just about read them on a flaky monument, overgrown with weeds, by a no-entry sign at a corner of the Church of San Giovanni Decolato. Nine in all. "Wretches pulled from the flames of their houses and extinguished here by cowardly Bourbon rage, 27th May 1860."

Otherwise Mundy was "forcibly struck by the efficiency of the barricades... Carpenters, bricklayers, stonemasons, ironmongers and artificers of every denomination, apparently under divisional leaders, were actively at work at the various depots preparing arms and materials for defence... thousands of pikes, pitchforks, swords... were placed out in the streets, ticketed and ready for issue."

Buttà witnessed the same activity and was furious: "What ignorance, what stupidity! If in one night the city could be barricaded in such a way that the troops would have suffered great losses attacking it, after a truce of a further three days wasn't Palermo going to be impregnable?"

No sooner was the second truce signed, the Bourbon chaplain complains, than "the usual suspects, Lanza's close friends Buonopane and Letizia, set off for Naples".

The purpose of these consultations, surmises *Chronicle of Events*, was to "have the responsibility for any eventual further bombardment fall upon the king".

But Lanza was certainly no friend of either General Letizia or Colonel Buonopane, and would later complain bitterly about their having gone over his head to get direct orders from Naples. What was the point of his being the king's lieutenant if the king had to be consulted before any decision could be made?

In Vicolo del Bosco, just five minutes from San Giovanni, we poked our noses through the doors of the dilapidated Palazzo Oneto, erstwhile home of the Prince of San Lorenzo, where Lajos Tüköry and other wounded garibaldini were given beds. There is a quiet courtyard with peeling stucco, parked cars, rusty scaffolding, high narrow balconies.

"I sent Doctor Walker, MD," – Mundy – "first assistant-surgeon of the *Hannibal*, to visit Colonels Tüköry and Carini. The leg of the former had been badly amputated... Both were much gratified at seeing an English medical officer."

Of course.

"Some garibaldini" – Abba – "were taken into the houses of rich families whom the people had reason to hate; without knowing it, these men served as a cover for their hosts."

Eight hundred wounded or sick Bourbon soldiers were embarked on ships for Naples that day. But not all was sweetness and light. On 2nd June, thirty Bourbon policemen were hunted down and massacred. Each victim "is subjected to torture" – *Chronicle of Events* – "then shot; the corpses are not spared from desecration – heads crushed with stones, eyes and teeth dug out."

"The massacre of policemen" – Giulia de Beaumont – "is never-ending, and sadly no one knows how to stop it."

"All attempts to save the lives of these men were unsuccessful" – Mundy. "The mob was implacable – many of them were stoned to death, and then torn to pieces."

"The things you hear" – Eber – "about the oppression of the police are almost incredible… thousands of secret agents had penetrated every home… even the most intimate friends were afraid of communicating their thoughts for fear of being denounced."

"This morning in the piazza of the Chiesa del Carmine" – Beninati – "the crowd killed six policemen and were about to burn the corpses. But a woman began to yell like crazy that Baby Jesus, in the arms of the Madonna over the door of the church, had turned his head away, not wanting to see such wickedness. Everyone was convinced they had seen the Baby's head turn. A miracle."

We could see Santa Maria del Carmine Maggiore from where we ate in the Ballarò market. Or rather, we could see the blue-and-gold tip of its bizarre and beautiful dome. After lunch, we visited the piazza outside the church, where stalls, crammed into the narrow spaces all around, were doing brisk business despite the stifling heat. "The men selling tuna in the streets are shouting louder again" – Eber – "a sign that the city is getting back to normal."

Certainly everyone's shouting loudly today, and there's plenty of tuna on sale, great blood-red wedges of it. "It's almost the only thing people are eating," Eber remarks, though Beninati never mentions eating fish. Above the noise of the men hawking their wares and the motorbikes weaving through the crowd, the façade of Santa Maria del Carmine is a drab baroque shape of crumbling grey stucco and brown underlying stone, with just one central ornament: a Madonna in a niche over the big double doors seems to be leaning out a little to show her child what's going on in the piazza below. Both she and Baby Jesus are pointing, as if at something that has caught their eye.

Inside, the church is as polished and sumptuously coloured as its façade is dilapidated and dull. Flanking a fifteenth-century portrait of the Madonna del Carmine, two thick, gilded helical columns are thronged with tiny white figures who seem to be climbing up the spirals towards the roof, while simultaneously involved in dramatic biblical scenes. It would be hard to exaggerate the wonderful detail of this stucco work or the energy it communicates. Every figure is moving or gesturing. Looking around at the saints in the panels of the choir stalls or an apostle's robe flapping beside a pillar, it occurs to me how often the Sicilian baroque creates this bustling interpenetration of crowd and building, as if the congregation were part of the structure, big-bellied gargoyles holding up ledges with angels dancing on top and men and women leaning out from walls and columns to blow trumpets, shoot off arrows or wave their scrolls. The architecture teems. "People came running from the streets" – Beninati finishes his story – "bringing candles and lamps, and all the women were weeping." Despite searching the walls for some time, we can find no plaque to record the murders that day or to celebrate the miracle, just a scrawled graffiti, "CONTRO STATO E POLIZIA" ("Down with State and Police").

Eber, the Hungarian, who was writing up the war for *The Times*, is often infuriated by the excitability and passion of the Sicilians, their loudness, their violence. This was his first visit to the island. But he sees a positive side: "However much theory teaches that a small disciplined force is superior to a disorderly mob, you could easily forget this before the spectacle of a wildly excited crowd transported to a state of mania." So he was pleased that during the truce many officers of the Bourbon army crossed the lines to visit friends or family in the city; they would realize the mob was up for a fight. Eber suspected Garibaldi had made this concession to the Bourbons deliberately.

Bixio shared Eber's aversion to the Sicilians, their rumbustiousness and volatility, which he felt was one with an alarming unreliability: "Bored by the prolonged truce, the *picciotti* are leaving the city in large numbers. Some of the barricades assigned to them are deserted."

Ippolito Nievo, who had been working on the administration with Crispi in Palazzo Pretorio, was similarly scathing: "Sicilian men are all women," he writes to his mother. "They love to make a noise and show off." "All thieves," he writes to his beloved cousin Bice.

Walking down the erstwhile Via Toledo, we were almost run over by a young woman dashing out from between the display stands outside a souvenir shop. A burly man rushed out after her yelling, "*Ladra!*" – "thief!" His white linen shirt was soaked in sweat. "Coward!" He cupped his hands round his mouth to shout louder. "Gypsy! Scum!" The woman – a slim, well-dressed figure – was already lost in the crowd.

Whatever his thoughts about the Sicilians, Garibaldi never complained. His instinct was always to harness whatever energy was around and make it work for the cause: there was no point in provoking hostility with criticism. During the second truce, he finally made a tour of the city – "on horseback, wherever it was possible to get through the rubble," says Abba; "on foot, among the immense crowd," says Eber; "in the evening," says Abba; "in the afternoon," says Eber.

But they agree on the reception he got.

"People knelt before him" – Abba. "They touched his stirrups, kissed his hands."

"People shoved forward" – Eber – "so as to touch the hems of his clothes."

"I saw women lift their babies to him" – Abba – "as if he were a saint."

"It was one of those triumphs" – Eber – "that seem too much for one man."

"We felt lost" – Abba – "in the midst of this endless multitude here to honour us."

"In the midst of this frenzy" – Eber – "the hero was calm and smiling, as when the bullets flew thickest."

Beninati reported to Sirtori that "a commoner" had told him she had seen Bavarian soldiers climbing into the attic of a convent that commanded a view of the barricades hemming in Del Bosco's soldiers. Near Porta Vicari. Garibaldi wanted to see for himself. "As soon as the nuns heard that the General was in the convent" – Beninati – "they came down and surrounded him, trying to kiss his hand." Twenty minutes later, when he came down from an inspection of the roof and the Bavarian positions, "they presented him with a big tray of cakes". Garibaldi didn't want to accept – perhaps they could be sent to the wounded, he suggested. "'Have no doubt, Your Excellency'"

– Beninati quoting the Mother Superior – "'that as well as the cakes we will send conserves and medications and bandages.'"

Eleonora, three of whose aunts on her mother's side are nuns, tells me that in Sicily nuns are famous for making excellent sweets and cakes.

"I've met a certain Sister Agostina" – Nievo – "who makes fantastic prickly-pear cream."

Eating cakes with nuns would soon become a staple of garibaldino lifestyle.

Meantime, other gifts flowed in to support the rebellion. "They're being kept in the entrance hall of the University" – Beninati. "Heavens, how much cotton stuff! How many woollen mattresses. How much wine!"

Priests were preaching in the streets. "The priest of San Giovanni dei Tartari" – Beninati – "with a big crucifix... was exhorting the people to fight, telling them this war was a holy war... I was moved to tears."

Thirty miles away, in Alcamo, the wounded Giuseppe Bandi, hitherto Garibaldi's aide-de-camp, also listened to a revolutionary priest at the funeral of a garibaldino, Crescenzio Baiguera, thirty-seven, who had died from gunshot wounds inflicted at Calatafimi. "The hour for revenge has struck," thundered the priest. "Fight for your country... God demands it!" "I thought I was dreaming," says Bandi, "then wondered: how long will this priestly passion last?" Before the year was out, he decides, "the priests would be cursing Garibaldi and his Thousand and Italy itself."

On 2nd June Bandi was well enough to join a group of seventy-two garibaldini who had landed at Marsala and were bringing 2,000 rifles and ammunition to Palermo. Not so Augusto Elia, whose jaw had been shot away protecting Garibaldi at Calatafimi. Still unable to speak, Elia was being fed through a tube in a private home in the small village of Vita, and still had many months of suffering before him. Bandi travelled to Palermo by carriage; immediately he gives the sort of details one doesn't find in other sources: that the Sicilians guarding the barricades in the city all had images of Santa Rosalia on the butts of their muskets; that foreigners living in Palermo raised the flags of their countries over their doors in the hope this would spare them from sackings and reprisals. At Palazzo Pretorio, he remembers, "before reaching the general, we had to cross three big halls packed with people speaking in loud voices."

"There is a continual back-and-forth of negotiators from both sides" – Eber – "discussing truce violations, suspicions, facts to verify."
"The convoy bringing food to the royal troops" – *Chronicle of Events* – "is constantly hampered by hordes of garibaldini."
"The [Bourbon] soldiers" – Eber – "wouldn't let through a convoy of flour [for the people of Palermo]... since the soldiers had set up a black market to sell what they'd stolen..."
"The Royal Palace" – *Chronicle* – "only has reserves for another two and a half days."
"As a reprisal" – Eber – "the rebels stopped one of the convoys meant for the royal troops."
"The storehouse with forage for the animals" – *Chronicle* – "has fallen into enemy hands."
"The mules of the convoy we intercepted" – Bixio – "were brought over to our side... General Colonna [Bourbon negotiator] must have seen them in the lobby of Palazzo Pretorio."

Certainly it's hard to imagine a huddle of mules when you enter this decorous building today. We're not used to animals in the streets any more, beyond a dog or two, or the well-groomed horses pulling carriages for tourists. But then it's also hard to imagine priests delivering fiery patriotic sermons. When we cross the road from Palazzo Pretorio to poke our noses into San Giuseppe, where the garibaldini slept, there are just a dozen or so people scattered up and down the shadowy nave, listening to the rosary over a P.A. system. Beside the door, a stone angel swoops down the wall to hold up the heavy bowl of a font. A small statue of San Giuseppe is illuminated by a blue neon halo. On the steps of a side chapel a young man kneeling to pray has a skull and crossbones on the back of his denim jacket.

On the ceiling of the church, hence very likely the first thing the garibaldini would have seen on waking, scores of airy saints and martyrs are going through biblical motions on dramatic storm clouds; each busy scene is framed in thick gilt scrolling, which again is largely made up of intertwining bodies. We take seats ourselves to soak up the blissful cool of marble floors and the lofty spaces above. Outside, the temperature is in the mid-thirties again.

"Tüköry – Beninati never spells the name the same way twice – complained to me that Palermo is too hot; but I think it's the heat of the violent fever that's burning him up."

Bandi had arrived at Palazzo Pretorio just hours before the second truce came to an end. As soon as he had fought his way through the three crowded antechambers and was admitted to the general's presence, Garibaldi comes to life again.

"Poor Bandi, you look like a miller."

Stripped naked after the battle of Calatafimi, the young lieutenant had had to borrow civilian clothes. Garibaldi ordered cash to be provided and sent him off to make himself respectable; half an hour later he was back with "a fine red shirt, a new cap and a magnificent silk kerchief with red and yellow flowers loosely knotted round my neck." A doctor had "refreshed" his wounds with new bandages, willing hands had fed him, and, if we are to believe his version of events, the convalescent soldier had barely sat down on the sofa in Garibaldi's office to resume his aide-de-camp role when General Letizia and Colonel Buonopane were announced.

"Only a few minutes to midday," Garibaldi observed. When this second truce was to end.

Letizia and Buonopane had returned from Naples the evening before. "Those two sad soldiers" – Buttà – "gave the king the gloomiest possible description of the royal troops and the most brilliant account of the state of the garibaldini."

It's not clear how Buttà could have known this.

"Filangieri," says De Cesare, describing another long meeting of the king and his councillors, "observed that the Sicilian insurrection had gone beyond the point where it could be subdued by bombardment, and warned the king not to give the order to fire, since this would only arouse the fury of liberal Europe."

"Late in the first watch" – Admiral Mundy, 2nd June – "General Letizia returned from Naples, but the orders which he brought were kept a profound secret."

"Garibaldi" – Bandi – "was sitting on a small armchair with another chair between his legs, on which he had laid several cigars, two or three oranges, an unsheathed dagger and several pieces of paper."

Bandi got up to leave the negotiators alone, but his colleagues at the door pushed him back in the room: "Keep an eye out – there have been death threats."

"General Letizia" – Bandi – "was a handsome man, and in his time must have been a smart young fellow and a favourite with the ladies.

Colonel Buonopane, on the other hand, was... heavy and tubby, at ease with himself, more than ready for a joke and a good laugh."

"As soon as hostilities resume" – these were the secret orders that Colonel Buonopane had handed to General Lanza on his return from Naples – "the troops will be ready to march with their arms – that is, to leave their present positions abandoning everything superfluous and cumbersome."

There follow two pages of meticulous instructions, describing how the troops at the Royal Palace and in Fieravecchia were to fight their way out of the town down to the port and embark on ships for Messina and Naples.

Given the detailed nature of these orders, it's difficult to understand why exactly the two officers had gone to Garibaldi to negotiate. Once again, the need to talk to the enemy revealed their disarray. Had they decided to fight it out, throwing all their explosives and manpower at the city, it was hard to see how they could have lost, or how Palermo could have survived complete destruction. But the king had still not given orders either to bombard or not to bombard. His subordinates were confused. Handling the negotiations entirely alone, Garibaldi was involved in a war of nerves at least as important as his generalship in battle.

"Gentlemen" – Garibaldi according to Bandi – "I'm sorry I can only offer you my second-rate cigars from Nice... But, *à la guerre, comme à la guerre*."

Garibaldi smoked cheroots, which he always cut in half. The Bourbon officials accepted their halves and "were prodigal with compliments".

"We're here" – Letizia – "because it's almost midday..."

"And now" – Garibaldi jumped to his feet – "don't you agree with me that this fratricidal war is as painful for us as it is for you?"

An appeal to their common Italianness.

"Who would deny" – Buonopane – "that no one wants to see these scenes?"

"So" – Garibaldi – "it's up to you."

Garibaldi's own decision not to budge from the city was being presented as a *fait accompli* beyond negotiation; all responsibility for further bloodshed would rest with the Bourbons.

Letizia said he would look favourably on a new armistice, but without a time limit.

"All right," says Garibaldi, and, "picking up his dagger" – Bandi – "he began to peel an orange."

In that case, says Letizia, he personally will depart again at once for Naples to tell the king how things stand and get definitive orders.

"Letizia's words had been more than clear" – Bandi – "but Colonel Buonopane jumped in to offer a lengthy commentary, having us understand that their soldiers were beginning to disobey orders and that the Swiss and even more the Bavarians had become real demons, just about obeying the officers who spoke in their own language, but getting arrogant and threatening with any superiors who spoke to them in Italian."

It seems extraordinary that a high-ranking officer would make an admission like this, but then perhaps they assumed Garibaldi would already be aware of the situation from the accounts he had received from deserters.

"In the time they had been idle in Fieravecchia" – Buttà – "desertions of both soldiers and officials had very much begun."

"To promote desertions among the royal troops" – *Chronicle of Events* – "a poster had been printed in German and French offering forty ducats to anyone deserting with his rifle and thirty for those without a rifle; and if the deserter didn't want to serve Garibaldi free passage to Marseille."

"This morning" – Bixio, 2nd June – "the general told me he knew that a number of Neapolitan warships were eager to come over to our side."

"Buonopane" – Bandi – "wound up by saying that if Garibaldi would agree honourable and discrete conditions... one might hope the truce would lead to... God knows what."

"You won't be surprised to hear" – Eber – "that the local people have a very poor opinion of the good faith of the Neapolitans, and see all these negotiations as an attempt to fool Garibaldi."

"While Colonel Buonopane was speaking" – Bandi – "Garibaldi had peeled his orange and opened it up, and now he stabbed a segment with the tip of his dagger and offered it to Letzia, saying 'For you, general', then another that he offered to Buonopane, saying 'For you, colonel'."

What a wonderfully droll assertion of power: Garibaldi was the one who could carve things up and share them round.

Far from being all in favour of Garibaldi, says the ultra-Bourbon Buttà, "many citizens of every social class... came to our camp in Fieravecchia to protest their devotion to the cause of the present order and the king."

Colonel Buonopane had accepted another piece of orange from Garibaldi's dagger and was reading out a list of truce conditions, when "right then, but really right then" – Bandi – "a long burst of musket fire exploded not far away and rattled the window panes. Letizia and Buonopane jumped to their feet, pale as death."

The hour had struck; it was twelve o'clock. The truce was over.

Garibaldi told Bandi to go and order the shooting to stop, and assured his guests, "you're in the home of a *galantuomo*" – an honourable man.

"These words were spoken as I repeat them," says Bandi. "Certain words you never forget."

Would guns really have started firing exactly at midday, so near to Palazzo Pretorio? Bandi published his book twenty-six years later, after becoming a successful novelist, a man used to telling a good story. And there are other problems with his account. Garibaldi was demanding that the Neapolitans leave the city of Palermo altogether as soon as possible, withdrawing to the plain north of the port, the very place to which, according to the secret orders Buonopane had brought from Naples, the soldiers were supposed to fight their way. Letizia said he would have to go back to Naples to get the king's approval for this. But Bandi claims that the meeting ended with the Bourbons promising to leave at dawn next morning, which was hardly possible. In fact, they didn't leave until 7th June, three days later, after another meeting between Garibaldi, Letizia and Buonopane on 6th June. Also, he writes, "The Bourbon officers had barely left Palazzo Pretorio when there was a loud commotion in the piazza: Nino Bixio had given Agnetta a slap in the face." But we know that that slap also happened on the seventh of June, not the third. The day of Lajos Tükory's funeral.

"This morning" – Beninati – "word got around that the Hungarian, Luigi Tukory, had died; not believing it and wanting to check, I went to Palazzo San Lorenzo; unfortunately it was true. I didn't have the courage to raise the funeral shroud."

"The funeral procession was forming outside San Giuseppe" – Abba – "and Bixio, who was extremely agitated, God knows why, flying into rages over the slightest thing, was organizing it." When Carmelo Agnetta turned up with his men, Bixio wanted to take them over. Agnetta, who had arrived in Palermo only a few days earlier on the steamship *Utile*, didn't know who Bixio was and said no. "It was as if Bixio had been struck by lightning; he let fly a slap across the man's face, and Agnetta went for him: a violent scene, very rapid, broken up at once; the two were separated, one man here, the other there. Garibaldi was furious."

"The coffin had to be carried all the way on shoulders" – Beninati – "because of the difficulty getting over the barricades."

"From the windows" – Abba – "flowers rained down on the coffin, on us – and from the flowers and the laurel leaves came a perfume that gave me an idea of a sweet death."

Afterwards, Garibaldi placed Bixio under house arrest and forbade him and Agnetta from fighting a duel until the war was over. "How will you ever command ten thousand men," he demands of Bixio in Bandi's version, "if you don't know how to command yourself?"

To return then to the meeting between Garibaldi, General Letizia and Colonel Buonopane on 3rd June, it's hard to know how much credence to give to Bandi's description. Perhaps he was mixing it up with another meeting. In any event, according to De Cesare's account, on the morning of 4th June, arriving in Naples after a ten-hour sea crossing, "General Letizia highly praised Garibaldi's manner of speaking and negotiating, and the king listened with curiosity and pleasure almost."

"The courage in battle of my faithful troops under your command," King Francis wrote that day to General Lanza, "deserves my complete approval." However, "the continuation of such acts of prowess... would only lead to further bloodshed... and reduce the city of Palermo to a heap of rubble."

Garibaldi's charisma had somehow travelled with Letizia and Buonopane and affected the young king. On 5th June, Francis sent this Order of the Day to be read to his troops:

The God of armies decides the events of war. Whether favourable or otherwise, the brave will always know how to save their military honour.

In other words, it was understood that Garibaldi would let the Bourbon army leave Palermo peacefully, with their weapons, without surrendering, hence with their honour intact. Along with this Order of the Day there was another letter from the king to Lanza personally, complaining that the first armistice had been unwisely made, since Von Mechel was within sight of taking the city, and that as a result there was now "no alternative but to lead the troops to another place and put them in a position to be useful".

But the real bombshell for Lanza came the following day when Letizia and Buonopane brought him their own joint letter, which the king had clearly agreed on.

> Your Excellency must not tell a living soul that negotiations are under way... the troops must only know that there is a truce to permit the evacuation of the wounded... if you were so ill advised as to betray this secret, the immediate and irreparable desertions would be fatal to our king... a terrible disgrace in the face of all Europe... you must not advance doubts or obstacles... these troops will be needed by the king for other actions on the mainland... we consider ourselves the only and secret arbiters of this extremely delicate and difficult affair... Garibaldi, for his part, will be discreet... Should Your Excellency seek to hinder our negotiations or betray their secrecy... we will immediately depart and never return, leaving Your Excellency entirely responsible for the whole situation.

Departures

That night I woke from a dream and couldn't sleep. I had been in bed in the house I grew up in, an old vicarage in north London, but rain was pouring through the window and roof, streaming down the walls, soaking my pillow and mattress. Running to my mother's room, I found her on the landing, dressed in white, sleeping in a white coffin. The Church, I protested, needed to invest some serious money in maintaining the vicarage, otherwise it would fall down around our ears. She replied that the Church had lost interest years ago: "We're on our own."

Waking, I sniffed the air for rain, but it was another warm, dry night in Palermo. Which reminded me I hadn't watered the landlady's plants. I climbed the stairs to the roof terrace, uncoiled the hose, opened the tap and began to soak geraniums and oleanders. There was a honeyed smell of water on dry earth, and a soothing sound of splashing in the quiet of the early hours. I realized the dream had put me in a good mood: just the crazy panache of dreams, sticking dear mum in a white coffin and washing away my protestant childhood in a shower of rain.

What did the garibaldini dream, I wondered? Or the *picciotti*? Or the Bourbon soldiers? In all the diaries and archives I've read and reread the only mention of dreaming is Bandi's account of his feverish nightmares after being wounded at Calatafimi: "The executioner with his axe, King Bomba [Ferdinand II] with flames in his hands, gaunt horses, furious dogs, skeletons and demons." Otherwise, there's not a single mention of a dream in literally thousands of pages. Perhaps the men were so exhausted they slept the sleep of the blessed, or so anxious they lay awake at night wondering whether the time hadn't perhaps come to desert, and how that would play out with their families, their futures: men stretched under palm trees outside the Royal Palace, asking: "Am I a Neapolitan or an Italian? Is this old house I grew up in doomed to be swept away, or will it weather the storm? And do I make my decision out of conviction or for convenience?" Which again reminds me that soon after we return to Milan I have my swearing-in ceremony to become an Italian citizen. Not exactly a desertion, since dual citizenship is possible, but nevertheless an important shift in who I am.

Or perhaps these men did dream – I coil up the hosepipe – but dreams were hardly worth mentioning when reality was so extraordinary as to seem dreamlike. Seen from distant mountains, wrote Nievo, Palermo was an "incredible dream". "Everything that's happened these last few days seems a dream" – thinks Beninati – "a real miracle of Santa Rosalia." Of the departure of the Bourbons on 7th June, "a neverending column of infantry, cavalry, carts", Abba says, "to us it seems a dream, but to them…" Well, a nightmare.

The soldiers would have passed close by our apartment here, since they went round the city to the north, outside the old walls and gates, rather than down Via Toledo through the centre. Leaning over the parapet, between a cactus and a jasmine bush, I can see the road they would have marched along. It's just a string of street lamps now, moths and mosquitoes fizzing in halos of light, the occasional flitting of a bat, three or four cats nosing at the rubbish beside a line of bins.

But what if things had ended differently? I lie back on the swing chair to consider. The premise that gradually took over the truce negotiations was that Palermo would be spared so that rebels and royals could fight it out elsewhere. Garibaldi had encouraged this idea, having little ammunition and no doubt sensing that the withdrawal of the Bourbons would give the impression of a major victory, and hence swell the tide that was running his way. So he readily agreed that the Bourbon soldiers could keep their arms and their honour and wouldn't be harried as they abandoned their strong positions to head for the port and board ship. Agreeing to keep these details secret cost him nothing, since it would be obvious to everyone there had been a negotiated arrangement. For their part, the Bourbons had lost Palermo in 1848 and promptly won it back – why couldn't that happen again? Certainly Admiral Mundy thought this was the most likely outcome: "The invaders were a handful of undisciplined men, and were opposed by a powerful and well-organized host. The success of the revolutionists… was impossible."

Six weeks later the two forces joined battle at Milazzo, a narrow peninsula on the north coast of Sicily, a hundred and thirty miles east of Palermo and twenty-five miles west of Messina. The peninsula, about four miles long and less than half a mile wide, was dominated by an apparently impregnable fortress. Neither side had planned the engagement. Major Del Bosco had been sent from Messina with 3,000 men to reinforce the Milazzo garrison, where a thousand soldiers were based. Behind him in Messina were another 18,000 royal troops. On the rebel side, Giacomo Medici, who had arrived in Palermo from Genoa in late June, had been sent on an exploratory expedition along the north coast; Medici had been fighting with Garibaldi one way or another since the two were together in Uruguay in the 1840s.

Initial skirmishes occurred on 16th and 17th July as Medici tried to seal the Bourbons inside the peninsula and Del Bosco tried to keep his supply route to Messina open. Both commanders called for reinforcements. In Messina, General Clary hesitated: like other Bourbon commanders he seemed anxious to delay a showdown until absolutely certain of victory. Garibaldi didn't think twice: he committed all available resources and set off to Milazzo himself, at once, by ship. "We had to win," he repeats over and over in his memoir.

On 20th July almost 6,000 garibaldini, mostly volunteers freshly arrived from the north, took on around 4,500 Bourbons, well equipped with cavalry and cannons and occupying strong defensive positions at the base of the peninsula. For more than eight hours the battle hung in the balance. Both Del Bosco and Garibaldi joined the fighting personally, Garibaldi narrowly escaping death from a cavalryman's sabre. Eventually, the arrival of the newly named *Tukory*, an ex-Neapolitan warship that had come over to the rebel cause, broke the deadlock, training its cannons on the Bourbon flank. Del Bosco retreated to the fortress, where he was surrounded, trapped and eventually obliged to surrender. "But victory was bought at a high price," remembers Garibaldi. "The number of our dead and wounded far exceeded the enemy's." Almost 800 garibaldini were lost, compared with 150 Bourbons. Days later, General Clary withdrew the royal troops from Messina, leaving Sicily entirely in rebel hands.

But let's imagine, I tell myself, rocking on the swing chair in the balmy Palermo night, that Garibaldi is killed by that Bourbon cavalryman, that the *Tukory* does not arrive in time, that General Clary sends substantial reinforcements – soldiers, artillery, warships – and that the royal troops carry the day, then march directly on an undefended Palermo. In a matter of days the rebellion is over. Bourbon power is reasserted. At this point the earlier decision to abandon

Palermo begins to seem wise: thanks to Letizia and Buonopane the city was spared further destruction, and meantime the decisive battle has been fought in conditions more favourable to a regular army, just as the elderly General Filangieri had always advised. Now Garibaldi can be criticized for not taking on the royal troops when he had the advantage of narrow city streets, an inflamed populace and an evident loss of nerve on the part of General Lanza; he should never have let his enemy march away uncontested.

On the other hand, if Garibaldi had more than five thousand men, all armed with decent rifles, albeit without cannons or cavalry, to commit to Milazzo, as well as two columns exploring the interior of the island under Bixio and Türr, it was because the retreat of the Bourbons from Palermo had brought a huge boost of morale for the revolution and opened the floodgates for the arrival of new recruits from all over Italy and abroad. Not to mention turning the trickle of Bourbon desertions into a flood.

It's pleasant relaxing in the mild night air, looking out across the rooftops to the dark line of the mountains above Monreale. One of the rewards for reading an awful lot about the same subject is that you have so much material for idle speculation. What if the king had granted a generous constitution in April, before Garibaldi arrived, instead of late June, after Palermo was already lost? What if a foreign power had come to his aid? France perhaps. Can we really imagine Italy today split into two nations, a southern and a northern? What would have happened in the First and Second World Wars?

But now, from alarmingly close by, comes the shrill sharp cry of the *civetta*, the small owl. It must be on the roof of the church across the street. Suddenly the air feels cooler. It's impossible to know how a complex situation will turn out – that's surely the truth of the matter. One plays one's hand and hopes for the best. The scandal of the Bourbon generals was that they held on to their strongest cards until the game was all but lost. "If you don't want to call them traitors" – Buttà for a moment puts aside his conspiracy theories – "call them cowardly and inept." And he adds, "Events in Palermo had deprived this government of the moral strength necessary to rule a people." He never wonders whether the dithering, desertions and general lack of cohesion didn't indicate there was something irretrievably rotten in the Kingdom of the Two Sicilies.

Returning to bed, I'm aware of our trekking clothes, trekking poles and trekking shoes laid out beside our backpacks near the front door. We're leaving early tomorrow. "I wear a red coat these days," writes Nievo to his cousin Bice on 24th June. "That makes me look like a Napoleonic general… But I keep my old rags in a room in memory of past miseries." His old rags were the civilian clothes he had worn, without a change, for the twenty-two days from Quarto to Palermo. For sure, our own moment of drama on the road from Marsala to Salemi – the heat, the thirst and the generous man who brought the bottle of cold water – seems a long way off now. Lying down to sleep, my mind is already moving on to all the things I'll have to do when I get home.

The end of the conflict in Palermo was hammered out between Garibaldi, Letizia and Buonopane on 3rd and 6th June. The troops began to move out of the city the morning of the 7th. What are we passing over in between? Antonio Mosto, commander of the Genoese Carabinieri, goes back to Parco, where his younger brother Carlo went missing in action on 24th May, finds the twenty-three-year-old lying where he had fallen, ten days dead in the burning heat, digs a hole and buries him on the spot. Several burnt-out palazzi on the Via Toledo collapse, crushing passers-by. La Masa complains to Garibaldi that Crispi is using his administrative power to put out an official version of the war that excludes him and his *picciotti* from the narrative. The famous statue known as the Genio of Palermo is retrieved from Santa Maria dello Spasimo and replaced in Piazza Fieravecchia; within hours, amid wild rejoicings, a Bourbon policeman is captured and killed beneath it, as if sacrificed to a deity. Beninati is appalled. Giulia de Beaumont confides to her diary her "surprise and fear" on hearing that the Bourbon troops will be camping around her house as they wait to be embarked for Naples: "It was not something we could sleep soundly with." Garibaldi is disgusted when he finds that none of the thirteen garibaldini captured at Parco and returned in a prisoner swap had been wounded – they'd simply given themselves up. "I'd have no regrets," he tells them in Bandi's version, "if the enemy had killed every last one of you." Going to Palazzo Pretorio to discuss truce details, Major Del Bosco is overwhelmed by the mob, and has to be defended by garibaldini with drawn swords. Crispi issues a decree announcing that "The children of those who die defending the national cause... will be schooled and fed at the expense of the state: girls to the age of sixteen; boys to the age of seventeen." Two newspapers, *The Official Newspaper of the Provisional Government of Sicily* and *Italian Unity* "are now being hawked in every street," writes Eber, "alongside the men selling tuna." The garibaldini are "filled with joy" – Capuzzi – when in a major speech Garibaldi tells them they will form the nucleus of a national army, "called to other battles and other glories". Bixio visits the wounded garibaldino Stefano Canzio and takes notes from the terrace of his host's house on the "military material" that the Neapolitans are moving from Castellammare to their ships in the harbour. In Naples, observes Raffaele de Cesare, "a curious metamorphosis is taking place: the once-hardline royalists have all become constitutionalists, while the erstwhile liberals have all pronounced in favour of a united Italy." Three Piedmontese warships arrive in Palermo, one bringing Cavour's envoy and Garibaldi's enemy, Giuseppe La Farina, who has orders to arrange for the immediate annexation of Sicily to Piedmont, while hopefully deterring Garibaldi from crossing to the Italian mainland. Musical bands flock into the city from the outlying villages, "kicking up a din", complains Bixio. Menotti Garibaldi, the general's son, joins in the street dancing. "You can see the happiness on everyone's faces," says Beninati, "except those poor people who've lost their homes and loved ones. They are many." "Between two and three thousand men were killed and wounded during the four days' struggle," reports Admiral Mundy, "and as many more are lying sick at the hospitals from exposure and want of nourishment." The day before, he reported, "theatrical entertainments on board HMS *Hannibal*, performed by the ship's company, and dancing till midnight."

We leave our flat at 7 a.m., following, as far as I have been able to work out, the route the troops must have taken from the Royal Palace round the north of the town to Porta Maqueda, where the Teatro Massimo now dominates, our packs on our backs. Fortunately, this is the same direction as for the airport. As ever, the sun is bright. "Sicily was never cheered by a sun more radiant than on that day," remembers Zasio. "The Royal Palace and gardens were packed with soldiers in tight columns" – Bixio – "while we formed a thin line around them." "When ten or twelve of us" – Nievo – "were present to watch the evacuation of the Royal Palace, we thought we were having hallucinations."

Nievo puts the number of the royal troops at fifteen thousand, "with cavalry, artillery and devilish quantities of equipment". Bixio at twenty-two thousand. Buttà at twenty-four thousand. Giulia de Beaumont at thirty-three thousand, "with prodigious artillery and thousands of cartloads of stuff". For Eber there were about thirteen or fourteen thousand, "with many women and children on the luggage carts".

On the corner of Via Papireto and Via Cappuccinelle someone has dumped a queen-sized mattress. Months ago, by the looks of it. A melancholy Arab song drifts among the laundry hung out in the narrow Via della Speranza. A woman places something in a basket lowered from a balcony. Then the scene changes as we reach the huge Palace of Justice, the city's courtrooms. Designed in Fascist times but not completed until the 1950s, this building is a good two hundred yards long. Relentlessly rectangular and symmetrical, it radiates grim, grey state power. To one side, the recently developed Piazza della Memoria, a sort of outdoor mausoleum, ascetic and anonymous, has the names of the magistrates killed by the mafia written in large black letters on broad concrete steps Giovanni Falcone and Paolo Borsellino are prominent, but there are many names I've never heard of. Perhaps thanks to centuries of being governed from afar, there are elements of Sicilian society that have always resisted state authority, arranging themselves in secret associations of one kind or another. Garibaldi had no doubt benefited from these forces in the first phase of his campaign; soon they would be his enemies ("to the point," writes Nievo "that we now have to play policeman with yesterday's allies!"). Looking about us, it's striking that there are no statues around the Palace of Justice – perhaps there was the fear that anything human would be dwarfed by its monolithic scale. In any event, we're glad to get beyond it into the busy morning traffic outside Porta Carini, where market stands are already piled high with oranges and persimmons.

"At every street corner" – Eber – "a party of garibaldini held back the crowd and gave a military salute to the passing troops."

"The retreating column included many top police officers" – Beninati – "and the people greeted them with a barrage of whistles."

Oddly, none of the sources I've read reflects on the scale of the operation involved here: making sure that all the roads along the route were sealed off and that there was no contact between the people and the retreating troops – above all, that no one started shooting.

Needless to say, Bixio was fretting: "Our first battalion only has 130 rifles, and our second 260. All the rest have been sold or stolen! So much for the discipline of the soldiers before whom eighteen to twenty thousand royal troops are retreating!"

Buttà was in denial: "The people were amazed to see our numerous, flourishing army shamefully abandoning a town it had conquered."

Nievo was scornful: "They left with their ears down and their tails between their legs."

Abba more thoughtful: "If they marched without pride, they did not seem crestfallen. The soldiers had fought."

"We marched with heads high and military dash," Buttà insists.

From his ship, Admiral Mundy could see Von Mechel's men marching along the waterfront, and his royalist sentiments rebelled: "It was one of the most humiliating spectacles that could have been witnessed, and I turned from it with disgust." In particular, Mundy was convinced that Garibaldi was doing everything possible to humble the Neapolitans: "At the entrance of the Toledo, the son of Garibaldi, mounted on a black charger, with a dozen red-shirted youths near him, took up a position in front of the principal barricade... doubtless the Dictator placed his firstborn in that marked locality in order that the vanquished hosts of disciplined men might defile before him, and their degradation if possible be made more apparent."

This seems to me quite wrong. Garibaldi's strategy was always to seduce the Neapolitans to the Risorgimento cause, not to humiliate them. Very likely he hoped the retreating men would want to don a red shirt themselves.

We stop for coffee at a corner of Piazza Verdi, opposite the big theatre and opera house. This is where the old Porta Maqueda used to be, and it was here that Garibaldi had sent his second in command, István Türr, and other chief officers, to greet General Lanza before he turned his column away from the city into the flat land by the sea. Again, as at every street corner, there was a full military salute. "General Lanza" – Eber – "seemed to appreciate this act of courtesy and saluted the garibaldini officers graciously."

What the Bourbons most resented, as Buttà has it, was retreating before men who weren't even real soldiers. "Do we have to surrender to those tramps?" he reports one officer protesting, and he himself mocks the "clownish appearance of the garibaldini". One moment he imagines them financed by Britain and Piedmont, if not themselves Piedmontese soldiers in disguise, the next they are so poorly kitted out and so slovenly in demeanour that it was humiliating to defer to them. "And yet," Buttà concedes, "if someone dared insult us, a single scornful gesture from the garibaldini accompanying us was enough to instil respect."

"Before the troops left the Royal Palace" – Buttà continues – "Lanza mounted his horse, the first time he'd done so since he'd arrived in Palermo." We remember that the general was seventy-two and seriously overweight. At the old city gate, somewhere in the middle of the present piazza, perhaps right where we're sitting, he and Türr went briefly over the agreed locations where the Bourbons were to camp until they could board ship. As a last guarantee of their security, Lanza was holding back seven key political prisoners, leading figures in Palermo, who would only be handed over when the final ship left.

We pay our bill and set off to follow them, at least the first mile or so, heading north along Maqueda.

"They appeared to withdraw in perfect order," writes Eber. "Indeed, it was as they withdrew that they appeared most formidable."

It's interesting that in the diaries of royalists, Buttà and Mundy for example, the idea of military discipline – the smart blue uniforms, the white criss-cross shoulder straps, shiny weapons and orderly marching – is taken as a token of moral superiority: a well-drilled, well-equipped army has a right to victory, at least when fighting tramps. Which is why, despite their radically different backgrounds and temperaments, both men show a certain bewilderment at the Bourbons' defeat. "It did seem rather a miracle," Eber concedes, watching the cavalry clatter by. "Nobody could believe it," chimes in Giulia de Beaumont, "yet we saw it with our own eyes." However, after a long analysis of Bourbon recruiting difficulties – the notorious ignorance of the peasant classes in Calabria and Campania and the liberal sentiments of the educated middle class – Eber concludes that, yes, "it was certainly pretty to look at, this Neapolitan army... it was held together in perfect order... only one small thing was lacking: a spirit."

Whatever the case, the Bourbon retreat proved a triumph of discipline on both sides of the divide: tens of thousands of men marched out of a city that they had bombed and shelled and sacked for days, causing thousands of deaths, without a single serious incident.

"The staff officers" – *Chronicle of Events* – "establish the appropriate outposts to guard against the enemy and assign buildings in which to place the battalions on a rota basis, since there isn't space inside for everyone."

It must have been the worst possible situation for Bourbon morale, to be stuck roughing it out in the fields, an area suggestively known as the Quattro Venti – the "Four Winds" – while the enemy rejoiced.

"Huge crowd celebrating on the beach" – Zasio – "singing patriotic songs and raising deafening cheers."

"Many foreign and Neapolitan soldiers deserted from the Quattro Venti camp" – Buttà – "Even a few army surgeons deserted and two military chaplains whom I shall not name."

"Shops have started opening" – Beninati – "the prices of wine and olive oil have fallen... Our urchins have learned Garibaldi's hymn."

Sent to Monreale to collect the families of soldiers who wished to sail with the troops, Buttà was finally bound to admit that the local people really were happy to see the Bourbons leave: "Everything was noise and orgies here; the acme of frenzy. Everyone embracing, in disorderly joy, shouting, 'We are free Italians.'" But Buttà was not in danger of changing his mind about the nature of the revolution: "Oh, the falseness of human discernment!" he comments. "Oh fatal illusions!"

The airport is officially called Falcone e Borsellino, though people refer to it simply as Palermo airport, or Punta Raisi, the promontory it is built on. On board, I'm lucky enough to have a window seat. The plane taxis east with the rugged chiaroscuro of the mountains above Cinisi to the right, then turns around to take off to the west. Looking behind I can make out Partinico, a pinkish stain under the dark slopes of the mountain that we climbed two weeks ago. And Alcamo too, which seems a mere stone's throw away. One imagines how excited Garibaldi would have been to have had this opportunity to study the landscape. Beneath us, the sea offers different intensities of blue in the blazing light. Not a ship is to be seen. One looks in vain for a glimpse of the Golden Bowl and Palermo itself, hidden behind Monte Pellegrino. In a few minutes the island is lost in a vast Mediterranean haze; we won't make landfall until we reach the coast of Liguria, whence the Thousand set out to assist the Sicilian revolution one hundred and sixty-one years ago.

"In a certain sense," Buttà consoled himself, "it was a pleasure in that camp to see so many generals who in peace time had been arrogant and haughty, bragging and swaggering, as if they could destroy all the armies of Europe with a mere flourish of their swords, now so humiliated, so despondent and crestfallen as to provoke, well, I'm not sure whether scorn or pity."

Born in Naso in the north of Sicily in 1826, Giuseppe Buttà stuck with Major Del Bosco's battalion right through the coming war, until the final capitulation after the long siege of Gaeta, sixty miles north of Naples, in February 1861. Briefly imprisoned and forced into exile in Rome, Buttà eventually returned to Naples, where he made his name as a writer of declaredly pro-Bourbon, anti-Risorgimento historical accounts. They were not censored and Buttà lived freely in the new Italy he loathed until his death in 1886.

"This is the first day," wrote Beninati on 19th June, when the last Bourbon troops sailed out of harbour and the seven political prisoners were finally released, "that one can shout without fear of being hit by a bullet or blown up by a bomb. The joy is on everyone's faces, everyone embracing each other. Right now all social classes have ceased to exist: we are all brothers, preparing flowers to throw over the liberated prisoners." It would be good to offer a word of biography on Antonio Beninati, but it seems we know no more about him than the brief description attached to his diary: "Notes jotted in pencil by Signor Beninati, old and modest patriot."

"The prisoners Baron Biso, Prince Giardinetti, Duke San Giovanni, Prince Niscemi, Father Ottavio, Filippino Prince of Monteleone and Duke Ceserò are standing in the middle of the troops," wrote Giulia de Beaumont the same day, getting the names wrong: it was Baron Riso, not Biso; Duke Notarbartolo of San Giovanni; and the Duke of Cesarò, not Duke Ceserò. But then she had only been staying in Palermo for a couple of months. "The sight of them moved us to tears, when they, pale with their sufferings and imprisonment, arrived under our windows and greeted us, being all acquaintances of ours." Still only eighteen, Giulia stayed in Palermo long enough to give detailed accounts of wild rejoicings, before returning at the end of July to Vicenza, where she assisted her husband Paolo Lioy with his many scientific publications and gave birth to two children. She died in 1900, aged fifty-eight.

On 20th June 1860, the very day after the Bourbons left, Giuseppe Capuzzi published his diary, *Memories of a Volunteer*. An instant book. "I promise to publish the sequel," he wrote "when the Naples campaign is over, unless of course it is written in the stars that I must seal my political faith with my blood." Capuzzi fought to the end of the campaign, served again in 1866 in the war against Austria, was involved in a duel with a colonel, and became editor of the local newspaper in Brescia. But he did not write the sequel. He died in 1891, aged sixty-five.

While other diarists moved on with Garibaldi to the conquest of Calabria and Campania, Ippolito Nievo stayed behind in Palermo to administer the revolutionary government's finances. "I'm half a Palermitano," he writes to his dear, alas married cousin Bice, on 11th September 1860. "People address me as 'Don' and I sip soft drinks and granitas as if I were born on Via Toledo or Maqueda." He also mentions "ice creams big as beefsteaks". On 4th March 1861, instructed to take the governments' accounts to Naples, he boarded the steamship *Ercole*, which sank in a storm that same night. There were no survivors. Nievo was twenty-nine. In 1866, when Bice was dying of tuberculosis, she asked to be buried in Ippolito's old red shirt. In 1867 his huge novel, *Confessions of an Italian*, a rich picaresque tale of patriotism and thwarted love, was finally published and eventually recognized as one of the greatest Italian novels. "There are rights," Nievo's hero reflects, "that can only be called such if you deserve them; freedom is not something you ask for, but something you take."

Fully recovered from his wounds, Giuseppe Bandi commanded a battalion at Milazzo. "Our victory there," he wrote years later, "still seems miraculous, but I have to say that right then it simply bewildered me. I was in Milazzo saying to myself, 'But how the devil did we get in here?'" Bandi fought with Garibaldi throughout the coming campaign, and again in 1866 against the Austrians at Custoza, where he was captured and taken to Croatia for internment. A novelist and increasingly right-wing polemicist, editor of two local newspapers in Livorno, he was stabbed to death by the anarchist Oreste Lucchesi on 1st July, 1894, just two weeks before he would have turned sixty.

"After the taking of Palermo," wrote Augusto Elia, captain of the *Lombardo*, wounded at Calatafimi, "when Garibaldi heard that news of my death was false, he sent his son Menotti to Vita with orders to bring me to Palermo... and when Count Cavour heard of my wound, he kindly sent the expert dentist Commander Oddo, of the House of the Prince of Carignano, to take care of my mouth." Three years later Elia would at last regain the ability to speak, and three years after that he was fighting with Garibaldi again in the war against the Austrians, and then again in 1867 against the French at the disastrous battle of Mentana. For twenty years he served as a member of the Italian parliament for his home town of Ancona, before dying in 1919, aged eighty-nine.

"Suspicious of the proposal that he delay his entry into Naples," writes Emilio Zasio on 6th September 1860, "a rather irate Garibaldi got to his feet and said: 'Let's go there now.' A telegram was sent for horses and to book the train. We left at eleven in the morning, and after long stops caused by the impetuous cheering crowd we arrived in Naples towards 1 p.m. A simply immense crowd had gathered there, yelling hurrahs at the top of their voices... Swaying handkerchiefs and hats, palm fronds and raised arms, frenzy and deafening shouts, and weeping – everything contributed to make this a new spectacle in the history of popular triumphs." One of only five men who accompanied Garibaldi in his daring entry into Naples, Zasio joined the regular Italian army in 1861, fighting first the brigands in the south, then the Austrians in the north. "Imaginative, impetuous, rash in love and ambition," says Abba, Zasio died after a brief illness aged thirty-eight, "the sparkle of his mind already extinguished."

"I (and I say it with calm and my head held high) hadn't given the slightest pretext to criticism of my activities," wrote Giuseppe La Masa. "It is only because fortune granted me the honour to further the liberation of my country more than any other that those who wished to discredit me were obliged to resort to calumny." No sooner was Palermo occupied than La Masa fell out with Crispi and Sirtori, convinced that there was a conspiracy against both him and the Sicilian people in general, though of course Crispi was Sicilian. He did not follow Garibaldi to Calabria and Naples. A member of the Italian Parliament throughout the 1860s, much of his energy was spent trying to establish a commission that would assess the facts of the Sicilian revolution and affirm his role in it. Struck by blindness, he withdrew from public life and died in 1881, aged sixty-one.

"Ten or twelve days ago," wrote Cesare Abba on 14th September 1860, "when I saw Naples from the harbour, I would have dived from the deck of the *Carmel* to swim there alone. Now that I'm here, though... well, it is huge, immense, so various as to leave you disoriented and so ostentatious as to be making a show of its poverty. I have never seen filth on display like this before." Giuseppe Cesare Abba fought the whole of the campaign of the Thousand through to the decisive Battle of the Volturno in October 1860. He fought again with Garibaldi against the Austrians in 1866, before settling down in Brescia as a writer and schoolteacher, dying in 1910 at the age of seventy-two. Wherever he went, Abba noticed women: "On the bridge of the *Carmel*," he remembers of that sea passage to Naples, "the ladies create an atmosphere of springtime. Two very beautiful young girls from Catania seem the stuff dreams are made of."

"I saw the burnt and mutilated corpses, their hearts torn out," Nino Bixio told the Italian parliament in 1863. Placed in charge of a column of men whose job was to cross Sicily and make the new government's presence felt, quelling the score-settling and violence that followed the Bourbon withdrawal, Bixio arrived in the village of Bronte on the western slopes of Etna on 6th August 1860. That was just two days after seventeen people, mostly interrelated members of the local elite, had been tortured and killed in a feud between opposing factions over the allocation of land expropriated from local landlords, in particular the descendants of Lord Nelson, who had been granted the most extensive estates in the area. "I had to have six people shot," Bixio wrote to a friend, "and these things are a torment to my soul." In fact, he only had five people shot, after a summary trial, though at least three of these were falsely accused. Praised for his severity at the time, all too soon the event would be seized on as proof that nothing had changed, and the new regime, by supporting the landowners, was no better than the old. Two weeks after the executions in Bronte, Bixio led the assault on Reggio Calabria, where he took a bullet wound in the hand, but in early September he was again in trouble when in a fit of rage he cracked the skull of a man who had disobeyed an order. Asked by various officers to punish him accordingly, Garibaldi remarked, "Find me another Nino Bixio and I will have this one shot at once." At the decisive Battle of the Volturno the general's leniency was rewarded: when the Bourbons breached the garibaldini's lines and seemed on the brink of victory, Bixio organized and led the counterattack, collecting yet another wound. In 1861 he fought a duel with Carmelo Agnetta, whom he had slapped in Palermo, and was maimed in one hand. "Punished in the hand that sinned," he observed, and the two became friends. Taking a seat in the parliament of the newly united nation, Bixio sought to establish a middle ground between left and right, but did little more than antagonize his old friends. In 1870 he was the only one of the garibaldini to be asked to take part in the assault on Rome that completed the unification of the country. But politics bored him, and he had money problems now. He built a ship, and in 1873 set off to the Orient with a cargo of coal. Contracting yellow fever in October, he died on board in December and was buried on a small island off the Vietnamese coast. He was fifty-two.

"I don't know," wrote Francesco Crispi in 1884, "how Europe will be governed fifty years hence. Meantime, I believe and am profoundly convinced that there will be no place at all for the divine right of kings. What great states can achieve as republics we can see from the example of France, but to give a nation lasting peace there is only one solution, the one Garibaldi arrived at: a king at the head of a democracy." Crispi was the administrative mind beside Garibaldi throughout the campaign of 1860. Surviving accusations of bigamy when he abandoned Rose Montmasson, nurse at Calatafimi and Milazzo, to marry the more aristocratic Lina Barbagallo, in the 1880s and '90s Crispi would be prime minister of Italy for some seven years. Among many other reforms, he abolished the death penalty and extended the vote to all literate males – but he also favoured colonial adventures in Libya and Ethiopia that would have dismayed Garibaldi. Italy's humiliating defeat against the Ethiopians at Adua in 1896 put an end to his long and checkered career. He died in 1901, aged eighty-two.

"Having reached the Strait, we had to cross it" – Garibaldi – "and cross it despite the extreme vigilance of the Bourbons", who had

80,000 soldiers on the mainland. Garibaldi organized for two ships to sail from Sardinia right around Sicily's west coast, meet him south of Taormina, far away from the Strait, and cross to Melito di Porto Salvo, on the very tip of Calabria. That was the night of 18th August. The Bourbon army continued to shy away from a decisive engagement. On 7th September Garibaldi entered Naples, 320 miles to the north. The king had fled to Gaeta, a further sixty miles up the coast. But the Bourbon army was still more or less intact, and at last launched a major counterattack. The two forces met on 1st October just to the south of the river Volturno, which runs from the east to the Tyrrhenian sea: 28,000 Bourbons, 22,000 garibaldini. Like Milazzo, it was a battle that hung long in the balance. "Our line was poor" – Garibaldi – "too irregular, too long." The front extended for about twelve miles. Fortunately for the general, the Bourbons attacked along the whole line. "Had they concentrated all their forces on one point," he confessed, "I have no doubt they could have been in Naples the same day with very few losses." But with the decisive contribution of Bixio the line held, the attack was repulsed, and King Francis's fate was sealed.

On 26th October Garibaldi met King Victor Emmanuel II, whose forces had marched down from the north, capturing the Papal State, though not Rome, thus thwarting any attempt by Garibaldi to take the Holy City itself: it was to be left with some surrounding territory as an independent Catholic state. Both men were on horseback, their armies behind them.

"The king held out his hand," wrote diarist Alberto Mario. "Garibaldi lifted his hat, under which he wore a silk scarf, tied under his chin, against the morning chill. 'How do you do, my dear Garibaldi,' says the king. 'Well, Your Majesty,' says Garibaldi. 'And you?' 'Fine,' says the king.'"

In his memoir Garibaldi merely remarks, "I placed the dictatorship conferred on me by the people in his hands, proclaiming him king of Italy."

Soon enough the two men separated, the king to eat a banquet in the small town of Teano, Garibaldi to "sit on a bench in a farmhouse, a couple of paces from the tail of his horse... where he ate a slice of cheese and a roll of bread". The thirty thousand garibaldini who had captured the whole of southern Italy were largely ignored. The king never inspected them, never addressed them, never wrote a message for them. "The idea was," wrote Garibaldi, "to enjoy the fruits of conquest, but to get rid of the conquerors." Having rejected the king's offers of a noble title, a generalship in the army, a castle and a ship, on 9th November at six in the morning, the former "dictator" had himself rowed out to HMS *Hannibal* in the bay of Naples to pay an unexpected farewell visit to Admiral Mundy, who was obliged to jump from his bed "hastily throwing on a few garments". Garibaldi invited the admiral to come and visit him in his cottage on the tiny island of Caprera. Then the two argued about politics. "No person of moderate observation," Mundy reported, "could be engaged even in a short conversation with this remarkable man without being struck with the clear, silvery tone of his voice." From HMS *Hannibal* Garibaldi went on to the American warship *Washington*, which was to take him to the almost uninhabited Caprera. With him he brought a few packs of coffee and sugar, a sack of beans, a sack of seeds and a barrel of dry herring.

It was never likely he would stay put for long. Elected to the nation's new parliament, in 1861 he turned up in red shirt and poncho to accuse Cavour of treating the garibaldini with contempt and planning a "fratricidal war". The prime minister had indeed explained to the French that Piedmont was invading the Papal States in order "to oppose the revolution personified by Garibaldi". Thus denounced in parliament, the excitable Cavour was helpless with rage and had to be taken outside while the sitting was suspended. Not two months later, aged fifty, he died from a recurrent intestinal illness.

Garibaldi was now both a national treasure and an embarrassing problem. Returning to his island home, he obsessively plotted irregular military operations to claim Rome and the Veneto for Italy, the one protected by France, the other still part of the Austro-Hungarian Empire; they were not powers with which the newly formed Italy wished to find itself at war. "Towering from the rocks of Caprera, the giant figure of Garibaldi casts his vast shadow as far as Paris," warned Costantino Nigra, Italy's ambassador to France.

In the summer of 1862 Garibaldi crossed from Sicily to Calabria with 2,000 volunteers intending to march north to Rome. Pressed by Napoleon III, the Italian army intervened, eventually tracking down the garibaldini in the hills of Aspromonte. Garibaldi ordered his men not to fire, but a skirmish was inevitable. Almost at once he himself was wounded with a bullet in the ankle that would cause him unspeakable pain for months to come. Imprisoned in the fortress of Varignano, near La Spezia, he was examined by celebrated surgeons from England,

France and Russia, until the bullet was finally extracted in October. It would be another year, spent almost entirely on Caprera, before he could walk without crutches.

Suffering and imprisonment only enhanced the hero's reputation in liberal Europe. Invited to London in 1864, he was met by a wildly enthusiastic crowd of half a million well-wishers. There were meetings with Palmerston, Gladstone and Florence Nightingale, and a moving reconciliation with Mazzini, who had both inspired Garibaldi's patriotism and opposed his readiness to work with the monarchy.

In 1866 Italy took advantage of the Austro-Prussian conflict to declare war on Austria in the hope of seizing the Veneto. Once again, a rehabilitated Garibaldi was given command of an army of volunteers, but, as in 1859, he was sent off to fight in the mountains of Trentino, not on the crucial battlefields of the north Italian plain. Making a virtue of necessity, he led his poorly equipped men to the only Italian victory of the war, and was preparing to march on Trento when, after the official army's costly defeat at Custoza, south of Lake Garda, the Italians sued for peace. Ordered to retreat, Garibaldi sent the famously laconic response: "Obbedisco" – "I obey". The Austrians, meantime, comprehensively beaten by the Prussians and aware that it had become impossible to hold on to the Veneto, ceded the territory to France, who then handed it to Italy. For the Italian government and King Vittorio Emanuele the outcome could hardly have been more humiliating. But Garibaldi's reputation was enhanced.

In February 1867 the hero had a daughter by the eighteen-year-old Francesca Armosino, illiterate wet nurse to his grandchildren. He was fifty-nine. Two more children would be born in 1869 and 1873, and the couple would eventually marry. But there was no question of Garibaldi abandoning his Risorgimento aspirations. In October 1867 he once again brought together a volunteer army in the hope of taking Rome and its now much reduced papal territories. As with Sicily in 1860, the move was prompted by a number of local rebellions suggesting the people might rise up. But it was not to be. The papal police crushed the attempted revolution in Rome, while a French expeditionary force equipped with new self-loading rifles routed the garibaldini at Mentana, some fifteen miles northeast of the holy city. Once again Garibaldi was confined to the fortress of Varignano for a few months while the situation cooled down.

At last accepting that the heroic phase of the Risorgimento was over, he nevertheless got involved in all kinds of popular protests and disputes, with the result that he found himself more or less under house arrest on Caprera, constantly watched over by Italian warships. In 1870, taking advantage this time of France's war with Prussia, the Italian army at last marched on an undefended Rome. Garibaldi was not invited to the party. But after Napoleon III had been taken prisoner by the Prussians and France had declared itself a republic, he travelled north to offer his services to the same nation that had defeated him only three years before. The French were now patriots opposing foreign tyranny. For four months, through the winter, barely able to walk or ride a horse, suffering from crippling rheumatism and arthritis, he led a multinational, ill-equipped volunteer army against the Prussians, scoring some of the very few victories for the French side of the entire war. "His campaign in France," reported Bakunin, "was a truly sublime example of greatness, simplicity, perseverance, heroism."

With the job of uniting Italy now complete, Garibaldi, started to write, producing a book of memoirs and three novels. His purpose, he explains in the preface of *Clelia, The Rule of the Priests*, was to remind Italians of the courageous compatriots who had died for their country; to spell out to the young what had been done and what remained to do; and finally, perhaps most importantly, "to earn some money to get by". The novels are wearisomely polemical and sentimental, but the memoirs offer an exciting, stripped-down account of the political and military events during the Risorgimento, as well as all kinds of insights into Garibaldi's character. "A tree is judged by the quality of the fruit it bears," he remarks at one point, "and individuals are judged by the benefits they can bestow on their fellow human beings. Being born, existing, eating, drinking and dying, these are things the merest insect can do. In times like those in 1860 in southern Italy, men are truly alive, and their lives in the service of others. This is the real life of the soul!"

In the mid-1870s Garibaldi became obsessed with the condition of Rome. Now the Italian capital, the city was plagued with malaria. Intuiting that this had something to do with the meanders of the filthy Tiber, Garibaldi campaigned to have it covered over to create a great Parisian-style boulevard. He had a scheme drawn up and presented it in parliament, without success. Only in 1898 would the disease finally be connected to the mosquitoes that thrived around the river.

Drawn into the quarrels of the political factions on the left – some reformist, some radically republican – Garibaldi urged them to unite behind a single achievable goal, and in 1879 founded the Democratic League to promote electoral reform. Universal suffrage, he declared, was "the principal, fundamental reform" and the natural continuation of the Risorgimento project. The whole purpose of achieving national sovereignty, he claimed, had been "to improve the lives of the poor and promote social justice and inviolable liberty". In 1882 the Italian parliament did extend the suffrage to all men over twenty-one who could read or write or who paid a certain amount in taxes; this meant 6.9% of the population was enfranchised, rather than the previous 2.2%. Universal male suffrage was not introduced until 1912, with women over twenty-five finally getting the vote in 1946.

All these activities were carried out despite crippling arthritis. "I got him on his feet," said his young wife, "changed him, bathed him, put him to bed and pushed his wheelchair." Despite serious financial problems, Garibaldi refused the offer of a government pension in 1875. He had always refused to accept gifts that might limit his political independence. Only when the left-wing political parties came to power in 1876 did he finally accept.

In March 1882 he was invited to go to Palermo for the 600th anniversary of the Vespri rebellion, when the Sicilians had taken up arms against the Angevin dynasty that ruled the island from France. His family warned him against the journey, but Garibaldi wanted to return for one last time to the scenes of his greatest triumph, the extraordinary days when the liberal tide rising across Italy and Europe was taken at the flood on the battlefields of Calatafimi, Palermo, Milazzo and Volturno. Met by huge crowds in Naples, he travelled on the recently opened railway to Reggio Calabria, then by ferry to Messina, then again by train to Palermo. Seeing the decrepit old man pass by in his carriage, too weak even to wave, many wept in the street. From his bed in a friend's villa he sent a last public message to his compatriots: "If Italy is respectful of the brotherhood of nations, it can show that, while never threatening others, it does not fear the aggression of any tyrant." Returning to Caprera, Garibaldi died in his bed, on 2nd June, aged seventy-four. His wish to be cremated on a heap of wood in his red shirt, on the island's remote and empty beach, was not respected.